Shark's Fins and Millet

SHARK'S FINS AND MILLET

By Ilona Ralf Sues

LITTLE, BROWN AND COMPANY · BOSTON

1944

To the Nameless Builders
of a free, democratic China

Contents

The Three Soong Sisters — Political Rivalry — Evacuation.

Illustrations

Shark's Fins and Millet

I

Flight from Geneva

THE WHALES were at the bottom of it all. My first impulse to go to China came from them. Not that I was inordinately interested in these marine mammals, but the League of Nations was entrusted with their fate. And as I lived in Geneva, where everyone and everything revolved around the League, I was naturally aware of the periodical meetings of the Committee for the Protection of the Whale. This small body of politicians and experts had the task of drafting a convention acceptable to all nations, which would prevent the extermination of whalekind by ruthless, gain-seeking fisheries.

Early in 1932 the League was at its peak. The Manchuria Incident, its first major political test case, was still on the agenda of the Council and of the Assembly, and the preparations for the greatest event in history — the Disarmament Conference — were in full swing. Hopes ran high. The flags of fifty-seven nations waved from the façades of the hotels on the Quai du Mont Blanc, indicating the headquarters of the various delegations. International private organizations and individual pacifists had come in swarms; no room was to be found in Geneva and for miles around it. In the new glass palace where the Naval, the Military and the Aviation Committees were to meet, special tall showcases had to be built to display the millions of petitions which poured in from all corners of the globe — prayers, wishes, demands that the Disarmament Conference lay the foundations for a lasting peace.

The League was proud — it had scored successes in several technical domains. The League wanted more people to know about its problems and achievements — millions of people, the whole world. It set up a powerful short-wave broadcasting station at Prangins, just outside Geneva at the foot of the Jura Mountains. Weekly broadcasts in many tongues were to rally all of mankind to that nucleus of the future world society — the League of Nations. Each week one of the problems entrusted to the League was to be explained comprehensively.

Sir Eric Drummond, the Secretary-General in person, inaugurated the Prangins sender on February 2, 1932. The details of the program had been kept secret to provide a greater surprise. I tuned in. Instead of the burning question of Disarmament, Sir Eric had chosen as his subject "The Protection of the Whale"! I turned the knob: "Damn it — I'd rather be in China."

But I did not leave then. Geneva held me, as it held thousands of others, with powerful clutches.

I worked at the Anti-Opium Information Bureau, a very small private organization, whose aim it was to make the League and the individual governments live up to their international pledges.

Opium was produced in the Far and Near East in unlimited quantities. All big colonial Powers had opium monopolies. The dope kept native populations calm and yielded appreciable revenues. In addition, there was unlimited manufacture of opium derivatives, such as morphine and heroin. Such drugs were invaluable to medical science, but the quantities needed for legitimate purposes were very small. Whatever was manufactured over and above the medicinal requirements went into the illicit traffic creating millions of addicts throughout the world. No country was safe. Clandestine factories and traffickers operated anywhere, frequently changing their centers of distribution. The police in many countries collaborated closely, endeavoring to track down the powerful international dope rings. But, to quote J. P. Gavit, this was like "trying to catch a million fleas with teaspoons."

The United States was the only big Power which had no opium monopoly. The manufacture of high-powered narcotics was limited to the country's internal use, whereas practically all other countries with well-developed chemical industries turned out tons of them to supply the world market.

The United States was the foremost and most consistent anti-opium champion in the world. It was responsible for the 1912 Hague Convention which called for the gradual reduction of opium poppy cultivation to the limits of legitimate medicinal requirements. If the Convention had been applied, there would be no drugs available in the world today for addiction purposes.

When the League was established, the opium problem was entrusted to its care. Though not a member of the League, the United States collaborated conscientiously with many of its technical bodies. It was represented on the Opium Advisory Committee and participated in every international conference. Two Americans were the spiritual leaders of the good fight waged against the omnipotent official and unofficial vested interests. One was hard-hitting, outspoken Stuart J. Fuller, Assistant Chief of the State Department's Far Eastern Division, who never missed a chance to show up any crooked maneuver. His merciless statements were classics hailed by the press, dreaded by the League Secretariat, hated by the Japanese. Everybody knew that Japan was systematically poisoning China — as a matter of national policy and to prepare the ground for an all-out conquest — but Fuller was the only one who would disclose the details of this crime in public. On his initiative the United States had made an unofficial two years' survey of the opium and narcotics situation in China and Manchuria (a thing Chiang Kai-shek was then still too weak to undertake). Fuller came to Geneva with all the proofs neatly typed out. He wiped the floor with the writhing Japanese. However, the outstanding feature of his international career was the rallying of all nonmanufacturing and nonproducing countries and welding them into a majority bloc – the "Victim Bloc" – to fight the battle against the "Old Opium Bloc." These latter could not get away with murder so long as he was in Geneva. But the Americans were there only during sessions. The dirty work of undoing the progress accomplished, of "editing" reports, of "cooking" records, of slipping weasel words into agreed-upon resolutions, was done in the months between the sessions.

That's where the Anti-Opium Information Bureau came in. We had to be on the alert constantly, watch every word, every move; the vested interests and the League's Secretariat were up to a new trick every day, to sabotage inconvenient international agreements. As soon as we learned of a novel one, we would tip off the press and the Victim Bloc, raise hell in one of our blue press notes or communiqués, or prepare a meticulously accurate paper for some ambitious delegate in search of a good nonpolitical speech, and get him to "spill the beans" on opium at the League's Assembly or the Council table. We did good work and were just as proud of the congratulations as of the invectives that were hurled at our heads.

The other American was a broad-shouldered, powerful fellow of few words and an iron fist – Harry J. Anslinger, United States Commissioner of Narcotics – the driving power behind the League's International Police Conference. The United States with its proverbial prosperity and tempting currency had always been a great attraction to clandestine dope traffickers. Prohibition and bootlegging had widened the possibilities. Anslinger did his best to protect the thousands of miles of coast line and southern border and mop up the traffic inside the country. But you cannot prevent malaria by swatting mosquitoes in your house. The swamps have to be dried up. Anslinger set out to dry up the swamps of the world. He placed his men in and around suspect factories and centers of clandestine distribution, watchful to catch the goods before they reached America. Some governments collaborated, others refused, still others did not even know. He did an excellent job, cracking down upon factory after factory. The most recalcitrant authorities of a country could not close their eyes and had to collaborate willy-nilly when faced with a public disclosure. But the world is large. Manufacturers indicted in France emigrated and opened factories in Turkey. When Kemal Pasha shut down three big, well-equipped "clandestine" concerns, they moved to Bulgaria. And when the Bulgarian Government finally "discovered" that ten illicit factories were operating in its territory, the enterprising gentlemen moved into the interior of China, where raw material was abundant and war lords complacent.

China loomed large as the biggest victim of her own opium and Japanese-imposed narcotics. There were said to be five million addicts in the Yangtze Valley alone. After Fuller's statement Generalissimo Chiang Kai-shek took matters in hand and stunned Geneva by adopting his Six-Year Opium Suppression Plan, providing death penalty for manufacturers, traffickers and addicts. The Old Opium Bloc publicly bemoaned the severity of the plan! Sure enough, six months later Chiang added a revenue-yielding opium monopoly to his radical Suppression Plan.

After years of tremendous effort on the part of the United States, the Victim Bloc and all people of good will, the League finally convened a conference in 1931 which was to limit the output of manufactured narcotics to legitimate quantities. A convention was signed which was perfect. It was so perfect that the whole world acclaimed it as the most far-reaching international agreement ever entered into. It was so perfect that not a grain of dope could be bought or sold in the legitimate trade by any druggist or pharmacist throughout the world without the proper national and international endorsement. The only trouble was that it did not affect the illicit trade! Fuller's proposal for a proper control of raw material, so long as production was not limited, had been voted down for some unexplained reason. The League gloried in its new international dope-bookkeeping activities and expanding budget. By 1936 the compiling of estimates and statistics in this field had dwindled down to tedious routine.

In reality the situation was hopeless. I had lost faith in a solution of the opium problem. The other international domains were just as gloomy. The "settlement" of the Manchurian Incident left Japan master in the Far East, with all countries vying in their efforts to supply her with the necessary war supplies. The Disarmament Conference petered out dismally. I had many Chinese friends, and their dignity in all adversity was the first thing that attracted me. When Mussolini invaded Ethiopia, I started learning Chinese. I was weary of the futility of public sessions. The whole atmosphere was vitiating. The sessions dealing with the Ethiopian Incident were nauseating. I decided upon flight, to escape suffocation. I looked around for a place where something constructive was going on, and found nothing nearer than China. I sold my couch, bought a Leica, packed my three C's — Cat, Camera, and Continental typewriter — and set out as a free-lance journalist. With me I took from Geneva a remnant of love for the human being and a bagful of seasoned skepticism.

I went to China totally unprepared. I do not believe I had read half a dozen books about it. I wanted to see things for myself, to be "the eyes and the ears of the man-in-the-street," to publish "Letters to Tom, Dick and Harry" as I went along. It never occurred to my impractical mind to obtain a contract from a publisher or an assignment from a newspaper. I had a verbal agreement with a London news-photo agency to send them the negatives of any interesting snapshots; they would sell them on a fifty-fifty basis. The agreement worked satisfactorily a few months, then the director was replaced and the new man made a practice of keeping say fifty negatives and sending me seven shillings sixpence as my share, which was rather annoying. So

I had to do some secretarial work or some teaching, now and then. Living is cheap in China and I am anything but ambitious.

The strangeness of this amazing country threatened to knock me off my feet, and it took weeks before I could get my bearings. Then I became so fascinated by everything I learned that I never thought of writing. Even today I think it is presumptuous on my part to do so.

This book is neither a study nor a travelogue nor a political treatise. It is a medley of everything, as unorthodox as life itself — an unconventional set of stories and anecdotes — a series of big and small events, of great and little people observed not through a high-powered microscope but with the imperfect, naked, sympathetic, twinkling human eye.

I was fortunate. Through no merit of mine, Madame Chiang Kai-shek played fairy godmother to Cinderella and chose me as a tool — a chisel, to be precise — in one of her sweeping reorganization schemes. This meant daily work with W. H. Donald, China's publicity-shy Richelieu, just across the road from Generalissimo's Headquarters.

I got my first glimpse of Chinese politics and government factions from Donald on Purple Mountain, before the Ming Tombs, during Jap air raids. From that lofty height I was parachuted into the midst of the Central Publicity Board, some sixty color-fast Kuomintang colleagues whose "rice bowls" I had tried to break. Kid-gloved bureaucracy catapulted me back into private life again. A good-will mission took me to Commander Chu Teh's Eighth Route Army headquarters, and curiosity made me proceed thence to Yenan, capital of the Communist Border Regional Government, where I met Mao Tse-tung and saw to my astonishment that democracy can work in China, despite all theories to the contrary expounded by people who wish to perpetuate the tutelage of the people by the one party in power. On my return to Hankow, I became English and French broadcaster for the Political Department of the Military Affairs Commission headed by Generals Ch'en Ch'eng and Chou En-lai.

It was a thrilling experience to live and work with people who make history, to see their real faces undistorted, unembellished by propaganda. And when I say "people who make history," I mean any representative of the spirit of free China: a leader in Headquarters, a Kuomintang official, a racketeer banker, a missionary, a people's educator, a soldier, a campaigning school child. I mean a Communist, a reactionary, a liberal, a fighter for democracy, a pro-Japanese minister. Every one of them counts. Every one of them is in China's tremendous struggle individually, a vibrating human being. Every one of them is part of this most stupendous phenomenon in history — China's United Front — a front where bitter foes stand shoulder to shoulder, ready to fight to the last breath for a free China. To every one of them Free China means something different.

I have endeavored to tell of my experiences as vividly as I have lived them. My only ambition has been to re-create each scene, each personality, so that the reader may get a whiff of the atmosphere. If I have failed in many instances it is because life and mankind and China are so much richer in color than words can tell.

To those whom the title *Shark's Fins and Millet* might puzzle, I wish to explain that shark's fins are the crowning delicacy of sumptuous official feasts, and that millet — a cereal which looks and tastes like London fog — is the rice of the poor in China's indomitable Northwest.

II

En Route for China

"I CAN amputate a leg, and take out an appendix, but bless my soul, I don't know how to deliver a child," said the ship's doctor in dismay, contemplating little Mrs. Hsu, who had just been brought into the ward.

The tourist class passengers in the Italian liner *Conte Verde* — mostly Chinese students on their way home after graduation — stood on the deck in small groups, discussing the situation with concern. Mr. and Mrs. Hsu had met and married in Rome, where she studied law and he political science. Three weeks ago they had both obtained their degrees and were now hurrying back to their families. Mrs. Hsu expected to have a quiet month with her mother before the child would be born. But because of either curiosity on his part or the excruciating heat of the Red Sea, the baby had apparently decided to come earlier.

The Italian doctor and the two nurses stood helpless at the bedside. Her pretty face distorted with pain, Mrs. Hsu held her husband's hand convulsively. They did not speak. He swallowed hard to hold back the tears. The situation was critical.

The door opened and a quiet, plain-looking Chinese girl stepped into the ward, and said in a matter-of-fact tone: —

"I have just finished a year's practical work in the maternity ward of the Berlin Charité Hospital. Will you entrust this case to me?"

Next day mother and baby were fine, and a week later Mrs. Hsu was again at our poker table.

Time had to be killed somehow to escape boredom; it was

impossible to read the whole day long. The trip was one of the most tedious imaginable. Usually a few hours' sight-seeing in the British Far Eastern ports constituted a welcome diversion, and we were all looking forward to this first glimpse of the Orient. But from Port Said to Hong Kong we did not see a single port — nothing but the immensity of oceans, now and then interrupted by some flying fish or by a lone native fisherman's barge. Had it not been for the terrific heat and for the glorious tropical sunsets which steeped the skies and waters each evening in a sea of fantastic, hallucinating flames, we would not have realized that we were sailing across the Indian Ocean. Something was wrong with the *Conte Verde:* her speed was irregular — she either steamed full blast ahead or lingered for no apparent reason, and she arrived at every port well after dark, when not a thing could be seen. . . .

(I had had my misgivings about booking passage with an Italian company. Italy had invaded Ethiopia and should be boycotted by every internationally minded person, and here was I, aboard an Italian liner! I was inclined to believe that I was rightly punished. But after all, I had chosen the Lloyd Triestino for two very important reasons: first, because the fare was exactly half of the price asked by ships of other nationalities, and second because Italian companies were less fussy about my cat than the British, for instance. British law stipulated that every animal which had not had the privilege of being born on the Isles was subject to six months' quarantine prior to entering British territory or boarding a British vessel. No self-respecting dog or cat could stand such treatment, least of all my Gueidze, who had spent his babyhood in my Geneva studio listening to so many conversations on international public law that he was perfectly conscious of the civil rights of a cat. . . .)

The passengers remonstrated. The officers and the crew offered unconvincing explanations, vaguely hinting at some engine trouble, though no one could give a valid reason for the erratic changes in the vessel's speed. At last the truth slipped out in a confidential whisper — there was nothing the matter with the engines, the trouble was British sanctions.

Sanctions? That magic word made me sit up.

The League of Nations Assembly had recently terminated its debates about Italy's invasion of Ethiopia. It was the last depressing performance I had attended in Geneva. Under the terms of the League's Covenant, government members of the League were pledged to put pressure upon any aggressor nation by applying economic sanctions destined to stop its war machine and thus to protect the victim nation by an act of collective security. Unfortunately the only countries interested in collective security were the ones attacked or those whose frontiers were menaced. The Great Powers and their satellites looked upon the matter from another angle. Governments were no philanthropic institutions and could not be expected to carry out their international obligations if these conflicted with their immediate national policies. There was no profit in sanctions, they only crippled a nation's trade. As a result, Japan, who had been branded as an aggressor by the League in 1932, never suffered from any interference by League members and could buy in the open market everything she needed for the conquest of China. The Disarmament Conference had ended in a pitiful fiasco in 1933. Hitler was rearming Germany with everybody's blessing in 1934. And there was no reason why, in 1936, Italy should not get away with her African venture. But, as hope is the last thing to die, people still believed that the League would stop Mussolini this time.

Discussions had gone according to schedule. Italy was duly recognized to be an aggressor. Then the seasoned representatives of the governments took the floor, one after another trying to wriggle out of the obligations which this verdict imposed upon their respective countries.

The U.S.S.R., China, a few weaker nations and public opinion demanded embargoes on oil, airplane gasoline, arms and war supplies, which would have stopped the war automatically. But embargoes on such valuable commodities would have interfered with legitimate business and affected internal revenues; and none of the Great Powers was prepared to make such sacrifices. As was to be foreseen, the majority bloc, headed by Great Britain, voted down the drastic proposals and substituted a noncommittal resolution which simply suggested that governments might, if they so wished, apply such minor sanctions against Italy as they saw fit.

Couched in the League's characteristic language, so full of weasel words, the resolution meant nothing and did not deceive the insider. It was just one more confirmation of the fact that the League was a fake, and collective security as dead as a dodo. No sanction had ever worked; neither would these.

Small wonder I was electrified by the news that Great Britain applied sanctions in the Indian Ocean. No one in Geneva would have believed it. The matter was worth studying.

All British ports had received orders to boycott the Italian merchant marine and give preference to British shipping. This meant a heavy loss to Italian steamship companies dependent upon Far Eastern cargo. And although the measure had no direct bearing upon the outcome of the Italo-Ethiopian war, it combined the advantages of being profitable to British interests, saving the Empire's face in the international domain, and appeasing to a certain extent that righteous and sentimental monster called "public opinion."

The Italians were angry, and retaliated by ordering their vessels to arrive at British ports in the middle of the night and to stop just long enough to take on the indispensable fuel, fresh water and stores — operations which seldom took longer than three hours' time. This prevented us passengers from spending good money on British soil and it reduced harbor fees to a minimum. Thus we were robbed of the pleasure of sightseeing. In the impenetrable darkness of the night, we could only imagine the presence of gorgeous temples, lofty snow-white government buildings, palm tree groves.

However, any pangs of conscience I may have felt on account of supporting the merchant marine of an aggressor nation were now dissipated. What did it matter that I would not see Colombo, Bombay and Singapore? The moral compensation outweighed the loss — I had come across the first piece of evidence that international justice was not an empty term but a reality. What were all the marvels of Oriental architecture to me, who had been waiting seven years in Geneva for this miracle to happen? The miracle was right here: A sanction that was taken seriously!

We had a number of interesting Chinese on board. One of them was Mr. Chu Hsueh-fan, who has since become prominent in Chinese-American labor circles. Mr. Chu had just made his debut on the international scene as China's first Workers' Delegate to the International Labor Conference. He was said to have been a worker himself and to have organized the Chinese Postal Labor Union, of which he was now chairman. Shanghai's 800,000 organized workmen had then elected him unanimously as their delegate to the I.L.O. Mr. Chu's English was then not as good as it is today, but he made two very comprehensive speeches at the Conference, one describing China's labor conditions and program for the future, the other giving the high lights of China's anti-opium campaign. The speeches received considerable publicity in the world press, and overnight his international reputation was made. From Geneva, Chu had toured France, Belgium, England and Holland, speaking at labor and seamen's unions and participating in conferences of the Second International. He was a modest, likable fellow who made friends everywhere.

Now he was returning home second class. Mutual friends had told him of my presence, and he looked me up immediately.

We spent many hours talking. The ship's food was bad, so as soon as we arrived at any port, Chu and I and half a dozen other friends would rush ashore to the best Chinese restaurant and get a decent meal. I thought it only normal that Chinese journalists were waiting at every landing to interview and photograph him. But I was somewhat embarrassed by his insistence that I should appear in every photo with him. He motivated this by the fact that we were colleagues in the anti-opium fight and told the journalists all he knew about me. None of my objections counted. I thought he wanted to give me a build-up out of sheer Oriental politeness, so I could not be too rude. Little did I know of the troubles which this unsolicited publicity stunt held in store for me.

Another interesting co-traveler was Gordon Lum. He had won an international tennis cup in England for China in 1935, and this victory was recorded in an imposing colorful square embroidered on his purple sweater right over the heart. He had been educated in the Philippines and the United States, and his personality was a perfect blend of Chinese sense of humor, American sportsmanship and the refreshing frankness of a college boy.

I shall never forget an anecdote Gordon told me. Two of his friends, uncle and nephew by the name of Liu, mighty war lords, fought each other fiercely for the supremacy of Szechsen Province. That was a few years before Chiang Kai-shek brought the whole country under his control. Gordon passed through that region and visited the nephew at his headquarters. The latter was delighted to see the famous tennis champion; he immediately sent an emissary to his uncle and proposed a three days' truce to celebrate this event by a great tennis tournament. Uncle Liu was just as much of a tennis fan and enthusiastically accepted the proposal.

The two hostile armies picked their best players, improvised a splendid tennis court in the middle of the forest. The troops fraternized, set up a joint jury, a joint entertainment committee, and the two Lius loosened the strings of their purses and provided the best food and wines that could be got in the province. Everybody enjoyed the break, and the match was a real success. And when the three days of feasting were over, the two armies resumed their former positions and the war went on.

In the course of that match, on serving a ball one day, Gordon spotted a round thing on a tree that seemed to him like a coconut. He had never seen a coconut on a pine tree before, and besides, this thing looked rather hairy. He looked up again, and realized that it was a human head nailed to the trunk.

"It gave me the creeps," he said with a shudder. "It took all my self-control not to miss the balls."

"Gives me the creeps, too," said I; "but why didn't you tell them to take it off?"

"Phew," he whistled, "such a request might have offended either the uncle or the nephew or both, and spoiled the whole feast. A trophy is a trophy and must remain where it is put. As a guest of honor, I could not make such a tactless remark. So I pretended that I hadn't even noticed the thing."

Though his tale was interesting from a psychological point of view, I was annoyed that a Chinese should go about telling such atrocity stories to foreigners, and I told him so frankly.

"This isn't precisely what I would call good propaganda for your country," I said.

Gordon was standing with his legs wide apart, his hands dug in his pockets. He looked me squarely in the face.

"Granted. But I don't make propaganda; it is a lousy way of distorting a truth. I told you a true story because I thought you could take it. Sorry if I have underestimated your sensitiveness. You'll have to get rid of this before you can tackle China. China is a tough proposition; it will either make you or break you. Don't close your eyes to anything, open 'em wide, and your mind too. Values out there are different — you can't measure them by Western standards. You think that you are a friend of China, but how can you or I or anyone tell whether it is not your own romantic dream of China that you are enamored with? Don't kid yourself. Go and look and try to understand. And only if you can go through China and take in all the beauty and grandeur, all the horror and misery she has to offer, and still continue to love her, may you have the right to claim, someday, that you are a real friend of China."

A few hours off Hong Kong, the news broke on board that Generalissimo Chiang Kai-shek had just arrived in Canton, ousted the Kwangtung Autonomous Provincial Government and General Ch'en Chi-t'ang, and was incorporating the province into the territory of the National Government. Simultaneously he was negotiating with Generals Pai Ch'ung-hsi and Li Tsung-jen, the overlords of neighboring Kwangsi Province, to fall into line with Nanking as well. Since 1934 Chiang had changed his policy of subjecting independent provinces by the power of his sword and had shown remarkable statesmanship by bringing the different war lords under his rule on a basis of mutual conces-sions. The pacification of the Liang Kwang — that is, the two Kwang provinces, Kwangtung and Kwangsi — was not only an important political factor but the crowning point of his daring program. If Kwangsi agreed upon a peaceful surrender — which was not at all sure, as it possessed an excellent army and aviation — the whole of China would be unified, leaving only the territories of the Red Army, which Chiang still expected to conquer by armed force.

Eager to see what a province in the process of pacification looked like, I decided to disembark at Hong Kong and go up to Canton, instead of carrying out my original plan of going to Shanghai. I hurriedly packed a small suitcase, coaxed Gueidze into taking his place in the wicker basket — a thing he detested — took my camera and typewriter, and let all the rest of my luggage proceed to Shanghai.

At the foot of the gangplank I found myself literally plunged into the arms of China, not two but hundreds of arms. I was surrounded by a seething mob of excited, yelling coolies, tugging at my skirt and sleeves.

"Hello, Missie, this way." "Missie, my ricksha best ricksha." "Missie, how many piecy luggage?"

"I want a motor car, I want no ricksha."

I had resolved never to take a ricksha in my life. A human being was not a beast of burden, and I, for one, would not have a Chinese pull me through the streets. One has one's principles.

The screaming was so loud that I could hardly hear my own voice. I tried to keep my chin up, bewildered though I was. . . . Gosh, I won't be swamped by this crowd. I can yell just as loud as they can. And they aren't going to notice just how lonely and lost I feel in the midst of this turmoil of half-naked Orientals and that forest of shiny ricksha shafts. . . . There seemed to be no way out; I was trapped.

"Missie, where you go?" "Missie, go hotel?" the coolies insisted, nearly pulling me to pieces.

I shook them off and retorted haughtily: "No hotel. I go Canton. Please, call a motor car."

"Okay, Missie, go Canton."

They grabbed the suitcase, the basket, the typewriter. I tried in vain to wrest it from those small brown clutching hands. They were a hundred to one. There was nothing to do but be brutal, I told myself. And with all the brutality I could muster, I shouted: —

"Damn you, let go, get out of my way. I want a motor car. I want no ricksha. Understand? No-o-o ricksh — "

I felt myself lifted into space and carefully deposited on a soft cushioned seat. Within a fraction of a second I was out of the forest of ricksha shafts, speeding along the streets of Hong Kong on noiseless wheels, my eyes fixed upon the rhythmically swinging back of my ricksha coolie, who ran hell-for-leather. A second ricksha behind us carried my belongings. Right and left four porters kept pace, panting and continuing their chatter: —

"Okay Missie — No ricksha, Missie — Missie go Canton."

They had won. I relaxed and leaned back. They stopped jabbering. The twilight descended upon the city. Here and there a light was turned on. It was wonderful to float along like this, fanned by the cool evening breeze, looking down upon this sea of animated human faces. At a turning I saw through the delicate bluish mist the soft contours of the Peak, Hong Kong's residential hill, scintillating with myriads of lights. A voyage on a magic flying carpet, across some beautiful island in fairyland. . . .

The little riverboat to which my six coolies had brought me was exquisitely clean and comfortable. The jovial fat captain spoke English. But he lost his power of speech as soon as I asked him how much I should give the men. I had a handful of English silver, no Hong Kong currency, and gave them three shillings — which, I knew, was more than ample pay. But they started to shriek again, raising an awful row. The captain would not come to my rescue — he gazed noncommittally across the waters.

"Well, how much do you want?"

"Missie, look-see hand."

I opened my hand and Number One coolie counted the coins in my palm. Seven shillings.

"Missie give all, be okay," he decreed.

I let the money glide into his cupped hands. After all, I had been beastly to them, and they had taken me here through fairyland. They deserved more than this, but I had no more change.

How those fellows brightened up! With many an "Okay, Missie" and "Good luck, Missie" they grinned and bowed their way back to the shore.

The captain gave me one pitying look which expressed all the contempt he felt for that nitwit of a foreigner who did not even know how to bargain! Then he turned on his heel and showed me into the ship's best stateroom.

III

Canton

CHINA, CHINA — I am in China, I repeated to myself next morning, before opening my eyes. But somehow the feeling of happiness was mingled with uneasiness. The boat seemed motionless; only the soft purring of the motor indicated that we were still advancing. No, I would not open my eyes before finding out the cause of this uneasiness. Let us proceed systematically, I pondered, half awake. China of my dreams . . . Canton . . . What was I going to Canton for? Oh, yes — to see Chiang pacify the province. . . . Immediately upon my arrival I would call on . . . Call on whom? Did I know anyone in Canton? No . . . Yes . . . No. . . . I recapitulated the names and addresses of the few letters of introduction stowed away somewhere in my luggage — they were all for people in Shanghai and Peiping. Nothing for Canton . . . And I had never given it a thought. Now I must needs do some hard thinking. . . . There was that American (what the dickens was his name?) who had spent an hour in our office in Geneva, some two or three years ago. A Chinese Maritime Customs official on furlough — a tall, thin, wiry gentleman with gray eyes, a sharp profile, and a dry sense of humor. He should be somewhere round here. . . . I congratulated myself sarcastically on my wonderful memory for personal characteristics, so utterly futile under present circumstances. A fine chance I had of locating this man in China! I racked my brain to recall his name. . . . L. K. . . . L. K. . . . L. K. Little? That's right. Now I am a step further. . . . He had spoken of Canton. Sure, but he had also talked about Peiping, in the North, and Wuhu, in Central China, and Yunnanfu in the Southwest. Where was he stationed today? The situation was funny, but I could not smile. Facts must be faced.

I opened my eyes and lit a cigarette. The mellow light of early dawn filled my stateroom, attenuating the luster of the highly polished mahogany wood paneling. What a relief — this warm, rich coloring, after the glaring whiteness of my cabin on the *Conte Verde*. How remarkably clean and shiny everything was kept. And there was a window — thank heaven, no porthole. I walked over to it, to catch a glimpse of that brown, pitiless China of mine. . . .

What I saw was so unexpected, so unbelievably beautiful, that I held my breath. Here was no landscape, no earth, no depth of perspective; nothing but a gorgeous Chinese screen woven of opalescent pale rose-and-lavender mist; and painted onto it, in the most delicate water colors, were little huts with thatched roofs — tawny, dreamy, lonely little huts looking down upon the tawny, dreamy river below. Our boat was passing alongside this magic screen slowly, leaving millions of pale rose ripples behind. . . .

"Gueidze," I called out, too thrilled to keep all the emotions to myself. There must have been a particular urge in my voice, for he jumped down from his armchair at once, crossed the cabin in a bound and leapt onto the window sill.

"*Gueidze, voici la Chine! As-tu jamais vu pareille merveille?*"

He sat straight, his bright green eyes staring at the unusual scenery, and acknowledged my question by wagging the tip of his tail. And like this we remained, shoulder to shoulder, two pals facing a strange land; I, with my elbows leaning on the window sill, wondering what the future held in store, and my black, shiny, furry companion with his little nose and long whiskers quivering in the attempt to smell what the air in China was like — until the steward knocked at the door and announced that we were nearing Canton.

*   *   *

On arrival, we were herded through a narrow gateway — some hundred Chinese men and women, mostly small business people, clad in black Cantonese silk and carrying the most heterogeneous collection of bundles and parcels, and I, the only foreigner, conspicuous by my insolently white dress. In a queue, we passed through the narrow Customs shack, where two quiet, efficient men examined our luggage. I feared that they might quarantine my cat under the new laws, but they only shrugged their shoulders at its sight and pasted the release labels on the basket. Instead they decided to quarantine my typewriter and my camera; in a mixture of English and Mandarin they explained politely that the "machines" were new and I would have to pay duty on them tomorrow, Monday, at the Hai-Guan, the Chinese Maritime Customs. It was an awkward feeling to part with my Leica, but their verdict was categorical — only Number One could exempt me from payment. Who was Number One, a foreigner? I asked. Yes, *mei-kguo jen*, American. And, with a spark of hope — was his name L. K. Little? Two hands jerked up simultaneously to the uniform caps, saluting; yes, it was Mr. Little. A weight fell off my chest. I asked the officials not to open the Leica and took a taxi to the New Asia Hotel.

The New Asia was a big, modern, seven-story building with a spacious entrance hall embellished with palm trees and fine Chinese rugs. All along the walls stood little tables flanked by two heavy easy chairs, and in front of every table, on the floor, stood a huge Chinese porcelain vase. Why on earth didn't they place these *on* the tables, I wondered. But a few seconds later I was shocked into understanding their practical use — they were cuspidors, over-life-size cuspidors! The hall was crowded — so crowded that I had to stand in a fourfold queue to await my turn at the reception desk, and could observe things in the meantime. Canadians were, to my mind, the world champions when it came to good marksmanship in long-distance spitting, but I had never dreamed of such prolific spitting in unison as I witnessed during my first half-hour in Canton. And the noise that accompanied — or rather preceded — each individual expectoration was simply terrific. I mention this first impression because the habit was so characteristic and widespread, and one of the very few to which I could not get accustomed during my stay in China. Now that I am so far away and memories have grown wistful and mellow by absence — now that I long to be back there — whenever the familiar *Khrrrrr-tfoo* sound strikes my ear, I feel homesick for China.

The young lady at the desk advised me in very good English that the hotel was full up but that — if I had patience to wait — a room might be freed in the course of the day. It was seven o'clock, Sunday morning. I sat down near the entrance and watched the endless procession of new arrivals. One of the countless white-clad bellhops poured me a cup of tea and kept replenishing it. I had never seen such crowds in my life — a real migration of peoples.

A stout, elderly, prosperous-looking gentleman came in, clad in a long gray silk gown, wearing a Panama hat and soft-soled black slippers. He turned round, uttered a few brief instructions to the flock of people following him in perfect order, and took his place in the queue. The flock stopped respectfully, waiting. It consisted of about half a dozen youngsters between twelve and twenty-five years of age, then came a portentous lady in black, surrounded by a half-dozen pretty maidens of all ages in gay colors; behind them was a respectable number of male and female servants carrying bags and bundles; the rear was formed by a few coolies loaded with household utensils of every description — there was even a cage with little singing birds among the lot. The head of this family worked his way to the desk and came back presently, hustling his group upstairs. I was amazed that so many people should find accommodation in a full-up hotel, and made a remark to the lean gentleman who occupied the other armchair at my table. He explained very kindly that the gentleman in gray was a high government official with his family, and that they had probably reserved their rooms beforehand.

Scores of similar groups, some larger, some smaller, entered the hall in the course of the day; they either obtained living space or filed out again in the same orderly manner to look for quarters elsewhere. My vis-à-vis informed me that the very same phenomenon could actually be watched in all Canton hotels, since the city was flooded with Northerners. Chiang Kai-shek had ousted the governor, General Ch'en Chi-t'ang, and with him the entire body of 20,000 officials, whom he wished to replace by men and women from the provinces which had remained loyal to the Nanking Government. The good news had brought some 50,000 people to Canton — prospective candidates, their kinfolk and servants. The scrambling for hotel rooms was surpassed only by the scrambling for the highly desirable government jobs. I was sorry for the fired 20,000, most of whom had probably never been interested in politics. Such radical procedure did not tally with my conception of pacifying and befriending a province. But I had to be satisfied with the explanation that things were always done this way in China.

Every now and then I worked my way through the crowds to the nice girl at the reception desk, reminding her of my presence. Gueidze was restless in his basket. Finally, at 4 P.M., my patience was rewarded.

I got a fair-sized room with a view on Canton's sky line — a sober profile of a prosperous city: solid blocks of concrete office buildings, with here and there the fancy red brick tower of a theater, or the majestic green-glazed roof of a temple with gracefully upturned gilded corners.

The room was clean and simply furnished. The large bed was impressive — a wooden berth resting on high bamboo legs, with a thin straw mat for a mattress; the sheets and blanket formed a neat roll against the wall; the pillowcase was beautifully embroidered. Right over the center of the bed dangled a maze of heavy muslin — my first mosquito-net — tied into a huge, artful knot for the daytime. There was a beautifully carved table against the wall, flanked by two armchairs, with the obligatory spittoon in front. And on the table stood a steaming teapot and four cups. I was informed that the management had succeeded in finding, among the scores of white-liveried youngsters, two boys who understood Mandarin and English, as I did not speak Cantonese. They would take care of me.

I went for a stroll. Strange splendor of China's Southern capital . . . Imposing wide, concrete-surfaced avenues, flanked by modern office buildings, banks, hotels, magnificently decorated shop-windows displaying gorgeous silk, daintily carved ivory, red lacquer, green and milky jade, sophisticated silver filigrees spun finely like cobwebs . . . Department stores, as in America . . . Then other shops — long, solid blocks of them — huge concrete cubes without façade — exactly like the open toyshops children find under the Christmas tree . . . Here a gigantic delicatessen store with legions of pressed salt ducks hanging from the ceiling — in fact, one can't see the ceiling at all . . . Walls covered with Cantonese hams — the most delicious and fragrant smoked hams in the world . . . Bunches of sausages . . . Heaps of sugar-cured bacon . . . Mountains of ruddy, red-legged crabs; pink shrimps, ready to eat, spicy, appetizing; barrels of golden, smoked fish; buckets of silver, salt fish . . . Tall glass containers with neatly curled — to the Western taste less appetizing — snakes . . . Preserved ginger and candied fruit that make one's mouth water . . . Mud-coated hundred-year eggs . . . Stuffed dates, nut candy . . . Here and there a maze of dried, nondescript delicacies which look like shrunk mummies of strange, antediluvian creatures . . . And, lingering over it all, enveloping, penetrating you, there is that undefinable, enervating, sensuous smell that makes your nostrils quiver. Crowds of customers gesticulating vivaciously

. . . Gaiety, laughter . . . Long masculine gowns — jet-black, snow-white, or wash-blue — mingle with the long, flimsy, flowery gowns of the ladies. . . .

I pass on. I am a drop in the stream of humanity flowing through the street. The next shop I notice is stacked full of coffins — enormous, thick-walled, heavy coffins, from the simplest, unpainted wood to the most elaborately carved and gold-trimmed. The place is deserted. Behind the counter, an old, solitary man is poring over a thick volume. . . .

Farther down a lunch counter, serving soup with meat balls and steaming stuffed dumplings out of huge cauldrons, beleaguered by an eagerly munching populace. Gowns are few. Working people — men and women — wear black, pocketless silk or cotton pants that stop high above the ankle, as if there were an acute shortage of material, and black or pastel-color vests. Ricksha coolies with nude, sun-tanned, sweat-polished torsos squat on the footboards of their light chariots, deftly handling their bowls and chopsticks, visibly enjoying the quick snack between two runs.

The stream of humanity rolls on, drones on. The noise is terrific — a symphony of human voices talking, shouting; of jingling bells; of whirring rattles, and squeaky trumpets, and clangorous gongs, and rumbling drums — each peddler has his own distinctive instrument to advertise his wares. And there are myriads of peddlers, one more picturesque than the other, selling useful and wondrous things — feather dusters, paper dragons, peanuts, boiling water, ear-swabs, performing humming birds, sliced melon, straw sandals, branches of fresh lichee nuts. . . . This orgy of sounds is the background, the accompaniment, to the shrill, impatient, urging leitmotiv of automobile horns. There are no traffic cops, no traffic regulations.

It was not easy for me to walk, and more difficult still to stop for a moment before any shopwindow. People surrounded me immediately, stared curiously, watched my gestures, appraised my clothes. At moments, I felt embarrassed and self-conscious; they noticed it in a flash and laughed at me — very much as children laugh watching the antics of an exotic animal in the zoo! What else could I do but laugh with them?

Across the street from the New Asia, children tugged at my skirt — the raggedest of ragged street urchins, their dirty little palms outstretched, crying, yelling, howling like professional beggars, to soften my heart . . . and making funny faces behind my back. Some of them had sore eyes, others were covered with eczema, but the majority seemed healthy, intelligent, peppy. I distributed all the coppers I had. They were delightful, and I could have adopted the whole bunch of those tiny tots with their big black sparkling eyes. They must have liked me too, for, after a few minutes of our acquaintance, my white dress bore a striking resemblance to the archives of a fingerprinting department!

Twilight is nonexistent in Canton. There is no transition between dazzling daylight and black night. The change is sudden. But the noise in the street does not stop. Oh no, it swells and rises, because the Cantonese pretend that the night is cooler! . . . Cooler? I was stifling under my mosquito net and took it off, preferring eventual malaria to certain suffocation. Now I had at least the benefit of the refreshing breeze from the electric fan on the table. I had nothing but hot tea to quench my painful thirst. No ice, no drinking water — a self-respecting Chinese hotel management does not carry such death-bringing liquids. The bottled lemonade tasted like lukewarm syrup and contained a formidable quantity of bubbles; I was sure to float through the air like a balloon, if I ever managed to swallow the ghastly concoction.

Miserable, I turned off the light and tried to pretend that the streets were quiet, that I had just had an ice-cream soda, that the people next door did not rattle with their mah-jong bones, that there was no major powwow in the adjoining corridor . . . that the thing whizzing round my room was probably nothing but a bat — bats usually flew round in circles, and I did not mind them.

I was falling asleep, when Gueidze's hunting spirit suddenly awoke, carrying him over the bed, over my body, chairs, tables and spittoon, in wild pursuit of the whizzing enigma. I swore. Something crashed against the fan. A grinding sound . . . *meeeow!* I sat up with a jerk, every hair rising on my head: Gueidze's paw? I turned the switch. No. Thank heaven, the cat was unhurt, sitting on the floor, blinking, and just as frightened as his mistress. But what was this on my bed? Cut-up parts of a big, brown insect — hard as a shell. A long, thin leg, sharp and dented like a saw — at least three inches long. *Brrr*, what a disgusting thing. I shook these mortal remains off the blanket and lay down to sleep. But as soon as the light was out, the whizzing began again; this time it sounded like more than one — his friends must have gathered for the victim's funeral, I concluded. Gueidze resumed his chase. I had to face the music and meet the guests. On went the light. Plums — big, brown plums flying through the air, with rigid wings and long, thin landing gears . . . miniature bombing planes . . . And, by golly — here was one of them power diving! Gueidze jumped and knocked it down. It ran fast toward me . . . A cockroach! Gueidze played Rugby with it. The other two flew out the window. The cat enjoyed the game, but not I. He turned his prey upside down — it was desperately treading the air with its three or four pairs of feet. I had had enough of it, but I dared not touch it, nor even let my feet down on the floor . . . I rang the bell. The door opened instantly, and nothing came in except a voice, a low voice asking in Mandarin: "What does the lady want?" "Come in," I ordered. "I am in your room," replied the voice. Was I really out of my wits? But no — presently a little round face peeped round the foot-end of my bed, barely four feet above the floor, and the smallest bellboy I had ever laid eyes on stood before me. "Oh," I gasped, "who are you?" "I am on night duty," he replied with adult dignity. "What's your age?" "I am eight years old," was the matter-of-fact reply; "what does the lady want?" I pointed to the struggling insect; I had never seen one like this before — could he tell me the name? But the kid would not be fooled; he knew I was scared stiff. He did not tell me the name but quickly fetched a dustpan and a duster. "*Ni bieh pa, ni bieh pa* (Don't be afraid)," he reassured me paternally, "it is quite harmless." He shoved the roach carefully onto the dustpan, on its back so that it might not run away. I felt crushed with shame. Here I was, a big, husky woman, trembling, squatting on my heels, comforted by a child! What a loss of face! But the little fellow had personality, poise and tact; he did not make me feel I had lost face. He asked me to lie down, tucked the mosquito net round my bed, bade me good night, and left. Four o'clock. A moment later I slept like a log.

I was having breakfast in my room next morning when the shooting started. First a loud detonation, like a cannon salvo, then a well-nourished machine-gun fire . . . It sounded quite near. Startled, Gueidze hid under the bed. How exciting! The Kwangsi generals must have decided to defend their province against Chiang Kai-shek's troops massed at the frontiers. It was thrilling to be in the midst of it! I ran to the window; some people were standing on the roof across the back yard; they did not seem particularly agitated. The firing stopped. I called the day-boy. Was Kwangsi fighting? How far was it to the front? No, said the boy, Kwangsi was still negotiating; the morning papers predicted an early peaceful settlement. Then what was the firing I had heard? Oh — the youngster giggled with delight at my ignorance — those were firecrackers; a marriage ceremony was being celebrated on the first floor. Gee whiz, but there must have been thousands of firecrackers! Thousands? he retorted haughtily — there were more than hundreds of thousands — it was a very rich man's wedding. . . .

* * *

Shameen was right across the creek — a well-kept park, not quite as large as New York's Central Park. One part of it belonged to the French, the other — where L. K. Little lived — to the British. There were beautiful lawns and many big trees. A shady oasis, so unlike the city in every respect . . . European houses, surrounded by gardens . . . A bank, a clubhouse, colonial villas, tennis courts . . . The Concession seemed almost deserted. Passers-by were few — Chinese and foreigners. They looked sleepy, self-important, and rather uninteresting — like Shameen itself: a safe zone, with nothing to wish for and nothing to fight for.

L. K. Little's cool, roomy, austere house was a haven of refuge, and he just as I remembered him — a tall, lanky colonial of the pioneer type, used to living alone, thinking a lot, and talking little.

A noiselessly moving boy brought refreshments — ice-cooled drinks! It was unconceivable that the temperature outside was 130 in the shade.

Commissioner Little considered himself a Chinese government official; he admired Chiang Kai-shek unreservedly as the greatest leader the country ever had, and dwelled at length upon China's unique development — thanks to the unification of the provincial governments under Nanking, to the rapidly growing mileage of railways and highroads, to the close cooperation with the League of Nations, and to the steadily improving health conditions.

He felt bitter resentment against anyone obstructing Chiang's work, and particularly against Governor Ch'en Chi-t'ang — who, according to him, was past master at any form of squeeze.

My usually taciturn host warmed up when talking about China, but his speech remained reserved and he weighed every word carefully. The strongest word he said was "swine" — it shocked me, coming from his lips — and he applied it exclusively to the Japanese. The Japanese had been, for years, waging a relentless underground campaign against the National Government, and Tokyo was spending huge sums of money to frustrate any attempt at China's unification. Dissenting war lords were financed in their anti-government campaigns. To break China's economic backbone, many millions of dollars' worth of Japan-made contraband goods were brought into the country every year under military escort who refused to pay customs dues and threatened the customs men who wanted to examine the shipments. In some instances such officials were shot "accidentally." Contraband goods comprised anything, from toys to morphine and heroin. Japanese consulates protected the smugglers, aided and abetted the drug traffickers, sponsored opium dens and white-drug huts throughout the country. The "drug huts" were not much bigger than a newsstand, all closed in, with a small opening for the customer to pass his arm through, to get a shot of dope. Two coppers (one copper is one third of a Chinese cent) was the average price per shot; any coolie could afford that much. But any new customer, or any person in whom the Japanese were particularly interested — promising youngsters, intelligent workers — obtained the poison free of charge. Japan was deliberately and systematically preparing a future military invasion by spreading drug addiction among all classes of Chinese society, undermining the people's health and morale.

This was true all over China, but with Ch'en Chi-t'ang consistently refusing to collaborate with the Chinese Government, the Japanese were particularly active in Kwangtung Province, endeavoring to use him as their tool, flattering and patronizing his regime, and flooding the province with propaganda material directed against Chiang Kai-shek. L. K. had found out that such material was printed in Japan, that it was brought to Canton aboard Japanese warships, that it was transferred into military launches just outside the harbor, which was not deep enough for seagoing vessels, and received ashore by a military escort, who took it to the Japanese Consulate General, whence it was generously distributed among the population. The Chinese Maritime Customs had no jurisdiction over Japanese subjects and could not interfere with military shipments. They were foaming at the mouth, determined to catch the Japs napping. The little customs launches zigzagged round the men-of-war patiently, doggedly, for weeks. At last they were rewarded. Either the Japs were too cocksure of themselves, or one of the shipments was too large for their own launches to handle; whatever the reason, one day they hired a native junk and ordered the Chinese to take a few cases to the shore. The distance was so short that really nothing could happen to the precious load. But L. K.'s men were waiting precisely for such a chance. Chinese craft are subject to customs inspection. In a jiffy the customs launch was on the spot, the junk headed for the customhouse; all cases were opened before the panting Nipponese arrived to claim their "military property." L. K. had to surrender the goods, but he kept the four cases with neatly packed pamphlets. The Japs could not account for these, neither did they attempt to do so; they explained that somebody in Shanghai must have packed them "by mistake"; they had never seen such books before and were not interested in Chinese literature! L. K. sent three of the cases to Sir Frederick Maze, Inspector General of Customs, and the fourth to Generalissimo Chiang Kai-shek, as *corpus delicti*. Both protested to Tokyo against such "unfriendly action." But Tokyo never gave a satisfactory reply.

L. K.* had not yet met the new officials of the municipality and could not introduce me to them, but he sent me in his car to an excellent contact man — Alfred Lin, Reuter's correspondent. After a few minutes' talk with this very amiable young man, I was on my way to my first interview with Chinese officials.

Leaving the busy thoroughfares behind, the car rolled smoothly through wide, tree-lined avenues. Part of the vast municipality

* Mr. L. K. Little was repatriated on the *Gripsholm* and has recently been appointed Inspector General of the Chinese Maritime Customs in Chungking.

compound was still in the process of construction, but the main building — a tall, lofty, dazzling white colonial palace, topped by a brilliantly red-and-yellow roof — was ready. A splendid piece of architecture, where Western utilitarianism and Oriental art were blended so harmoniously that they enchanted the eye.

A sober interior — high ceilings, wide marble stairs, tiled floors, an austere waiting room with large windows overlooking a beautiful landscape . . . Sun Yat-sen's and Chiang Kai-shek's photographs on the wall . . . A heavy carved table in the center, surrounded by four armchairs — teakwood inlaid with white-and-black veined marble — hard but exquisitely cooling to sit on.

One of my usual spells of irrepressible shyness crept up to my throat. Who was I, anyway? A nobody, interested in Chinese reconstruction. I represented no one, and no one had sent for me. Was I entitled to take up their time? How would they receive me? What would they be like? I felt stiff and awkward.

I did not have to wait long. A man entered the room swiftly — a very handsome young fellow with a clean-cut, intelligent face. His elegant sportsman's figure was enhanced by the perfect cut of his white linen uniform. The elastic gait, the graceful, well-rounded movements, were those of a man of the world and a *charmeur*.

"Colonel Li Fang, the Mayor's secretary," he said pleasantly, with a genuine American accent. We shook hands and, for the fraction of a second, I felt that he was sizing me up. Then he perplexed me by acting terribly old-fashioned Chinese. He insisted, with many ceremonious bows, that I should not sit in the armchair I had chosen but in the one on the opposite side, which was the place of honor. All chairs looked alike to me; I assured him lamely that I was a very modest person. But he went into a flowery tirade on the deep meaning and the high ethical value of Chinese traditional politeness, and on the relative importance of chairs, dependent upon whether they were facing the door or the window. A distinguished guest like me had to face the door! He actually made me change places and took the lowly seat I had just abandoned. This performance did not make me feel any easier. While explaining very stiffly the reasons for my visit to China, I searched my memory frantically for anything I had ever read about the Chinese official code of behavior. Alas, all that came back to me was that, if a person of rank offers you a cup of tea, you must receive it with both hands, and that an official visit is ended when your host touches his cup with one hand. There was no tea, and I was paralyzed by the thought of probably committing blunder upon blunder.

Still more disconcerting was the fact that Colonel Li Fang's obsolete conventionalities did not seem to fit in with his personality. Was I such a poor judge of human beings? Nonsense; intuition was the only reliable feeling on earth, and it worked the same, the world over. I racked my brain to solve the mystery, while he was telling me of his extensive travels abroad. He spoke English, French, German and Russian with remarkable ease and his ideas were absolutely up-to-date. Puzzling contrasts . . .

Mayor Tseng Yang-fu was quite different — a stocky, jovial, vivacious man, whose cordial welcome dispelled all my nervousness. Li Fang made a brief exposé of my aims and left us.

Mayor Tseng had studied in Pittsburgh and saw things from an American angle of approach. He was an engineer by profession and by temperament. He had been appointed Mayor of Canton with a mandate to collaborate in the reconstruction of Kwangtung. "It is a dream that has come true," he said; "throughout the years of studies I dreamed of reconstructing my native province." But he was a practical dreamer. He had gone into the problem with all its many details, and his desk was full of projects and blueprints. "Shall I tell you some of my plans?" I was enchanted.

Tseng pulled our chairs to a huge map on the wall, studded with pins and flags. He was a fascinating talker. We traveled on future railroads across fertile plains — improved cotton fields and rice paddies. We blasted tunnels through mountains all covered with priceless camphor trees — Canton's future source of income.

Mayor Tseng's pet idea, however, was the utilization of Kwangtung's waterpower — a gigantic power station would electrify not only the province itself but a good part of South China, and, possibly, even Indo-China. Every village would be able to afford electricity. *Post tenebras lux.* It would raise the standard of living. It would help large-scale development of industry, mining . . . The blueprints, the projects, were there, worked out in detail.

This interview with Mayor Tseng had opened new horizons to me. Up to then, I had met only Chinese diplomats, journalists and students in Europe. Their views on reconstruction were highly theoretical. Here was the first man who knew his facts and figures — a realist with initiative and vision. He had injected live blood into the problem and made it palpable.

Mr. Tseng Yang-fu is now China's Minister of Communications.

Colonel Li Fang's office, where later throughout my stay in Canton I used to drop in almost daily, was small and modestly furnished — a desk, a settee, a few chairs. But, facing each other, on high, daintily carved ebony pedestals, stood a pair of beautiful large eggshell-colored vases of the Ming period. When I admired them, Li Fang smiled moodily: —

"They may seem out of place here, but we Chinese are such queer people — beauty is indispensable to us, even in our everyday life. In Europe, these vases would occupy a place of honor in any museum. They would be soulless, impersonal exhibits. Here they live, they are my companions. Their presence is an inspiration to my work, and when administrative routine grows too vexatious, the purity of their lines is a pleasant reminder of the real values in life. . . ."

We chatted a while about Europe and mutual friends abroad. Then he called a few friends together — colleagues who could be helpful to me — and we went to a restaurant to celebrate my arrival. Though he called it modestly an informal, simple dinner, to me it was my first big Chinese feast. The number and variety of dishes seemed inexhaustible. I know of nothing more pleasing to the eye and to the palate, more sophisticated and more stimulating, than the Cantonese cuisine (as served in China, well understood; for chop suey and the whole range of non-descript, gruesome concoctions sold abroad for foreign consumption are unthinkable in China). The climax of the dinner was a big silver bowl carried in ceremoniously and placed in the center of the table on a silver tripod — shark's fins. Everything else was served on low plates and platters. Shark's fins: the queen of Chinese delicacies, official China's most official viand, served on special occasions to feast dear friends and honored guests — Colonel Li Fang enlightened me gracefully, filling my bowl as though he were performing a rite. Everybody had something to say about shark's fins. Many sharks must be killed, at the risk of human lives, to fill a silver bowl. . . . Only the privileged few could afford the luxury. . . . Millions of common people were ignorant of the taste of this gastronomic treat.

The contents of my bowl did not look at all exciting: transparent fishbones swimming in a thickly gray broth. But oh, the flavor of it! Superior to anything I had ever tasted in life — a subtle, voluptuous poem . . .

Fiery wine, served hot in little cups, accompanied the meal, warming the heart, kindling thoughts, loosening our tongues. Colonel Li Fang made a flowery, witty toast. Someone else followed suit. My turn came. I got up and thanked them, and told them I had never made a speech before and dared not attempt to make one now. But I wanted them to know my sentiments; they could be summed up in two sentences: "Down with unequal treaties," and "Long live China." A moment of surprised silence, then applause. "Long live China," they repeated, and "Long live Poland." Li Fang hugged me impulsively. "You are O.K.," he cried, "I adopt you as my Polish sister." Whereupon we all drank "*Can-pei*," which means "Bottoms up." Then anecdote followed upon anecdote. Jokes exploded like fire-crackers. A charming, noisy, happy atmosphere — Li Fang, with an unbeatable sense of humor, always in the lead.

Then, to their merriment, I parodied Li Fang, as he had received me that morning. He watched me, bursting with laughter. "Now tell me, Chinese brother of mine," I asked, "why did you scare me like this?"

"Who scared whom?" he laughed. "Goodness, you should have seen yourself! This is what you looked like — " He stuck out his chest and posterior, held his head very stiff, and pulled a face like a frustrated old schoolmistress. "*Watch your step,* I said to myself, *here is another of those righteous, unbearable English reformers, who come here to civilize us 'barbarians'!* Well, I know from experience that, when such a creature crosses your path, there is only one charm that works. . . ." He half-closed his eyes, raised his shoulders, put on that disconcerting, supercilious mandarin grin, and singsonged: "The charm of romantic old China . . . it is *so* disarming . . ."

He was irresistibly funny. "*Sacré comédien!*" I laughed.

"*Il n'y a que la comédie pour rendre notre vie un peu plus supportable,*" he retorted. "Now you know why I pulled that stunt this morning? Thank heaven, I was mistaken. Here's to good-fellowship — *Can-pei!*"

Next day I met T. T. Hsiao, director of the official Central News Agency, who happened to be in Canton for a few days, to keep up with Chiang Kai-shek's pacification *démarches*. He treated me with impersonal amiability, promised every assistance, and vanished.

A short time later, a sunny lad entered my hotel room. He wore a Western-style light Shantung suit and a sun helmet.

"Hello," he greeted me, American college boy fashion, "I am Francis Yao of Central News Agency. The boss has assigned me to act as your guide. May I take off my coat and

Col. Li Fang, Ralf Sues and Dr. T. T. Hsiao with members of
China's Central News Agency

Ricksha-Schoolbus   Wheelbarrow-Schoolbus

pour us a cup of tea?" He did it, taking my consent for granted. "Let's talk things over before we start. What do you want to see in particular?"

"Everything. Living China — minus cocktail bars, foreign clubs, dancing — "

" — and flying cockroaches," he completed my sentence with a roguish smile.

"Who told you?"

"Where's the cat? Hello, Gueidze, you big, black devil!" The cat came to welcome him, rubbed against his leg. "You see? I have even learned his name. And, by the way, you'll have to change that name, if you don't want to get into trouble. You can't travel through China with a black cat called 'Devil'! Folks are superstitious; let a child get measles in your neighborhood, or anyone meet with an accident, they will blame it on your four-legged 'evil spirit,' and you might get into a hell of a mess."

"What shall I call him?"

"Call him Guei-Guei, it's almost the same sound, and he'll listen to it, and it means 'Little Precious' or 'Little Darling.' This big monster should be flattered to get such a sweet name!"

"O.K. Thanks for the suggestion. What else do you know about us?"

"I know that Guei-Guei feeds on chicken exclusively, and that he must have fresh sand twice daily. I know that you are crazy about the beggar children across the road, that you don't know a firecracker from a machine gun, that you had a two hours' interview with the Mayor, dinner with Li Fang and his crowd. I know that you are against unequal treaties, that you are a friend of China, that you have a sense of humor, that you have come on your own, to write about China as you see it."

"Congratulations, Mr. Yao," I said, overwhelmed. "This is a remarkable report, so accurate and concise! Are you a detective or a newspaperman?"

"You can call me Francis. I am nothing but a plain, ordinary newshawk. And you need not congratulate me, because it was really a cinch to find out about you — it didn't take more than ten minutes. Hsiao gave me the gist on the official part of it; and when I came to the hotel, I just had to ask one of the bell-hops quite casually, 'What's that foreign devil upstairs like?' and I had the whole flock of them around me, telling me all the secrets of your private life! You don't realize what you are up against in China — four hundred and fifty million of the most curious people in the world; you see, we Chinese are interested in people. As the only foreigner in this hotel, you are quite a sensation. Those kids watch you day and night, they know every step you take, every word you say. They can imitate your gestures — no detail escapes their attention. Don't imagine that you are ever alone or unobserved; they are ever present, eavesdropping, peeping through the keyhole. They can't help it; curiosity is an integral part of our national character. Mind you, it is not maliciousness, just an irresistible urge to get at the bottom of things. They get to the bottom of your trunks too, I am sure — all servants do — locks are no obstacles; there is not one that you can't unlock! You might as well get used to the idea right away — they have probably studied every single one of your belongings with meticulous thoroughness, and may know them better than you yourself."

"Oh, stop it, Francis, this is awful!" I laughed — amused, but feeling pretty uncomfortable. "Now those rascals know my hidden vice, which is a secret even to my best friends — I never sew anything when I can pin it."

Francis had a pleasant, frank way of talking about people and things. I felt as though I had known him all my life. He was reliable, his facts were accurate, his opinions unbiased. Wherever we went, he was received like a friend. And he was just as much at home with high government officials, university professors, industrialists, shopkeepers, workmen, and the ricksha coolies at the university campus, with whom he would chat once in a while.

He was twenty-nine, married, father of three children and a fourth one en route. He spoke of his family with great tenderness, but, like the majority of Chinese, never seemed to be home much. His father seemed to have had a grudge against the government and had exiled himself to Macao. Francis had neither the family backing nor the pull in the Kuomintang indispensable to making a career. He could have made use of his personal contacts, joined the Party, and secured a good position in the administration; but there was no servility and no ruthlessness in his make-up, and bureaucracy was the last thing he aspired to.

Francis had studied journalism in Canton's Lingnan University and at Yenching University in Peking, with Chinese and foreign professors. He had never been abroad. It was amazing to hear him talk on any subject concerning Europe or America — one had the impression that he had spent years over there. He kept abreast of everything that was going on in the world; he seemed to know the streets of Rome and Paris and London just as well as the American skyscrapers and swing and crooning creations of the past ten years. Not that he ever tried to show off — he simply knew. He had edited one of the Yenching U tabloid papers. Then he organized the Canton broadcasting service. Then he got stuck with the Central News Agency, where his talents were not made use of because Mr. Hsiao's vulnerable point was flattery, and Francis lacked that particular talent. All this I learned in the course of time, and not from Francis. We remained friends throughout my stay in China, and as events moved on and moved north, I roamed with him through the streets of peaceful Shanghai, we lived through the bombings of Nanking, and we shared our war experiences on the roof of the *China Press* Building at Hankow during Japanese air raids. We would lose sight of each other for weeks or months, and then meet again and discuss things, as if we had seen each other yesterday. Francis was the finest fellow one could meet. We both loved and enjoyed the rough-and-tumble vulgarity of the streets, the perfume-sodden atmosphere of singsong houses, the clear, limpid air of the fields, the green mountain slopes and the monotonous "*Hei-ho, hei-ho*" of the burden-carrying coolies. And he was a gourmet — not only were his tastes refined, but he knew the intimate secrets of any culinary ingredient, the specialities of every province and restaurant and wayside inn, the flavor of every tea, the bouquet of every wine . . . I think of him with deep gratitude as one of my dearest friends in China.

We started out by calling on the Kwangtung Reconstruction Commission. A young commissioner was appointed to accompany us, whenever we wanted. A motor car was placed at our disposal. The whole transaction did not take five minutes. Efficiency, quick action, and total absence of red tape. Such qualities are rare in any administration. Least of all had I expected to find them in China. We visited the Government Textile Mills outside Canton: wool, cotton, and silk manufacture on a large scale, employing many thousands of men and women. Modern English and American machinery . . . Remarkable organization . . . Looking at the neatly clad girls deftly manipulating whirling spindles and rapidly shifting looms, I admired their machinelike precision. One involuntarily visualized China's colossal potentiality as a future industrial power.

The director, a slender, quiet, elderly gentleman, showed us around. He was particularly proud of the dormitories. I peeped into the girls' rooms — they were tiny cubbyholes, each housing two or four occupants, kept very neatly, but there was positively no floor space: a girl's bed was, at the same time, her chair and her table. Yet they told me that this was a model dormitory! Elsewhere factory girls had to sleep on straw in filthy quarters. The director had had a stone trough built all along the front of the building, with hot water flowing through it from the factory, and the girls were really happy over this unprecedented modern installation, for now they could rinse their dishes and do all their laundering right outside their doors. He had also provided for a little garden with trees, where the workers could relax and have their luncheon. They worked twelve hours a day, seven days a week, and their average wages amounted to twenty Chinese dollars per month. I was dismayed; not later than three months ago, China's delegate had told the International Labor Conference that the Government had introduced the forty-eight-hour week. . . . The director shook his head — this statement had probably been made to save face. In reality he had had to put up a hard fight to arrive at the present schedule; most other factories had longer working hours.

Next we went over the near-by Government Cement Works. I mean that literally. Three kilns were in operation, the fourth was being built, and the engineer in charge was so proud of it, and so eager to show us every bent and valve of his pet installation, that we did more climbing and crawling in one hour there than I had ever done in my seven years in the Swiss mountains. Francis and I emerged from this practical lesson resembling two mudcakes powdered over with coal dust! But we knew the entire process of cement manufacture, and we were happy to have met this fine, young pioneer, who worked shoulder to shoulder with his workmen at expanding the plant and increasing the output. His ambition was to surface all of Mayor Tseng's future highroads in Kwangtung Province, whose country roads were in poor condition; yet only the most urgent repairs could be undertaken, because pressure from above made most of Canton's cement go to Shanghai. And concrete imported from Hong Kong was expensive and paid high duty!

We saw other plants working full blast, feverishly expanding, directed by levelheaded, conscientious men who realized that all progress made in their factories meant a step forward for China. Fertilizers for China's impoverished soil . . . Beer for China's parched throats. . . .

We visited municipal kindergartens, primary and secondary schools. The young educators were all mindful of the old

Chinese proverb: "If you plan for a year, sow grain; if you plan for ten years, plant trees; if you plan for a hundred years, grow men." The children were kept immaculately clean, outdoors or in large, airy classrooms. They were regularly examined by attending physicians and nurses; there was a biweekly dental service, and seasonal vaccination and inoculation to prevent epidemics of smallpox, cholera, typhoid. Minute statistical records and graphs were kept in the well-equipped dispensaries. Much time was devoted to outdoor games and physical training. Great stress was laid upon a modern, practical all-round education, rather than upon the memorizing of the works of the Chinese classics and upon calligraphy which, until a few years ago, had constituted the major part of the curriculum. In the higher grades, boys and girls could choose the profession which appealed to them most. Laboratories, engineering classes, workshops, were at their disposal — with students of chemistry, agriculture, and similar subjects, or skilled mechanics, carpenters, and the like acting as instructors.

There was only one drawback — schooling was not free. The minimum charged per month per child was six Chinese dollars. No coolie, no workman, no petty merchant could afford to keep even one child in school; and Chinese families are very large. . . . Thus the feudal spirit was still prevalent even among those young citizens of the modern Republic. Like shark's fins, education was accessible only to the privileged classes.

"Bamboo wireless" is the technical term given to the incredible rapidity with which news travels in China. One day old friends called on me — Mr. Chen Yin-fun, one of the most capable members of the League of Nations Opium Section, and his wife. They had learned of my presence through the "bamboo wireless." Mr. Chen was on furlough, and on the point of resigning from the Geneva institution, because he had found a more satisfactory job in Canton: that of the Dean of the Faculty of Law at Sun Yat-sen University. Not that it was better paid — the salary was one fifth of what he was earning in Geneva — but he felt China needed him.

I was delighted to see them again, and the very next day Mrs. Chen and I set out to get a cool Chinese dress for me. We bought six yards of Cantonese black silk, which is non-transparent, delightfully cooling, and "impregnated" — that is, it washes like oilcloth and need not be ironed. "*Maintenant couturière*," said the little lady, whose French was rather fragmentary, and sang the praises of her dressmaker.

Mrs. Chen believed in the beneficial effects of physical exercise and abhorred waste of money — she would not hear of taking a ricksha. So we walked in the baking heat for a solid hour, the molten asphalt sticking to our heels, farther and farther into the ever narrower growing lanes, where small shopkeepers did business at more accessible prices than the swell establishments along Chungshan Road.

I was nearly fainting, when Mrs. Chen finally led the way through a narrow door into a large loft. The place was cool but so dark that I had to do some blinking before being able to see the interior. Then I opened my eyes much wider than usual. About a dozen boys between sixteen and twenty, clad in white union suits, were sitting at two long tables littered with colorful tissues. Each of them had a piece of work in his hands. They looked like a busy lot, but, at this moment, hands, scissors, needles were immobilized in mid-air, and twelve pairs of eyes stared at me in utter amazement. A foreign woman!

"*C'est ça, votre 'couturière'?*" I asked my guide flabbergasted. She beamed up at me: "*Si, si, couturière.*"

The boss wore a long, dark gown; he approached us with dignified composure. He and Mrs. Chen looked at my silk and discussed the terms. The tailor boys resumed their work, looking up as often as they could, and jabbering excitedly in low tones. Their tongues moved as fast as their needles.

Mrs. Chen had told me that she never paid more than three dollars for the dressmaking. Now she was flushed and embarrassed: the man asked one dollar more; she was so sorry — would I consider paying four dollars? Of course I would, but I was curious to know why he was charging more? She asked him to explain the reasons. He did so, elaborately, and she translated every word conscientiously. There really was no necessity for her going to this trouble, for his facial expression and the gestures which accompanied every sentence were sufficiently eloquent in themselves.

He turned me round, as if I were a mannequin. His hand followed the curves of my body, pausing here and there to emphasize a distressing prominence. "It is very difficult to make a dress for a foreign woman," he said. "A Chinese lady has a straight body — a dress hangs properly on her. But look at this top frontside . . . special provisions have to be made to take care of this. And look at this bottom backside — all round, and how round! Very complicated to make a dress fit such a figure . . . A great misfortune that your friend is a cripple — most foreign women are cripples . . . Our establishment charges one dollar more for a hunchback, and this here is more aggravating — there are several hunches. . . ."

I tried to keep a straight face, but this was more than I could stand. The boys watched and listened eagerly — giggling and puffing with laughter, and poking each other's ribs. My little lady was crimson; she thought I must be terribly hurt. I burst out laughing, and told her that I had never enjoyed anything more than this amusing scene. It was certainly worth the extra dollar! We all ended up by laughing heartily. Then Number One took my measurements in the boys' wardrobe — the only place where privacy reigned.

As promised, my first Chinese dress was ready twenty-four hours later. It fitted like a glove, and yet it disguised my "hunches" and made me look taller and slimmer — it was really a masterpiece of a first-class *couturière*. I felt cool, lighthearted, and thankful.

* * *

On September 1, 1936, the New Life Movement was officially inaugurated in Kwangtung Province. The entrances of all gambling establishments — many hundreds of them — were nailed down with boards. And the rattling of mah-jong blocks stopped abruptly everywhere.

National banners, New Life scrolls and streamers waved from the houses. The walls were plastered with slogans advising the population how to behave to become worthy citizens. Crack troops paraded through the streets. Crack orators spoke at street corners, motion picture theaters, schools. There were patriotic pageants, songs, theatricals.

One could hardly recognize Canton. Thousands of spick-and-span, eagle-eyed policemen unremittingly demonstrated to, and upon, the people of Canton how good and beautiful they must be to become perfect citizens in the old, Confucian sense. They regulated the traffic! It was no easy job: shouting and sweating, they pushed the solid masses of pedestrians from the street onto the chockful curb. And the Cantonese learned the astounding theory that the street was destined exclusively for vehicles! And that vehicles had to keep on the left side of the street and pedestrians on the left side of the sidewalk.

Policemen stopped thousands of men and women, ordering them to button their garments. Every button, if you please — never mind the heat — the New Life Movement forbids open collars.

"Mister, put your hat straight on your head — you may not wear it in your nape — it is unworthy of a Chinese citizen."

"Mister, throw that cigarette away — a decent Chinese does not smoke in the street."

"Lady, you so-and-so — you just spat on the street, I saw you do it! Who ever thought of such a thing, spitting in public! Don't you know that spitting is detrimental to the health of the nation? The New Life Movement forbids you to desecrate the soil of your ancestors. . . ."

No one dared disobey, for the policemen had strong, agile

fists and authority to use them for the good of the country. And they were democratic, too: the law applied to all Chinese, rich and poor. I saw them beat up some beggars and quite a number of ricksha coolies, because they had dared to appear in public wearing rags. Some were sent home to "change into a more proper apparel"; others were put in prison.

The police penetrated even into restaurants and tea houses. "Hey, you, over there, sip your tea noiselessly — don't you know this is one of the most important rules of the New Life Movement? How shall we ever become a great nation, if our table manners are obsolete?"

This unusual way of introducing a new era had something disquieting about it. However, my Chinese friends assured me that all this would blow over as soon as the Chiangs left South China and the banners were taken down. The people did not take to the New Life Movement; it did not appeal to their common sense, it only appealed to their sense of humor.

Sun Yat-sen's *Three Principles of the People* carried in them the promise of democracy and a better standard of living. The New Life Movement made no promises, not even that the people would get "a pie in the sky when you die."

The New Life Movement had first seen the light of day in the hectic year of 1934, which marked a turning point in Chinese history and a change in Chiang Kai-shek's policy. Almost overnight, the battling war lord had embarked upon the road of enlightened statesmanship. The task before him was colossal: to unify 450,000,000 people into a nation — to shake up the dormant, corrupt, self-glorious administration — to modernize China's life.

The first point was relatively the easiest. He undertook to pacify the country by means of persuasion rather than by the sword. In China everything can be arranged by means of negotiation. There were no fundamental differences of opinion between Chiang and the governors of the various provinces. They

all wanted a strong national government, provided they were
assigned a part in it, and provided that their personal interests
were safeguarded. And, almost without exception, they agreed
upon the suppression of the Chinese Red Army and the eradication of Communism — two items which stood topmost on
Chiang's program. Nevertheless it took considerable skill and
patience on his part to arrive at a compromise, in each case,
which would ensure not only smooth working but active collaboration with Nanking, and under Nanking's guidance. He
scored success upon success in this diplomatic field, in a record
time unprecedented in history. Province after province rallied to
the national flag; the national forces were swelled by the in-
corporation of former autonomous armies, and participated in
the anti-Red campaigns directed by the Generalissimo in person.

The left wing of the Kuomintang, many patriots and patriotic
organizations and the Chinese intelligentsia and student body
campaigned for the cessation of civil war and demanded armed
resistance against Japan. But the mind of Generalissimo and of
the governmental majority was set on fighting the Communists
first. Opinions contrary to this policy were suppressed as subversive activities. The "you-can-do-business-with-Japan" theory
was upheld by many outstanding politicians and businessmen
and military leaders. The invader was constantly gaining ground
and met with no opposition.

In 1931, at the outbreak of the Manchurian Incident, China's
delegate to the League of Nations Council, Dr. Sao-ke Alfred
Sze, had submitted the "conflict" for settlement to the League,
and gave assurance in the name of his Government that China
would not fight. Young Marshal Chang Hsueh-liang had received orders from the Generalissimo to withdraw his troops
without offering resistance. In 1932, General Tsai Ting-kai's
19th Division, who so gallantly defended Shanghai, received no
reinforcements and had to retreat. A year later, Japan had been
further appeased by the Wang Ching-wei–sponsored Ho-Umetsu
Agreement, which gave the Nipponese virtually a free hand in

North China. Notwithstanding this critical situation, Chiang Kai-shek had concentrated upon internal issues.

His headquarters feverishly issued orders and projects intended to push China forward in every domain of her national life within the shortest time. The ambitious plan was to accomplish within ten years what it had taken any Western country centuries to accomplish. For lack of a constitutional government, the planning and a good part of the execution lay in the hands of an anonymous brain trust, composed of foreign and Chinese experts and missionaries, most of whom had more good will than practical experience. Despite this haphazard combination, despite hasty and sometimes not very mature planning, and the shortage of trained personnel, there was remarkable progress. But the shortcomings inherent in a one-party government which ruled without the participation of the people confined this remarkable progress to a few experimental centers. And it was difficult for a man with Generalissimo Chiang's background to approach the problem in the same way as Dr. Sun Yat-sen, the revolutionary, the Father of the Republic, the democrat. Chiang Kai-shek believed in discipline and spoke to the people like a military instructor.

Having decided upon China's Renaissance, Generalissimo took the customary step of preparing his declaration of policy, the New Life Movement. It was based on four of the Confucian principles, and was expressed in Chinese in four simple characters: *Li, I, Lien,* and *Chih.* The translation into English is much more involved; there is an extensive literature on the subject. One of the varying interpretations, given by Madame Chiang, reads: —

First is *Li,* which, in the ordinary and most accepted form of translation, means courtesy. And by courtesy is meant that which emanates from the heart — not a formality which merely obeys the law.

The second is *I,* which, roughly translated, means duty or service, toward the individual's fellow man and toward himself.

The third is *Lien*, meaning clear definition of the rights of the individual and of the degree in which those rights may be enforced without infringing upon those of others. In other words, honesty. A clear demarcation between what is public and what is private, what is yours and what is mine.

The fourth is *Chih*, which denotes high-mindedness and honor.*

In the same article Madame Chiang explained that: —

Each nation, according to its lights, has sought to find a way out of stagnation into normalcy. Italy has its Fascism, Germany its Nazism, the Soviet Union its first and second five-year plan, and America its New Deal. The primary aim of each is to solve the economic problems involved and to bring material prosperity to the people.

It is not believed that China's lights were at their brightest at the time these four principles were revived as a way out of stagnation into normalcy. The New Life Movement did not herald a New Deal; at best, it could be called a code of ethics. It appealed to a few scholars, to Christian missionaries, and to a handful of chivalrous juvenile enthusiasts, but not to the wise old realist, the Chinese commoner.

Analysts, economists and ordinary people who failed to see how the four principles were to solve China's economic problems were referred to the "Forty-four Practical Rules" issued by New Life Headquarters: *Li*, for instance, teaches tidiness and cleanliness in dress and habit, because

. . . it was felt that if a man were sloppy and careless about his personal appearance, about his bearing, and about his general conduct, he would also be untidy in thought. Or, to put it in another way, it was recognized that there is ground for thinking some truth exists in the Neoplatonic theory that outward beauty is a manifestation and a forerunner of inward and spiritual beauty.*

* "New Life in China," published in the *Forum*, June 1935.

However, though unworkable in itself, the New Life Movement had its appreciable advantages. It was an excellent medium for propaganda abroad. It afforded an ideal to which the youth could aspire. Nonpolitical in character, it was a convenient whip which could be cracked over the heads of objectionable officials and party members. And, last not least, it served as the invaluable magician's hat out of which Generalissimo and Madame could conjure up any reform or organization without having to pass through the slow-motion administrative procedure.

Northbound for Shanghai on the *Hai-Li*, a trim little coastal steamer built two years before in London . . . The "first class foreign" on the upper deck had luxurious cabins and sitting rooms. It was fenced off from the lower deck by heavy steel bars, and each of the two doors was guarded by a fierce armed soldier. But I traveled "second class Chinese." Mine was a four-berth cabin — four planks, each covered with a thin straw mat. No bedding. No floor space. I had reserved a lower berth, but another woman occupied it, so I climbed on an upper berth and yanked Guei-Guei's basket up. A storm of protest came from another companion — she could not bear the smell of a cat. So I chose the coolest corner for Guei on the upper deck, made friends with the Chief Engineer, and Guei traveled like a prince.

One thing I shall never forget is a storm while I was on the *Hai-Li*. A night of howling tempest, frantically screaming women; a deckful of pitifully writhing human forms, brown distorted sweating faces in the flickering candlelight — audibly seasick, visibly seasick over their wretched bundles and ailing neighbors . . . And above this nauseating atmosphere that filled our ears, eyes and nostrils, the high-pitched, disemboweling sound of a Chinese fiddle — a young poet, two cabins from mine, poured all his heart's rapture over the unleashed elements into his two-stringed *peepa*.

*   *   *

We stopped a day in Swatow, and Miss Wang took me to see some friends who had a big embroidery business. The owner was a youngster who had started a small workshop two years before and now owned two big factories, employing thousands of girls and worrying for fear that he could never fill the rapidly increasing orders he received from all over the world, particularly from the United States. All factories were working full blast.

I was curious about the unusual quantity of wooden cases filling the halls and courtyards and marked SWITZERLAND or BELFAST, IRELAND. The explanation was simple: the cases came from Switzerland with bales of batiste, and from Ireland with bales of linen. The Chinese cut and embroidered the material into thousands of gross of dainty handkerchiefs and doilies, packed them neatly into the readdressed cases and returned them to Europe where they were sold as Swiss and Irish embroidery.

All this was possible because Chinese labor was so cheap — a topnotch skilled girl earned twenty to twenty-five Chinese dollars a month, a mere farthing. Customs duties were exorbitant. In addition there was the return freight and insurance. Yet it paid the importers to have the work done at the other end of the world. The magic label *"Made in Switzerland"* on a high-class Chinese embroidery increased the market price approximately tenfold. As a net result, the once prosperous Appenzell, Switzerland, industry had gone to pieces; within a year's time practically the whole population of the district was reduced to starvation. The maidens of Appenzell in their colorful national costumes, who used to sit at their windows in long rows, busily embroidering and singing, disappeared. They went to earn a living in the overcrowded towns. Only old people stayed behind, loathing "those dirty Chinks" who had robbed them of their prosperity. And the young Chinese girls, bent over their tambour frames twelve hours a day, underpaid, underfed, never so much as noticed that prosperity had shifted to Swatow.

IV

Shanghai

THE PORT OF SHANGHAI was different from the other Oriental ports. There was no gaiety. People had hard, bitter expressions, and there was no exuberant noise. A woman in black pants and a white blouse, and with an old-fashioned knot in her nape, was the captain of a fleet of floats. She barked shrill, brief orders. Her crew executed them deftly. In a few minutes the floats were lined up, made fast, forming a pontoon over which the *Hai-Li* passengers went ashore.

Let other people sing the praises of Shanghai. Granted it was a great modern city, a prodigious industrial and commercial center — the New York of the Far East, so far as buildings and business, air-conditioned hotels, restaurants, swell bars and dancing are concerned. But New York's grandeur — the sweeping gesture of a giant sure of himself, a giant who can afford a carefree smile — was painfully absent from Shanghai. The city was cut up into several areas which hardly resembled one another — the International Settlement, the French Concession, the Chinese cities. But the atmosphere in all of them was identical. Cold, hard, conceited faces. Everybody seemed to despise everybody else.

Shanghai was not a city where East and West shook hands. It was a jungle where cutthroat met cutthroat. A beautiful Shanghai society girl summed up the legal situation with a disdainful smile: "Only imbeciles have to abide by the law. No intelligent person is poor in Shanghai." Of course this may be true in any big city, but nowhere was corruption so apparent.

* * *

I was staying with Aimée and Dr. Frank B. Millican, veteran Presbyterian missionaries who had lived thirty years in Shanghai. They headed the Christian Literature Society and the Christian Broadcasting Station. They were saintly people, as unworldly as one could imagine, and knew absolutely nothing of Shanghai's gayer or darker side — not even the name of a night club or a café. To them every human being was a sinner, but a potential follower of Christ, and as such they treated him with patient kindliness. When I think back, I still wonder how they tolerated a visitor like me. I seemed to do everything they did not do. I tuned in to jazz music, I smoked, I drank whisky, I used words that made their hair stand on end, I sometimes even came home after 10 P.M. They suffered in silence.

Bishop Logan H. Roots of Hankow dropped in one day. I had met him in Geneva with the Oxford Group. In China he was less Groupy and more human — a grand old gentleman, slim, with twinkling blue eyes, a fine smile on his thin lips, and the most unassuming, modest attitude I ever saw in a bishop. And that means something in China, where bishops are not a rarity. I met a dozen of them within a few weeks. Their rank equals that of a governor of a province. Bishop Roots was a kindly soul who loved all human beings quite indiscriminately. He asked everybody's opinion and was eager to learn from everyone. He never dabbled in politics. He knew practically all people who had been members of the government during the past forty years, and had a particularly great admiration for Chiang Kai-shek, Madame, the H. H. Kungs. Like most missionaries of high rank, he was aware of current events, official and otherwise, and always emphasized only the best side of the present government — not only because such policy was in the interest of missionary organizations but also because of his personal loyalty to the Chiangs, who had tremendously bettered the lot and the standing of missionaries and whom he believed to be a real power for Christianity in China.

I had been waiting for him, as he had promised to introduce me to W. H. Donald, Chiang Kai-shek's Number One adviser, that legendary Australian of whom every white man said only that he was "O.K." No one seemed to be able to give any details, except that he had come to China as a very young newspaper reporter and had, for the past thirty years, been adviser to a number of leading personalities, at the Imperial Court and under the Republic, and lately to the Young Marshal, Chang Hsueh-liang, whose father Chang Tso-lin had been the last powerful war lord of Manchuria. Donald had the ear of the Chiangs, and Donald was the person anyone who wanted to know something about China must meet.

Bishop Roots and I walked over to the Cathedral talking about China's opium situation. While the Bishop phoned to arrange for an appointment, I played with a litter of puppies on the church lawn. Donald was a busy man, and we did not expect to see him for a few days. But presently the Bishop came out in excited hurry: "Ralf, Mr. Donald wants to see you right away." He hurried me into a ricksha, gave the coolie the address of the hotel, and off I went alone. The Bishop had another appointment and could not accompany me.

The first adjective I found for Donald was "volcanic." The whole question of opium was obnoxious to him. He did not want to have anything to do with it. He talked for an hour. The flood of words was breathtaking. I could hardly put in a question, from time to time. He stood before me or paced up and down the small room — tall, broad-shouldered, with a strong, ruddy face and curiously streaked gray hair, a willful chin, a determined mouth and extraordinary, world-conscious eyes that look right through people and things and cannot be fooled.

Accustomed to the finely chiseled Geneva speeches and international diplomatic drivel, I was flabbergasted to hear a man in so high a position talk sense with brutal frankness and a remarkable plainness of expression. He did not give a damn whether people liked it or not. He would not stand for anything that was not on the level.

If I wanted to know why Donald was through with the opium problem in China, here was the reason: Generalissimo had asked Donald's opinion, and Donald had advocated ruthless suppression. "You've got the armies and you've got machine guns — mow them down, every damn son-of-a-bitch who refuses to pull up the poppies and poisons the nation with opium and drugs." Generalissimo agreed and published his Six-Year Opium Suppression Plan, with death penalty for all offenders. Then Donald fell ill and stayed almost a year in a Hong Kong hospital between life and death. When he came back to Nanking, the whole opium policy had changed. Some blighter or other had persuaded the Generalissimo to add an Opium Monopoly "for better control," and to reduce production gradually, instead of suppressing it radically. Donald got as mad as a hornet. He told the Generalissimo that he was through with opium and would attack the Government's policy in the press, and he did. When Chiang Kai-shek established the Farmer's Bank, backed by Opium Revenues, Donald wrote scathing articles in China's English newspapers. Madame translated them to the Generalissimo. Generalissimo did not like it, but it was part of their agreement: Donald had safeguarded his journalistic liberty. If he did not like a thing, no one could stop him from publishing the fact. The Chiangs could kick him out, if they chose, but they could not make him pull his punches.

I left him quite overwhelmed by his candor. Could I come again to learn something about China's reconstruction? "Sure, just call me up and I'll give you all the dope you want."

I let a few days pass, then called him. "Would it disturb you if I drop in for a moment?" "Of course, it would disturb me. People always disturb me," was his sonorous answer. Intimidated, I stammered that I would try some other time, but he laughed: "Come over right away, we'll have a snack and a chat."

A tall, slightly stooping man with curly fair hair was taking leave of him. He accompanied him to the elevator, came back and said: "That was Lossing J. Buck. He came up at three o'clock for a five minutes' chat; it is seven now." Professor Buck had been described to me as the most taciturn man in China. "Oh, is he such a great talker?" I asked Donald innocently. He gave me a quick, inquisitive glance and grinned. . . . "No. I guess he is such a great listener."

This confession revealed the whole fellow in a flash. Quick reaction, candid self-criticism, good-humored admission of his peccadilloes. Donald was O.K., I repeated to myself after the others. More than that: *il a de l'envergure* — it takes a lot of personality to smile at oneself as one smiles at others. Donald was quite different this time. Opium was out of the way. I wanted to know about China's reconstruction and the Chiangs, and Chang Hsueh-liang, and why and how he had left him and joined the Chiangs. After having reassured himself that I did not work for any newspaper agency, and would not rush into print; that I was nothing but a free-lance journalist, that is to say a queer somebody who might never find a publisher, and that I was listening with interest, Donald let loose and talked till midnight. We did not have the promised snack — neither he nor I ever thought of dinner. Donald was the most fascinating talker I had ever heard. He spoke with the simplicity and the enthusiasm of a college boy to whom life is one big adventure, and with the fine skepticism of a gay old philosopher who understands humans and sees through their most secret motives. He knew the value of words — he chose them but did not mince them. I had the impression of turning the pages of a richly illustrated picture book on China's contemporary history. In a few colorful words he would paint a person with his chief characteristic and those little details that count. Or he would describe a situation so that it remained in one's memory, unforgettable. People said that he bragged and that his language was unbearably rude. Of course he bragged, but about one and one thing only: his absolute, unconditioned independence. I believed him then, and I saw later that it was true. Donald was the only person in China who could tell everybody what he thought, and get away with it. He made ample use of this extraordinary privilege, especially with the Chiangs and round Headquarters, because he believed in them and in their ability to build up China.

Donald had known the Soong family when May-ling was still a little girl; she sat on Uncle Don's lap and he would tease her by pulling her tresses. He had come to China from Australia as an enterprising young journalist, so poor that he could not pay his passage but worked his way across as the cook's helper. He was lucky in Shanghai. One of the big dailies was looking for a thing unheard-of in Shanghai — a reporter who neither drank nor smoked. Donald had those rare qualifications and got the job. Sometime later he was sent to Peiping to interview a minister at the Imperial Court. He was not admitted into the palace. The gatekeepers chased him away. He managed to penetrate into the garden. The guards kicked him down the stairway. He tried another and yet another entrance. Finally he sat down on the wide marble steps leading to the palace and refused to move. He would damn well get the interview. He waited for hours. A fat mandarin came down the stairs and wondered what the foreign youngster wanted. Donald enlightened him and expressed in unambiguous terms what he thought of the treatment inflicted on the foreign press by the Imperial Court. The mandarin led him into the palace; as in a fairy tale, he was himself the minister. He listened to Donald's views on what should be changed in China and was so taken by his opinions that he asked him to stay as adviser. Advisership seemed to be his real vocation, and adviser he remained to a number of leading personalities in turn. He did not "hold" a job. He lived it. He loved it. It was part of China's history and so intertwined with his own existence that he was incapable of writing a personal letter even to his brother in Australia; it invariably degenerated into a China letter. Donald knew the just value of things, also the value of money. But money did not interest him. The highest he ever earned in China was

NC$1000 per month,* which was about the salary of a foreign
stenographer. He was quite satisfied when his expenses were
paid and when he had a couple of dollar bills in his pocket. With
the economies he had made in China in forty years he had had
a yacht built for himself, a small yacht but so perfect in every
respect that he got sentimental every time he mentioned it. It
lay in Hong Kong and had been there for two years — he longed
to be on it. "If ever I am kicked out of China, I'll do nothing
but yachting," he would say with a sigh.

He had a deep affection for Young Marshal Chang Hsueh-
liang. He did not say it with so many words, but he described
the "young fella" so that one simply had to like the brilliant
young idealist — a sterling character, loyal, courageous, and a
man of heart. (Three months later, when the Young Marshal
captured Generalissimo in Sian, all China was tearing mad and
the Government demanded his death. He sent a wire to Madame
vouching with his head that nothing would happen to the
Generalissimo. No one in Nanking and Shanghai trusted him.
I believe I was the only one in Shanghai who had implicit faith
in his word. I had nothing to go by but this talk with Donald.
The American Consulate General was standing on its head,
expecting Chiang's death, revolution, civil war. The United
States Treasury attaché, M. R. Nicholson, shouted that I was
plumb crazy when I offered to bet ten to one that Chiang and
Chang Hsueh-liang would return to Nanking arm in arm. Of
course it was pure cussedness on my part to predict such an incredible thing; I did it on the principle that "*pour prouver il
faut exagérer.*" I was just as dumbfounded as all the others when
it really happened. But Mr. Nicholson never could get over the
fact that I had "prophesied" the event.)

The Japanese — always watchful not to let any brilliant young
Chinese grow up — had applied to Chang Hsueh-liang the
methods that had proved efficacious in the case of many another:
they inured him to the use of drugs. The practice was to have

* Chinese National Currency dollars.

W. H. Donald and Madame Chiang Kai-shek

a pretty geisha or singsong girl, or a Japanese doctor or dentist, introduce morphine or heroin into the house. An addict took less interest in the affairs of his country, and could easily be managed through the intermediary of the agent who kept him supplied. In the case of the Young Marshal it was a Japanese doctor. He made him smoke opium to cure an attack of indigestion. And when the young man wanted to get rid of the smoking habit, he was given "anti-opium pills" which were nothing but morphine — ten times more powerful than opium. He had begged Donald to help him. Donald demanded unconditional obedience: the young fellow agreed in advance to everything, and Donald turned him over to Dr. Miller, an American physician, who did a wonderful job. After weeks of seclusion, where only Donald and the doctor kept him company, Chang Hsueh-liang emerged a different man. As a "reward" Donald took him to Europe, where they had a wonderful time together. (I remembered the comments made in Geneva by many people who had known the Young Marshal; he had never looked fitter and had regained his spirit, his punch and his brilliance.)

Sometime later, Generalissimo and Madame asked Chang Hsueh-liang and Donald to accompany them on a three-day flying trip. They were both very fond of the Young Marshal; the relationship between him and the Generalissimo was that of younger and elder brother. Donald thought the idea very good but the time limit insufficient. In his witty, challenging way he told the Chiangs they did not know enough about China and the people they were supposed to rule; that they thought in the terms of Shanghai and the Eastern seaboard. He would show them their country, if they wanted, but it would take more than three days. Madame was fascinated, and Generalissimo agreed. The trip took three months. Donald showed me his large map with a network of neatly traced red, blue and black lines covering a good part of China — every flight was recorded and numbered. Donald poured forth reminiscences. Part of the time they were "chasing the Reds" — the Red Army trekking to the Northwest from Kiangsi Province, and battling its way across some 3000 miles, pursued by the Kuomintang troops. Donald's pointing pencil would stop. . . . "Here we got one of the worst lickings . . . Headquarters were trapped and we had to run for our lives. They nearly got the Generalissimo then. How they do it, beats me. They had no food, they had no money, and their ammunition was so scarce that they had to count the bullets. They were fighting us with a few hundred rifles and a dozen light machine guns, with sabers, spears and pitchforks. The government troops — crack divisions, well equipped and trained by German instructors — blasted them out of town after town with light field artillery. They could not hold anything, they could not dig in anywhere. And then when we thought we had them beaten for good, they would make a comeback in even greater numbers than before. They would attack us on the roads, outflank us, cut off our lines of communication, carry off our supplies, encircle us. We had a hell of a time getting out of the mess, waiting for reinforcements."

Donald was full of other stories, too — contacts were made with officials in the various provinces, problems were discussed, differences ironed out. Or the little party would stop at most impossible, out-of-the-way places, spend a night at an inn or in a temple, talk with the common people. There is no doubt that this trip really laid the foundations for Chiang's unified China.

Here is one characteristic little incident: Somewhere in a remote village they met a man who had the national flag tied round his hips like an apron. Astonished at the indignation of the strangers, he explained placidly that he was a butcher and that this piece of cloth came in very handy, as blood showed less on a red background. Chiang foamed and wanted the man hanged there and then. Donald chipped in: The hanging of one butcher was not enough. Something more had to be done to rehabilitate the flag. Instead of a hair-raising performance which would have only local effect, Chiang might use his power to order obligatory flag raising ceremonies throughout the country. Not the butcher but the Government was to blame for his ignorance. The people were loyal to their families, to their village, to their province, but did not know the meaning of a national emblem, of patriotism. Chiang saw the point and issued the order. After that day, every morning and night, school children, students, soldiers, officials and organizations rallied round the flagpoles to salute the symbol of China.

During that trip Madame had come to rely upon Donald for help and advice. On their return, she asked him to become her adviser. His reaction was truly Donaldesque: "What? Adviser to a woman? To the most capricious animal heaven ever created? Not on your life." Which made Madame redouble her efforts. She even got the Young Marshal to agree, though his heart was heavy. Generalissimo did not like the idea at all. However, "*Ce que femme veut, Dieu le veut.*" Madame arranged a lunch just for three. She usually interpreted, as Generalissimo spoke no English and Donald had refused to learn Chinese. But on this occasion she did not have much to interpret, as the Old Man maintained silence. Foreign food was served; Donald refused to eat "Chinese" or to handle chopsticks. Over the dessert, Generalissimo finally turned to Donald and asked him with condescending mockery how he would go about reconstructing China, if he had the power.

"First, I would shoot everybody who spoke about 'saving face.' Second, I would shoot everybody who said '*Meiiou fadze*' ["It cannot be done"]. Third, I would shoot every damn fool in the administration," was Donald's reply.

Generalissimo meditated; his face broadened into a grin. "Then I would have to set up an arsenal in every village."

The ice was broken. Generalissimo joined forces with Madame, and Donald moved to Headquarters. They never called him "adviser." They called him "friend." And I do not believe they ever had a better and more loyal one.

To hear Donald talk, Madame had started and was carrying on the vast reconstruction program single-handed. He described her working day: From 5.30 to 6.30, prayers and Bible discussion with Generalissimo. After breakfast, work at her desk — an enormous correspondence to take care of. A model Christian, she rallied all missionaries to the cause. She interpreted at all important interviews for her husband. She was the soul of the New Life Movement. She was the very spirit of the two Chiang Kai-shek orphanages for the Children of the Heroes of the Revolution in Nanking. She was Chairman of the Aeronautics Commission, and had put order into the air force. Just now she was conducting a relentless drive to get airplanes as presents for Generalissimo's fiftieth birthday on October 30. Chinese in the country and overseas were contributing anything from coppers to millions, and an appreciable number of planes had already been donated or were constructed. Mussolini had sent a superb bomber.

Madame was interested in everything, he said, she helped in actively improving the morale of Generalissimo's officers' corps at the Officers' Moral Endeavor Association. She was responsible for the setting-up of the Economic Research Bureau, which studied the country's resources in detail. She lashed out mercilessly at every act of corruption in the administration, arousing the wrath of a good many members of the Kuomintang. She was the living link between the Generalissimo and the West, and if relations with Great Britain and the United States improved steadily, Madame was the one who should be thanked for it.

Donald beat the most bewitching talkers to whom I had ever listened in my life. His enthusiasm carried one away. Had I come from anywhere else but Geneva, I should probably have accepted everything he said about Madame blindly, and swelled the stream of international propaganda by some gushing articles. As it was, my keenest interest was aroused and I promised myself to see all the manifestations of her activity which Donald had recommended.

When leaving Geneva I had vowed never to look into opium matters again. I would look for reconstruction work and human interest stories, but would leave the narcotics question severely alone. After all, Chiang Kai-shek's Six-Year Suppression Plan, started two years before, was now in full swing. He had pledged himself to eradicate dope in China by the end of 1940. It was a colossal undertaking and nobody knew how he could possibly bring it to a successful end. In many provinces the sovereignty of the Nanking Government was still only nominal. National and provincial officials were used to getting their share of opium revenues. The Japanese had been poisoning the Chinese people with tons and tons of morphine and heroin for the past twenty-five years as a matter of national policy, preparing the ground for future military conquest. China's own opium producers and merchants were too powerful for the Government to cope with. Chiang's police force was insufficient to handle so vast a problem. Besides, any trafficker could escape justice by moving into a Foreign Concession. There were five million addicts in the Yangtze Valley alone, and many more in the rest of the country. They were to be registered and forced to undergo compulsory treatment, and there was capital punishment for those who would relapse after having been cured, as well as for dope traffickers and manufacturers. But the facilities for such mass registration were meager, and the National Health Administration, still in its infancy, possessed neither the hospitals nor the beds nor the indispensable medical personnel. Notwithstanding these unsurmountable obstacles, Generalissimo had made a commendable start; the area under poppy cultivation was reduced in several provinces under his jurisdiction. A few hundred thousand addicts had been registered, a few thousand cured, and a few hundred people executed for illicit transactions. Stuart J.

Fuller, United States representative on the Geneva Opium Advisory Committee, had congratulated the Chinese Government upon its energetic and successful efforts. In view of the situation, I felt that, in fairness to Chiang Kai-shek, he should be left alone until 1940, and, in fairness to myself, I should be allowed to look at the brighter side of China and, for once, to ignore the obnoxious narcotics question.

However, I had counted without Shanghai. My reputation as anti-opium crusader was well established before my arrival. The photos of Chu Hsueh-fan and of myself, taken by those Chinese reporters at Colombo, Bombay and Singapore, had appeared in many papers. I had the definite impression that Chinese official circles suspected that I visited China for the purpose of prying into the secrets of this unsavory problem. They did their best to keep every scrap of information from me. On the other hand, Shanghai's international officials and diplomatic officers, with a number of whom I had had correspondence from Geneva, went out of their way to give me the high lights of the situation. They were only too glad to show and tell me all the things which they could not very well embody in an official report to the League of Nations. Those men were reliable sources of information, as they had been following developments very closely and had proof for any statements they advanced.

The greatest defaulters in the set-up were the Japanese in China, about seventy-five per cent of whom participated either directly or indirectly in the manufacture, sale and distribution of morphine and heroin. This was officially sanctioned and sponsored by Japanese consuls, and truckloads or trains carrying narcotics from factories in Shanghai, Tientsin, Hankow, or from ships were convoyed by Japanese soldiers to the centers of distribution. There could be no doubt that the demoralization and slow poisoning of millions of Chinese were part of Japan's national policy, preparing the ground for a future military invasion. The cynicism of it was that the victim paid ready cash for his own poisoning.

Under the extrality rights provided for by the unequal treaties between foreign powers and China, foreigners in China were tried by their own national consuls, Chinese living within the International Settlement or any of the foreign-policed concessions were tried by the local international or foreign courts, and only Chinese living under Chinese jurisdiction were tried by the Chinese authorities.

The difference in the sentence passed by the various courts was, to say the least, amazing. Under Chinese jurisdiction, capital punishment was meted out for the manufacture, sale, transport and distribution of drugs. Addicts were given compulsory treatment; if they relapsed into the habit later, they were shot. In the International Settlement, any of these offenses was punished with twelve years' imprisonment, addicts being disintoxicated before starting their term. The Japanese never arrested anyone for narcotic offenses, but if any Japanese or Chinese, arrested by any of the other police forces, was handed over to them for trial, they had to deal with the case, for the sake of saving their international face. However, fines were never higher than ten yen, and the longest prison term hardly ever exceeded three days!

In the French Concession, which was a haven for gangsters and for every form of illicit transaction, hardly anyone was ever arrested. It was the "sphere of interest" of China's Opium Tsar and Master of Shanghai's underworld, Tu Yueh-sen. He lived there, had a seat on the Municipal Council, and maintained the very best relations with the French authorities, whose sojourn in China he rendered more agreeable by means of very generous gifts, appropriate to their ranks. From the captain down to the cop, the men in the French Concession Police were receiving bonuses averaging three times their salaries. This must have helped them to close an eye to their benefactor's activities.

He was by far the most powerful man in China, and the Government itself had to count with this power. Tu was the acting chief of two combined secret societies, the Green Circle and the Red Circle. Foreign law-enforcement officers called them bandit organizations, but a number of missionaries and even some very level-headed Sinologues maintained that the Green Circle at least used to be a very respectable high-class fraternity, and that the great majority of its members still adhere to the principles of human decency. The society has millions of members in all walks of life, and I know a few of them whose moral integrity is beyond any shadow of doubt. No one could tell me how Tu Yueh-sen had obtained control over the Green-and-Red Circle, but he had certainly succeeded in introducing the fiercest elements of gangsterdom into its ranks.

Tu was a combination of Al Capone and Rockefeller. He was one of the most important pillars of Shanghai's financial, social and political life. He controlled an ever-growing number of banks, was the chairman of the Chinese Ratepayers' Association, owned factories of all descriptions, financed rural and urban reconstruction projects, advanced money to big landowners, and to small farmers through the medium of co-operatives. Outside of Shanghai, and particularly for foreign consumption, he was known under the generic term: "the Shanghai bankers." Without the support of the Shanghai bankers, Chiang Kai-shek and many of the men in the Government would never have been able to reach their present positions. They had largely financed Chiang's fight against the various war lords, his break with the Communists in 1927, and the ten year long anti-Red campaigns. Now he controlled Shanghai's labor and unofficially policed the French Concession for Chiang, "mopping up subversive elements."

Tu financed opium production in China, imported Iranian opium by the shipload, financed narcotics manufacture, and had a rake-off from practically every dope transaction in the country. In addition, he was the Chinese partner to the powerful international drug ring which had begun to extend its activities to the Pacific Coast of Canada, the United States and Latin America.

There was no anarchy or disorder in Shanghai's underworld. Every racket was perfectly organized, had its own businesslike department and responsible head. There was no free-lance stealing, murder or kidnaping. A stolen watch could be retrieved from the competent department on payment of a "remuneration." Tu Yueh-sen was the boss of it all; gambling, prostitution, blackmail and other vices and rackets were all sources of his revenues.

People who dared oppose Tu met with a fatal accident. In some cases, where higher personalities were involved, he was more considerate; the person would receive a casket with Mr. Tu's compliments; usually so delicate a reminder would bring about the desired agreement.

Government officials or important personalities coming to Shanghai had to pay a "protection fee" for their safety.

Madame Chiang had persuaded the Generalissimo to ignore this rule when they were newly wed. They traveled incognito. Soong May-ling — young, unruly, and proud of her new position — had decided that her husband had sovereign power in China, Shanghai included, and need not respect the dictates of a gangster. Two hours after their arrival — Generalissimo was out on business — a beautiful limousine with a pretty maid called for Madame, to take her "to her sister." Madame left, and never reached her sister's house. On his return, many hours later, Generalissimo smelled a rat and shook with anxiety. Propriety would not permit of personal inquiry, so he called on his brother-in-law, T. V. Soong, renowned for his great talent as mediator.

T. V. phoned the Master of Shanghai and was courteously informed that Madame Chiang was safe and in perfect health; that she had been found motoring alone with only a maid accompanying her through the streets of Shanghai, a very imprudent thing to do; that she had been escorted to a comfortable villa, and surrounded with the respect due a lady in her elevated position, but that, notwithstanding all this, she showed signs of displeasure and refused to take any nourishment, solid or liquid. Tu deplored the fact that the Generalissimo had found no time to arrange for suitable protection for himself and Madame — a very dangerous omission in a big city like Shanghai. Would Mr. Soong come over and arrange jointly with him the customary formalities required to assure the safety of his charming sister, and would he then escort her back to her husband, who was probably full of anxiety? T. V. rushed over, settled the formalities, and brought Madame back to Generalissimo. No publicity was given to this incident, but for years to come the Chiangs avoided Shanghai.

When Generalissimo promulgated the Six-Year Plan, in 1934, the opium merchants were highly displeased.

T. V. Soong was appointed Director of Opium Suppression in Shanghai. He handpicked and uniformed the first two hundred of his crack special police for the purpose. But the lads never had a chance to show their talents.

T. V. was shot at by gunmen while he waited for a train. He escaped injury only by discarding his white Panama hat, which the rascals were taking as a target, and by hiding behind a steel girder.

The very next day he also discarded the honor bestowed upon him. The special police was disbanded, and the uniforms sold to the highest bidder.

Something had to be done about Shanghai, the Generalissimo decided, to bring it into line with the New Life Movement. In a modern metropolis people should not be shot at in bright daylight or kidnaped for ransom. Also, a *modus vivendi* had to be found with regard to opium. After some negotiations, a solution was found. Tu Yueh-sen agreed to stop kidnaping and to transfer other rackets underground. In exchange, he asked to be appointed Director of the Shanghai Bureau of Opium Suppression. Chiang agreed.

Sometime later, when Madame Chiang Kai-shek had suggested to the nation that the most appropriate present for the Generalissimo's fiftieth birthday (October 1936) would be airplanes, Mr. Tu contributed a beautiful factory-new plane himself. His picture with the airplane on the Shanghai airdrome appeared in all newspapers. The most beautiful of his four wives performed the christening ceremony. The ship was called *Opium Suppression of Shanghai*. I could not help smiling at Tu Yueh-sen's sense of humor.

The mastermind's latest ambition was to be recognized as a full member of China's élite. The *China Year Book's* "Who's Who" carried the following notice about him in its 1936 edition: —

Born 1887; native of Shanghai. Most influential resident in Shanghai French Concession; well known public welfare worker. President, Chung Wai Bank and Tung Wai Bank, Shanghai. Managing director, Hua Feng Paper Mill, Hangchow. President, Shanghai Emergency Hospital and Jen Chi Hospital, Ningpo. Founder and Chairman, Board of Directors, Cheng Shih Middle School, Shanghai. Councillor, French municipal council, 1931–5. Decorated by the National Government for munificent contributions towards flood relief and purchase of aeroplanes.

Among a host of social functions he also attended the regular Sunday Prayer Meetings in Finance Minister H. H. Kung's house. The missionaries of all the different denominations hoped eventually to bring him into the fold of their respective Churches. My sweet old friend Aimée Millican prayed ever so often that he might see the light someday and become a power for God. I found the same hopeful spirit in Wang Kwei-son, a young social worker to whom Tu Yueh-sen had entrusted his model rural center and eight orphanages. Young Kwei-son was a charming, open-faced lad and loved his work. He assured me that Mr. Tu was a very generous, "heroic" man; the day he found Christ he would give up opium and all other gangster rackets. I visited the rural center and three of the orphanages. One of the things which struck me most was that Tu advanced money to the co-operative at twelve per cent, while other banks took eight per cent interest. The other thing was still more remarkable: Kaochiao was the only place in or around Shanghai where I saw an anti-opium advertisement. It was a huge white painting on a red factory wall featuring a man with a pipe and a legend: how detrimental *ya-pien* was to the human health!

I was learning fast in Shanghai, and one of my most valuable sources of information was a man whose name I may not divulge for obvious reasons, and whom I shall call "Dick." Dick was one of the highest officials in Shanghai's international hierarchy. He had spent over twenty years as a foreign government's official in a number of Chinese ports. He was an uncompromising realist, hard as nails, immaculate in his appearance and official dealings, shrewd, cynical and merciless in his condemnation of corruption wherever he came across it.

There was another aspect of the problem I was interested in, namely seizures and the disposal of confiscated narcotics. Governments were pledged to test such drugs, destroy them if they did not come up to the medicinal standard, or convert them into less harmful substances, like codeine, for instance. As an alternative, confiscated narcotics could be kept as government stocks for emergency purposes, such as war. How was this resolution carried out in China?

Dick took me over to the Chinese Maritime Customs to find out for myself. We were taken down to the vaults — a privilege seldom granted to a stranger. An official piloted us through thousands of bales of silk and cotton, through thousands of cases of manufactured goods of all descriptions — which constituted only an infinitesimal fraction of the colossal volume of contraband with which Japan was flooding China to break her economic resistance.

There were only two seizures in the narcotics safe. One consisted of 113 kilograms of morphine cubes, about the size of and as innocent-looking as sugar cubes, neatly packed in shiny tin containers. They had been seized in two suitcases, with nothing but a suit covering them, so sure was the trafficker of escaping detection. The man and the drugs came from Tientsin. The man had escaped. The maximum dose of morphine administered for medical purposes is one third of a grain; a kilogram equals fifteen thousand grains, that is to say forty-five thousand doses. The shipment of 113 kilograms represented 5,085,000 doses.

The other seizure consisted of two large wooden cases containing heroin in powder form, packed in one-pound paper bags. The printing on the bags was Japanese. Heroin is obtained by transforming morphine, without any loss in weight; it is four times more powerful than morphine. Its use is prohibited in the United States.

The heroin shipment was not even camouflaged. The brazenness of the traffickers shipping hundredweights of this deadliest of high-powered narcotics across the world, as if it were sugar, was appalling. Both shipments were evidently intended for Europe or the United States.* What would become of them now?

Dick was grim and silent. I asked to see one of the responsible Commissioners of Customs.

"What is the routine now of disposing of these confiscated narcotics?" I asked him.

"Up to 1932, we used to destroy them . . ." he said reluctantly.

"I know," I interrupted impatiently, "they were burned in a public place under the auspices of the Chinese Maritime Cus-

---

* The recent trial of Murder Incorporated established the fact that these shipments were the property of the Lepke-Buchhalter gang.

toms. That, at least, was a guarantee that none went back into the illicit traffic. But what is the present practice?"

"We have to turn them over to the Government for destruction or conversion. . . ."

"To Nanking?"

"No, to the local representative — the Shanghai Opium Suppression Bureau."

"To Tu Yueh-sen?"

He nodded.

"What do you suppose he does with the stuff? Destroys it?"

"We have a good idea what he does with it. But this is beside the point. We can't go against official regulations."

The Chinese Government's Maritime Customs Service men were risking their lives to confiscate illicit narcotics shipments and had to turn them over to number one trafficker, to dispose of them as he saw fit!

Dick and other friends had warned me that my mail would probably be censored by Tu Yueh-sen's men, although the Post Office was nominally under a French Commissioner. They said I should take my letters down to any of the outgoing steamers, if I did not want them opened. I was curious to see whether this was true. I wrote a scathing letter about Tu and dropped it into a regular letterbox.

Two days later, Mr. Chu Hsueh-fan called me on the phone. He apologized for not having looked me up earlier and offered to show me some factories, labor unions, and his Labor News Agency, as I was so very much interested in the fate and the organization of the common people of China. As he was the head of Shanghai's Postal Labor Union, I wondered whether his sudden reappearance had anything to do with my letter. Did he know of Tu's censorship? Would he warn me?

We went through a number of factories — the most interesting place, however, was the Labor News Agency, where Chu was the unchallenged boss. It was located in a weird old three-story building that must once have served as tenement house. Steep, narrow stairs, a very poorly furnished editorial office, where he and two other men worked, and a number of bare, dismal rooms, with an occasional bench or two.

The secretary brought me a copy of the *News Bulletin* just off the "press" — not a printing press but one of those obsolete white screen pads which the office boy has to moisten with a brush, fastidiously "printing" one copy at a time.

The bulletin was a little over post-card size and consisted of four to six pages covered with handwritten Chinese characters. It was still moist. I could hardly believe my eyes at this, Shanghai's one and only Labor *News Bulletin*.

"What is your daily issue?" I inquired.

"It depends on the contents," was Chu's reply. "Sometimes we send out six, sometimes eight, seldom more than twenty copies. I told you before that we are a very modest little agency, quite unpretentious. Our overhead amounts to a few pennies' foreign currency. Subscription fees from all Chinese Shanghai papers cover the cost. There are hardly any profits. But all papers carry our news. We deal exclusively with labor items, and we are the only agency of this kind in China. What we discuss is wages, prices, management, current events, resolutions taken by guilds and unions, improved equipment, and the like — also strikes and settlement of differences, whenever they occur. This has news value. But we do not stop there. We are the only people who defend the Shanghai workers against exploitation."

"So this is the headquarters where Shanghai's strikes are organized?" I jested.

Chu smiled back: "Not quite. . . . I would not go so far as to call it organizing. All we do is listen to their grievances, and if their claims are justified we do our best to get them a better deal."

I could not help remembering a description of labor conditions Dr. Victor Hoo had made one day, privately, in Geneva, with reference to Tu Yueh-sen's power and social activities. He said that when, in 1932, all of Shanghai was on strike, the Government asked Tu to help; Tu just snapped his fingers, and every worker went back to his machine.

Was Chu his man, or was he organizing labor against capital? Whatever it was, the more I saw of this earnest, kindly man, the better I liked him. And the name of the Tsar never passed our lips, though the very air seemed saturated with his presence.

I wondered all the way home at the amazing things I had seen. A few pennies, a good deal of human kindness, and they had Shanghai's labor firmly in their grip. Who were they? My curiosity was at bursting point.

There and then I sent out my second trial balloon — I again wrote to Europe slamming at Tu Yueh-sen for the opium racket, and dropped it into the regular letterbox, just to see whether the Post Office would again react.

Two days later, Mr. Chu called unannounced in person. He seemed stern and preoccupied. We spoke about all kinds of things, but the conversation was lagging. We both knew that all our words were padding, and I felt sorry for Chu, whose slumped shoulders and sloppy posture were so unlike his congenial, composed self. He was weighed down by an unusual embarrassment, and Chinese etiquette would not permit me to ask a direct question.

At long last he pulled himself together, sat up straight, looked me in the face and said: —

"You must go see Mr. Tu Yueh-sen."

I was stunned. This was more than I had bargained for. For the sake of face, I tried to smile, but felt that the thing I had conjured up was a sickly idiotic smile. I was afraid.

"Why . . ." I stammered, "where do you get this idea? I had never thought of seeing Mr. Tu."

"You no can write book on China reconstruction without go see him." This unpleasant mission evidently impaired his

English grammar. "Mr. Tu very powerful banker man, industrialist, do very much for China. Great man."

That was enough provocation for me to get back on my bearings.

"I have heard many people here say so," I said in a confidential tone, "but you know what his reputation is abroad. He has a very bad name so far as traffic in opium is concerned, and that was the field I was interested in for many years past. Surely you would not suggest that I talk to him on this subject?"

"You must not say one word about opium. He no like people speak opium. He now director Opium Suppression. He once smoke himself, now all educated, he study very much, with professors economic, international affairs. He now no more smoke, no more addict. Very great man."

"Well, it would surely be a great honor for me to see him, but honestly I don't know what to talk to him about. . . ."

"You will ask him three questions," said Chu with authority: "First you will ask him about his history — and he will tell you. He was very poor boy, he work very hard, become position, become great economic power. Then you will ask him what he done for society in China, and he will tell you. Then you will ask him how he see China's future, and he will tell you."

There was no hesitation, no searching for words — he reeled it off like an order he had learned by heart. I felt quite dizzy.

"I shall have to think it over. . . . Do you believe such an important man will receive me?"

"He will receive you. Then you will write a series of articles in French and English papers about Mr. Tu and his work. People abroad must learn about his part in reconstruction of China."

I said I would let him know after I had decided, and he took his leave, not without hinting politely that the sooner I saw Mr. Tu, the better it would be for all concerned.

I felt as scared and excited as a kid having opened the tiger's cage. Aimée was the first to hear my story. She was in ecstasy over the wonderful opportunity I would have to bring this man nearer to God! I felt like screaming.

"If you want to come along and keep tabs on the interpreter, you are welcome," I growled. She took it as a wonderful Christian challenge, and agreed.

Wang Kwei-son, Tu's social worker, came that evening, and I asked him whether he knew Chu Hsueh-fan.

"Not personally," he replied, "but he is Tu Yueh-sen's favorite student."

"Student?" I gasped, "but Tu is an illiterate. . . ."

"Not quite. He studies hard and can already read and write a few characters."

And with his sunny, good-natured smile Kwei-son explained to me that "student" meant really follower, disciple, that there were about 5000 of them in Shanghai alone. Mr. Tu was always ready to give intelligent, poor boys a hand. In China, where education was expensive and where no boy without means and without political pull could succeed in life, it was an age-old practice for heads of cliques or secret societies to pick their followers among the young, pay for their education and place them in good positions. There was hardly any branch of China's international, political, economic or social life where Tu's students did not hold good positions, and he could depend on their lifelong affection and loyalty. Chu had been down-and-out, as poor as only a Chinese worker can be. He dreamed of organizing labor unions that would fight for improving the lot of the workers. And he had all the qualities to make a labor leader, but not the ghost of a chance to succeed. Then Tu heard of him, took him on as his student, and he made good. Through him, Tu was the benefactor, the leader, the master of Shanghai's labor. Working conditions had improved very slightly, but they had improved. Then 800,000 workers had unanimously voted that Chu should be sent to Geneva as China's workers' delegate, to the International Labor Conference.

When I told Kwei-son of Chu's visit and suggestion, he grew thoughtful.

"*Hm* . . . if the chief has sent for you, you must go. What are you going to tell him?"

"Frankly, I am scared at the thought of seeing him. But if I go, I'll talk about opium, I think."

"He won't like it. But he should be told the truth. He is very sensitive to criticism. It might be a challenge to him to stop the evil practice, and he is strong enough to put an end to it. The interview won't take more than fifteen minutes — then he gets nervous and leaves the room. He is very nervous — always afraid of being bumped off. He is not a happy man."

"Kwei-son, would you interpret for me?"

"Yes, if they consent."

"And you would translate every word I say, no matter how harsh?"

"I will. So help me God. Maybe God will use us both as an instrument to make a better man of Mr. Tu."

The Millicans were the Shanghai nucleus of the Oxford Group,* and as such a stepping stone for members of the Group's International Team. The political activities of the International Team were rather obscure — even shady, in the opinion of some people.

Realizing the power of psychoanalysis as an attraction to people and as a valuable source of information for the International Team, the O. G. had worked out a perfect scheme which embraced public confessions before large audiences as well as regular heart-to-heart "sharing" with a more advanced Group partner. There was the obligatory "quiet time" and "listening to God" directed and guided along proper channels by disciplined members, before any statement in public. But the personal sharing was as free and as searching as any professional psycho-

* Aimée, now in the United States, has formally disassociated herself from the movement. Frank is in a Japanese prison camp in Shanghai.

analysis. Minute records were kept of such "sharing"; they were either incorporated into reports sent to the Group's national headquarters, and thence to the International Headquarters in London, or they were gathered in by the untiring touring members of the International Team, and reached Brown's Hotel in London directly. I know from experience that most of these reports were sent in good faith by enthusiastic Christians who did so in witness of God's infinite Love and Greatness, and to show how He took care of the most varied problems of the human heart. But the fact remains that in this way Brown's Hotel was in possession not only of a complete picture of activities in the various countries but also of detailed accounts of the actions, leanings, state of mind and state of soul of O. G. members and prospective members — which was more than any secret service could boast of up to the time when Frank Buchman hit upon this ingenious idea. The O. G. was financed by "God"; its official approach in China was to establish friendly relations between China and Japan.

While I had my Tu Yueh-sen fever and was trying to make up my mind whether or not I should see the fellow, Irv Phelan, of the International Team, was stopping over in Shanghai in the Millicans' "Ash Room." Handpicked for the job of "contacting" the tops in the Chinese and the Japanese Governments, Irv had the winning personality of a tall, handsome, manly young American businessman, and a way of making you feel that you could be quite chummy with the Lord. In fact, Irv and the Lord patted each other on the shoulder when they had their "quiet time" powwows. He had been recruited by the I. T. only a short time before, in California. He had not had time to go so Groupy that one could not rely on his judgment.

I asked him whether I could do some "sharing" with him, and whether he would care to give me sound, common sense advice, untinted by Group doctrine. He agreed laughingly.

"Have you ever heard of a guy by the name of Tu Yueh-sen?"

His face was a perfect blank. "Tu . . . how much?" he asked.

"Well, never mind his name. What's he got to do with you?"

I gave him the high lights, and Irv listened sympathetically. He did not open his mouth once, until I mentioned, at the end, that Tu had allegedly given up opium smoking. Here, quite unexpectedly, Irv's eyes narrowed, his features hardened: —

"That is a lie," he said hotly, "that guy has never given up smoking. He and his whole darn family are addicts. They've got a couch and a pipe in every room."

"What," gasped I. "How do you know? You said you had never heard his name before."

"Never mind details. I have been through his villa in his absence."

We sat in silence.

"Cheer up, old girl, you're in a hell of a fix," he resumed; "you've got to go through with it. There is no place where you could hide from Tu Yueh-sen, so make the best of it. Think of the interesting experience. Good luck to you."

I never learned in what capacity Irv had "visited" Tu's house, but it was gratifying to know that there were Americans interested enough to penetrate even into the lion's den.

W. H. Donald said I had invited trouble, and I had better go and see the blackguard. He knew him only by sight, and there was no love lost between them.

Dick and my friends of the International Police were worried. There was no way out; I had better make up my mind quickly. But I could come to no decision. If I did not go, he would have me shot, and if I went and refused to write the propaganda articles he wanted, he would also have me shot.

Finally the boys grew impatient and tried psychotherapy: Dick and Pete, of the Narcotics Police, showed me Tu's Shanghai at night. It was a horribly depressing tour from the lowest Hongkew slums to Tu Yueh-sen's palatial Lido. But I remained undecided.

Soon after, Dick called me on the phone: "The International

Police are going to raid a few heroin dens this morning; would you like to join the party?"

I had refused twice before, on the plea that I had imagination enough to picture the misery of drug victims, without actually seeing the horror; but this time I accepted the invitation.

The black lacquered police van looked like the hearse used by orthodox Jews in Poland. Our car followed at a distance of about fifty yards. Pete and another officer in mufti were with me. They did not want to expose me to any possible shooting. Informants had reported a few small heroin-smoking places. I should not be astonished, they said, if every addict claimed that he was taking the drug because he was sick — that was the usual excuse. The penalty was twelve years' imprisonment, after compulsory disintoxication.

There was no shooting. The van led through the poorest quarters of Hongkew district. Narrow, winding lanes crammed with ragged, haggard people who had filed out to look at the intruders . . . A silent, curious mob with fear and distrust and contempt in their eyes. They stood motionless but for an occasional sluggish half-step backward when our fenders brushed their clothes.

The policemen entered a house; one of them returned after a few minutes, signaling to us that it was safe for inspection.

The façade had given me the illusion that it was a house. But once past the threshold, one had the impression of finding one's way through a garbage bin. The place was pitch-dark, filled with penetrating, unbearable stench of filth, mold, rotting wood, cooking and poor humanity — the hall a tiny doghouse with moist, slippery walls — the screeching staircase narrow, the ceiling so low that we practically had to crawl on all fours. Here and there a step was missing. The policeman flashed his light. Windows were nonexistent; no ray of sunshine from without. We saw a sickly yellow light flickering through a chink just on top of the stairs. It went out.

"Light that candle again, God damn you!" bellowed someone's voice; the Chinese policeman repeated the order. A match struck, and a trembling old man's hand relit the stump. The flickering light filled the cubbyhole of misery: four blackened walls, three low berths — unplaned boards on short bamboo legs. Three men — or what used to be men — two addicts, thin as skeletons, with rags barely covering parts of their bodies, and the proprietor, a poor old beggar himself in his tattered filthy remnants of a gown; he was the one who had relit the candle. Now a policeman was handcuffing those poor old trembling hands.

Usually the questioning was done by subaltern men, but today Pete questioned the wretches for my sake.

The old man remained stoical. He was seventy, death was near anyway. If there is prison ahead, let it be prison. He smoked opium himself, but had never touched heroin. Yes, he sold heroin. He did not remember how long ago he had engaged in this business; he had no other work. He could not tell from whom he bought the heroin. "A man in the street." No, he would not be able to identify him. Neither did he remember the price he paid. To help his memory along, Pete said the prison term might be considerably reduced if he disclosed the source of supply. The old man's eyes narrowed with disdain. He had told them all he knew; he was ready to face prison.

Pete turned to the others: one was about twenty-five, the other over thirty. They whined and squirmed. They were sick and had to take heroin for their stomach ache. After some threatening they produced their pipes and a few rough-surfaced pink pills.

The younger man had worked at the Post Office; they had fired him and all other opium smokers when the government regulations were published. Some richer colleagues went to the doctor's and were disintoxicated. He was afraid of a hospital. Opium was too expensive, so he took to heroin. He had sold everything he had. He had left his wife and two children many months ago, because he could not feed them. He carried parcels at the docks or begged in the streets to get enough money for the drug. The older man's story was practically the same, only he had been a policeman before.

Both were so emaciated they could hardly stand on their feet. It was horrible to see the handcuffs click round those parchment-covered wrists. All three were led away.

We raided four dens in all. They were all very much alike, and so were the victims. Vice? No, the most abject poverty and despair. Life? No, a half-naked, cock-eyed existence some-where in no man's land, bordering on human society — human society with polished brass buttons and shiny, tinkling hand-cuffs and gloomy prisons. Well-being? Social security? Happy home life? No, nothing but bitterness to eat. A friend? Yes, the drug peddler — the kindly man who sells them oblivion and courage and happy daydreams for a few coppers. Human beings — the living dead — detached from all earthly belongings — with not a pair of pants to call their own — clinging with all the life that is still left in them to a coarse little bamboo pipe — quintes-sence of happiness. . . .

And the few coppers go to a man like Tu Yueh-sen, who controls many banks and is a great philanthropist.

One of the places we raided had windows and some Western furniture. The only person in it was a slim lad of twenty-three, with a terrified look and disheveled hair, clad in a singlet and white shorts. He was a student, spoke excellent English and French. Tears rolled down his cheeks as he replied to Pete's questions with folded hands. He came from one of China's most respected families. "I won't tell you my name, but if you find out, for God's sake don't let it be known. My father would die of sorrow. He does not know I am an addict. Nobody knows — I am hiding from my family and from all my friends. I have sold my clothes to buy drugs. . . . I am ashamed . . . I am so ashamed of myself," he sobbed.

Pete was visibly touched by the boy's pathetic appeal. He

sent a man down for some clothes while he asked softly for details. The boy replied, weeping. Like most of his fellow students, he had a contempt for drugs and would not believe any intelligent educated person would ever smoke. He fell in love with a young co-ed, they got engaged, but her parents had promised her to someone else, and took her home. Heartbroken, he went to a swell bar, and drank liquor for the first time in his life, and saw Western dancing with taxi-girls. The alcohol made him sick; he was disgusted with life. Some gay strangers came to his table, asking why he was so gloomy. They took him along, hitting the high spots. They made him try heroin once, twice. It helped him to forget his heartache.

"I was an imbecile," cried the boy, "but I am not a criminal, I am sick. I *must* be cured. Please, take me to a hospital. Don't lock me up in jail until I am an old man!"

We were on the point of leaving when the boy began to cry again. He held onto the little wardrobe with both hands, screaming frantically: —

"Please, take me to a hospital. Please, don't put me in jail!"

Pete said calmly: "Now you be a man and keep your chin up. They are taking you to a hospital first. It will be damn hard in the beginning; withdrawal is hell. But you look as if you had the necessary will power. That's a lot. When you are released as cured, there will be a trial. I'll see the judge. I can't promise anything, but he may let you out on probation."

The boy stepped forward and looked up at Pete like someone awakening from a terrible nightmare and perceiving a ray of sunshine.

"Probation . . ." he whispered. "Probation . . . Life? . . . I'll make good, sir . . . I'll make good. . . ." He started to thank Pete, but Pete was in a hurry, and the two of us left the room precipitately.

"We've got to treat 'em rough," he commented gruffly as we groped our way down the obscure alley. "Sure," said I.

There were other filthy, dimly lit two-by-four dens, doped

skeletons, clicking handcuffs. In the last one we saw, I reminded Pete that I had not seen any of the men actually smoking and wanted to know how they smoked those pink pills. Policemen were taking the addicts to the van. Pete ordered that one of them remain — the one nearest to us, a dull-eyed symbol of misery, a wreck despite his thirties.

"Give him his pipe and tell him he can have a smoke before he goes — the lady wants to know how it is done."

The addict took the paraphernalia with the distrustful look of a hunted animal.

"Give him a pinch of tobacco."

An agent inserted some tobacco into the pipe, which looked like a lady's cigarette holder with a small bowl at the end. The addict placed the pill on the tobacco, pressed it down slightly. Pete gave him a light.

"Lie down."

The fellow understood. He let himself drop gently on the wooden plank as if it were a bed of roses and took one whiff, then another. He stretched comfortably and smiled up dreamily to the curling smoke. Then he turned away from us, and we could only see his profile, the half-closed eyes, and the deep, relaxed breathing.

We stood motionless, spellbound. The very atmosphere of the dreary place seemed changed. The cold, steel-sharp reality of police arresting criminals had faded into the background before a warm, pulsating caprice of life . . . a doomed man had banned desperation and was enjoying the last fleeting minute of freedom. Police, prison, punishment and everlasting hell — nothing mattered. He lay there in the soft golden candlelight, and inhaled the blessed fumes of happiness and serenity.

A policeman raised a questioning eyebrow. Pete whispered in reply: "Let him finish his pipe." And we sneaked out on tiptoe.

That morning's expedition was too much for my nerves. Something snapped within me. I gave vent to my bitter disappointment, to my utter disgust with the Narcotics Police. Why did they hound these unhappy, defenseless creatures? Why didn't they have the guts to get the big fellows who were making millions out of this misery?

"We can't lay our hands on them. They are too strong for us," Pete said grimly.

We drove in silence to Dick's office.

"Well, did you have an interesting time?" Dick asked.

"Extremely," said I. "Now I'm going to see that bastard."

"Oh," said Dick, and I caught him winking contentedly at Pete. "I'm glad you've made up your mind at last. I was seriously worried that Tu might get impatient and arrange an interview without your consent."

I telephoned Chu Hsueh-fan.

"I should be very glad if you could arrange an interview with Mr. Tu Yueh-sen."

Chu laughed pleasantly: "Everything is already arranged for tomorrow morning. My chauffeur will call for you at eleven."

"That's fine. May I bring my friend Mrs. Millican along?"

There was a pause. "I think there will be no objection to Mrs. Millican. Is she going to interpret for you?"

"No, but she'd love meeting Mr. Tu. Wang Kwei-son is willing to interpret — is that all right?"

"Perfect."

Dick and Pete were visibly relieved that a solution was in sight.

"Still afraid?" asked Dick.

"No — not after what you have so kindly shown me today. Darn good psychology on your part. Thanks for that final push."

Flattered, Dick grinned shrewdly. "What are you going to talk about?"

"Opium and narcotics exclusively. I have jotted down a few points already. Would you care to look at them and make a few suggestions?"

"Certainly. But let's attend to one little detail first, while Pete is still here: where will the interview take place?"

"Search me — I don't care. Chu's car will call for me at 11 A.M."

"At 128 Museum Road?"

"*Mhm.*"

My two friends looked at each other. Pete nodded and took leave of us.

It did not take Dick and me long to prepare some twenty questions. Not that we harbored the least illusion that Shanghai's mastermind might trip up on any of them; but we were curious to see how he would parry the thrusts.

When I was leaving, Dick said casually: "By the way, I don't believe Tu will have you murdered in his own house, but it might be advisable not to eat or drink anything that is offered to you there, to avoid a possible indigestion."

Aimée was thrilled at the prospect of visiting the great potential convert, and that night we offered an extra special prayer for guidance and for the salvation of Mr. Tu Yueh-sen's soul.

The clock was striking eleven when Mr. Chu's chauffeur knocked at our door. Aimée, Kwei-son and I got into the very modest motor car, which took us to the French Concession — 143 Avenue Edward VII — a small, modern, elegant red brick building — golden letters above the entrance: THE CHUNG WAI BANK. . . .

We had not spoken a word, and I was a bit tense going up in the elevator, which seemed armor-plated, to the second floor. Pale green walls, no door. The liftboy, or rather lift-bodyguard, pressed an invisible button, and the wall slid apart unveiling two of the toughest guys I had ever laid eyes on — huge fellows with bulging pockets, bulging muscles and fierce, brutal faces — and the one on our left who bent over to inspect us was one eye short. The whole thing was so grotesque that it set my sense of humor a-tingling. I felt like a person suddenly relieved of stagefright by magic. I was perfectly at ease and whispered to Aimée: "Isn't this simply grand?" Only then did I notice how pale and scared she looked. But she managed to smile back and press my elbow.

Mr. Chu welcomed us. The spacious reception hall looked like a hotel lobby with little nests of tables and armchairs along the walls, each half-concealed by palm trees — nooks for highly important conferences, affording privacy and, at the same time, permitting the eye to watch over the whole room. One group seemed to consist of well-to-do businessmen discussing their affairs. The rest of the people present — a dozen at least — were so obviously unorthodox that even Aimée's naïve and unpractised eye recognized them as gunmen or bodyguards.

A sheet of paper, covered with Chinese script, lay on the table. Mr. Chu handed it to Wang Kwei-son for translation. Kwei-son glanced at it, and while Chu and Aimée talked, he said to me in a low voice: "The replies to the three questions you're supposed to ask."

"Put it down," said I in the same tone. And the sheet resumed its place on the table.

We were still standing. "Mr. Tu Yueh-sen," announced Chu, stiffening respectfully, his eyes fixed on a door behind me. I turned, and we all watched the man approach. His picture had appeared in many papers, his features had never seemed to me particularly prepossessing. Now I was struck and fascinated by every detail of the man's person: a gaunt, shoulderless figure with long, aimlessly swinging arms, clad in a soiled, spotted blue cotton gown; flat feet shod in untidy old slippers; a long, egg-shaped head, short-cropped hair, receding forehead, no chin, huge, batlike ears, cold, cruel lips uncovering big, yellow decayed teeth, the sickly complexion of an addict. . . . He came shuffling along, listlessly turning his head right and left to look whether anyone was following him.

We were presented. I had never seen such eyes before. Eyes

so dark that they seemed to have no pupils, blurred and dull —
dead, impenetrable eyes . . . I shuddered. Childhood memories
flashed back; Polish peasants had told us that witches could be
recognized by their abysmal eyes which did not reflect your
picture. . . .

He gave me his limp, cold hand. A huge, bony hand with two-
inches-long, brown, opium-stained claws.

Mr. Tu assured us of his pleasure in our visit. I said the pleasure
was entirely on our side. Then we sat down — Tu on my left,
Aimée on my right, Kwei-son and Chu facing me.

Fearing that I had only fifteen minutes to do it, I went straight
to the point. I said that there were many questions I should like
to ask Mr. Tu in regard to China's reconstruction problem, in
which he was playing so preponderant a part. However, as Mr.
Tu was well aware, I had worked seven years with the Anti-
Opium Information Bureau in Geneva and could not resist the
temptation of asking his authoritative opinion on the opium situation in China.

Chu Hsueh-fan's face darkened with anger, but he dared not
interrupt. Kwei-son translated. Tu frowned for a fraction of a
second, and looked at each of us in turn, as if disbelieving his
own ears. But he replied with complete composure that he was
not an authority but a very modest government official in Generalissimo Chiang Kai-shek's Opium Suppression Commission.
Generalissimo was the Inspector General. . . . Mr. Tu repeated
the official explanation: that a properly run monopoly, with
every addict registered and rationed, and opium sold only to
holders of government opium certificates, afforded the best
means of control. The Indian opium monopoly had furnished
ample proof that the opium trade could be regulated, to the
best interest of the state.

India, I retorted, was ruled by white men who considered
themselves superior to every other race and sold the drug exclusively to natives and to local Chinese. No white man could
be registered as a smoker! From their point of view, they were

selling poison to an inferior race. But in China the monopoly meant legalized poisoning of China's own nationals! So no parallel could be drawn. Furthermore, India had set no time limit for the cessation of her monopoly, which was run like a regular excise bureau. According to the Royal Commission, it yielded up to twenty-three per cent of India's annual gross revenues! Chiang Kai-shek, on the contrary, had set a time limit. But if revenues ran high, would not there be a tendency to perpetuate the opium monopoly? There were already signs of such a possibility. The newly established Farmers' Bank — one of the four government banks empowered to issue currency — was guaranteed only by Chiang Kai-shek's word of honor and by the country's opium production.

At this point, Tu's eyes became animated as he looked into mine quizzically. Obviously surprised and amused that I spoke so freely of a fact which the Government endeavored to keep secret, he wanted to know whether it had been discussed in Geneva. I replied that the news did not seem to have leaked out abroad.

Tu took Chiang's defense. Generalissimo, he said, had tried to eradicate poppy production by military force, but had met with armed resistance from the poor peasants, who defended their precious crop for fear of starvation. . . . Facing failure, Chiang was by-and-by persuaded that gradual reduction under an opium monopoly was the only solution. And there was no doubt that his intentions were sincere.

I said I was sure Mr. Tu would agree with me that no poor peasant earned money enough in his lifetime to buy a machine gun. To my knowledge, the armed clashes had occurred at the outskirts of huge estates owned by wealthy landowners who had armed and trained their own farmhands. China's opium trade was better organized than any government institution, probably because it was financed and marketed by Shanghai's big businessmen — bankers and opium merchants. I had a great admiration for the Opium Merchants' Association, but I only wished they would instead concentrate upon organizing China's export trade of silk, tea, tin, tungsten, tung-oil, in the same efficient manner. It would be more patriotic. I was very sceptical of their co-operation in Chiang's Opium Suppression project, and Chiang was certainly not equipped financially and militarily to force their hands.

A boy served tea for the men — hot water for the ladies, as tea is often considered to be too strong for delicate persons! Aimée and I ignored the cups, but we could not help noticing that Tu Yueh-sen drank his tea out of a small golden teapot. The cover was kept tight by a little golden chain, and the mouthpiece was so narrow and curved that nothing could be inserted into it from without. "He is afraid *we* might poison *him*," flashed through my mind, but I was too preoccupied even to crack a smile.

Tu was just saying that Chiang was at present the strongest man in China, and could do everything.

He can do nothing against the Opium Merchants' Association, said I. All students of the opium problem know that, in this domain, the power lies in the hands of "the Opium Tsar of China."

I paused for confirmation or denial.

Tu looked at me attentively: "Yes, I am the head of China's Opium Merchants," he acknowledged moodily.

I appreciated his frankness, and described to him how the whole of Geneva was in uproar when Generalissimo had appointed the Opium Tsar head of the Shanghai Suppression Bureau!

A fleeting smile made Tu's face quite human. He himself must have considered the appointment a huge joke.

There were pessimists, I continued, who maintained that Chiang's whole Opium Suppression was nothing but window dressing. Geneva experts had plucked his first financial statement to pieces. They had multiplied the number of addicts by the quantity of their daily opium ration, then by the price per ounce, and proved it in black on white that China's opium revenue must have been five times the amount alleged.

The accusation was unjust, retorted Tu. Chiang had told the truth. He did not get more than twenty million Chinese dollars. The opium merchants handled the production, the purchasing and pooling of stocks, transportation, packing, distribution — in short, the business end. They collected the revenue and assessed a percentage to Chiang's Opium Suppression Inspectorate which they deemed adequate.

(It was my turn to be surprised, though I did not show it. We did not know to what extent Chiang Kai-shek's hands had been tied. In his endeavor to establish internal peace, he had farmed out the opium interests. Geneva had no inkling of this. To us, Generalissimo was the Inspector General of Opium Suppression; little did we know of his difficulties.)

Then I told Tu Yueh-sen that I was more concerned over the white drugs situation than over opium. In my opinion the production of opium should not be suppressed or even curtailed so long as the Japanese were free to flood the country with morphine and heroin, and so long as the Chinese Government had no jurisdiction over foreign concessions, where Chinese and foreigners could conduct their illicit trade with impunity. An opium smoker deprived of his ration would turn to the far more deadly white drugs. I hoped that Chiang Kai-shek's power would grow, and I was sure that the next war would do away with unequal treaties, foreign concessions and extraterritoriality. Then, with the whole country under Chinese jurisdiction, Chiang could go to the root of the evil and court-martial the Japanese and the Chinese dope manufacturers and traffickers, instead of having to mete out capital punishment to the victims of those villains.

Tu agreed that the Japanese dope traffic was formidable and had spread its tentacles far inside China, and that opium was far less harmful. He also spoke of the gigantic smuggling campaign Japan was waging against China — a continuous flow of trains and shiploads of contraband goods of every description entering under heavily armed military escort, swamping all markets and refusing to pay customs duty. . . .

I said I had seen the last two seizures at the Custom House. Could Mr. Tu enlighten me as to what happened to such seizures? I turned my head to see his face, and met his eyes ablaze with anger. I had drawn blood. The dead eyes had come to life — they were intelligent, passionate, cruel. A thrilling sensation to look into them . . . beginning of a duel. I did not flinch. The eyes dulled down again, as he turned to Kwei-son with the stereotyped reply that seized narcotics were burned under official supervision in public places. He was astonished that I had not seen the many photographs of such destruction, which had received wide publicity in the world press.

That was past history, I parried. According to new regulations, Shanghai seizures were turned over to the local Opium Suppression Committee. How did Mr. Tu dispose of them?

He said he shipped them to Nanking, where they were destroyed by the National Government.

This was a good enough version for the League of Nations, I spoke deliberately, but Mr. Tu knew perfectly well that it was not the truth. Every grain of the hundreds of kilograms seized went back into the illicit traffic. And this was by a damn sight worse than the opium monopoly.

Tu's clenched fist crashed down on the table. Teacups tingled. Alert bodyguards craned their necks from under their palm trees.

I protest, he bellowed: this is a lie! Everything is being destroyed except a small part, which the Government keeps for emergency stocks.

Emergency stocks! I cried — In case of war there won't be a grain of morphine available for the wounded. . . . Morphine was too valuable a commodity to be stored for public welfare. Mr. Tu was Director of Opium Suppression. The least he could do was to protect his countrymen from manufactured narcotics, if for no other reason than that white drugs competed with opium!

Kwei-son's interpretation was from the very beginning a masterpiece of artistic reproduction. He listened keenly, eager-eyed, flushed, and translated every sentence Tu or I said, using our own inflection, emphasizing the very same words, almost imitating our gestures. I had never done better teamwork with anyone. We were both ready to go to the limit to break through Tu's panzer plate. But there was a difference: Kwei-son radiated such convincing warmth when speaking to him — an apostle trying to convert a beloved sinner. I was cool, and determined to let Tu know what the world thought of him. If there was to be any killing, there should be at least a good reason for it.

I felt for the first time that my years in Geneva had not been lost. The many speeches I had written for delegates had fallen upon deaf ears in that sterile atmosphere over there, but they had prepared me for this moment. Here was reality; here was my first and only chance in life to plead for China's millions of living dead. Their tears and blood and coppers had made the man before me Opium Tsar. The heart-rending scenes of the day before were so vivid in my mind they made me eloquent and aggressive.

I gave a description of the horrible things I had seen. Then I spoke to Tu about himself, about his constructive work in factories, about his rural center and the orphanages, about his Labor News agency, about the Lido, about his numerous patriotic contributions to China's social welfare.

He was visibly pleased.

Mr. Tu did not realize, I continued, to what extent he was in the international picture. Many people considered him a great patriot and a very good man. Many others thought he was a dark character, a very bad man . . .

Down came his fist again with a bang. He did not care about public opinion, he cried.

"But both camps agree as to one point," I proceeded undismayed: "namely, that Mr. Tu is a most powerful man, and that he alone can do away with opium and drugs in China."

Kwei-son must have had a moment's nervousness, as he slipped up on this sentence and did not translate it. But Aimée chipped in immediately: "Kwei-son, dear, you must not have heard Ralf's last sentence." She turned to Tu and gave him the Chinese version. She had been listening there so quietly, her hands folded as in prayer. . . .

I hastened to explain that Mrs. Millican really was not concerned with opium but with Mr. Tu's soul. She would very much like to know Mr. Tu's attitude towards Christianity.

With a friendly smile, he replied that he was very much interested in Christianity. He was also interested in Buddhism, in Taoism, in Mohammedanism — in fact in every religion. But he did not give preference to any of them in particular. . . .

After this intermezzo, I resumed the offensive. Mr. Tu had accumulated great wealth and power, I said. He could now afford to take a different road, and build the greatest thing a man could build for himself and for all his descendants: a worldwide reputation as a benefactor of mankind. Up to a few years ago, Chiang Kai-shek's name had been one of the very worst in history. He was living it down rapidly; the world was already thinking of him in terms of "wise statesman" and "Builder of China." And Mr. Tu was the only man who could accomplish a task equally far-reaching: the eradication of narcotics and opium in China. Such an action would have a world-wide repercussion. It would explode the hundred-year-old imperialistic lie that Chinese could not do without the pipe. China could then demand that all foreign opium monopolies stop selling opium to her nationals. It would be a colossal thing for China's prestige. Overnight, Mr. Tu would become the sensation of the world — the hero, the patriot, the great philanthropist who sacrificed millions of dollars of profits to save his country from shame, and millions of human beings from misery and degeneration. . . .

Kwei-son aiding, I talked myself into enthusiasm. We appealed to his ambition, to his heart. Naturally, it was cheaper to build orphanages. . . . Charity was always cheaper than grandeur. . . .

I rose. The others followed my example. Tu thanked me in a very friendly way and said he would have a special opium report prepared for me. He insisted I should come back for another chat. I looked at Mr. Chu, whom the interview had made angry and unhappy; I had spoken on the one subject he had asked me to avoid. I felt sorry on his account; the least I could do was to save his face. Very politely, I bowed to Tu, and apologized for having spoken exclusively about opium.

"If time had not been so limited, I should have asked Mr. Tu to tell me how he had become so powerful, what he had done for the Chinese society, and how he saw the future of China. I hoped that Mr. Tu did not consider me rude for not having asked these questions."

Chu Hsueh-fan heaved a sigh of relief.

Tu accompanied us all the way to the cyclope-guarded door, chatting pleasantly. He promised to think the matter over, and we departed.

Aimée went home. Kwei-son and I had a snack at some old teahouse. The lad was swayed by the interview and Tu's interest.

Then I rushed to Dick's office. Usually I had to await my turn, but this time the excited office boy greeted me with a peremptory "Boss's orders: walk straight in." I stepped in proudly — but it did not last. Dick was every inch the old colonial official, and raging mad. I got the most colorfully expressive scolding I had ever received. They had waited for me. Dick hadn't had his lunch. The interview had lasted an hour and a half, I stammered meekly. He knew it, but when I had gotten out of there safely, what in Satan's name did I mean by walking off with one of those gangsters? Where had I disappeared to? Pete and his men were fine-combing the whole district to find me or my body. . . .

Just then the phone rang and Dick bellowed into the receiver: "She is here. It was just a matter of having tiffin with the gang's apostle."

Then he smoothed his neatly parted hair, apologized and listened to my detailed account, snorting maliciously and gloating now and then. We both agreed that nothing would come out of the whole thing but that it was good to have it off my chest, and not to be obliged to write the series of articles boosting Mr. Tu's civic exploits.

Aimée, of course, was of a different opinion. She called me her "pagan saint," and although I asked her not to talk about the interview, she "shared" the thrilling experience with every blessed Oxford Group team. The result was that, for months to come, every white person I met would tell me in appropriate mellow, hollow tones how wonderful it was to be used as God's mouthpiece!

When the war broke out in 1937, and the Japanese occupied Shanghai, Tu Yueh-sen moved to Hong Kong and transferred his opium and drugs headquarters to that British Crown Colony. American and Canadian authorities were frantic as increasing quantities of contraband narcotics reached the Western Hemisphere, but they could do nothing. Hong Kong's authorities declared that their crime-suppression budget was insufficient to combat the illicit traffic. Thus Tu Yueh-sen was just as safe and happy under the British flag as he had been under the French flag in Shanghai.

When Hong Kong fell, he flew to Chungking. It is problematic what will happen now to the National Government Mandate promulgated in Chungking on February 19, 1941, which provides death penalty for every category of narcotic offenders, from the poppy producer to the owner of a hypodermic needle, and destruction by fire of all confiscated opium, narcotics, poppy seeds and even "of caffeine, milk sugar and quinine alkaloid and other substances which are identified with the exclusive use of manufacturing narcotics."

There is, however, another side to amazing Mr. Tu Yuehsen: he has not relinquished his hold on Shanghai even today, after five years of Japanese occupation. He is a patriot; like all loyal generals, he has joined China's United Front and mobilized his army — the populace in the city and guerillas round Shanghai. The Green-and-Red Circle, with its respectable citizens in all walks of life, with its students, with its sprinkling of trigger-men (don't let us call them gunmen for the duration), is an ideal anti-Japanese Fifth Column. No Japanese, no Chinese traitor, no arsenal, factory or railway is safe. Young, ardent members of a special patriotic organization, "Blood and Steel," risk their lives daily serving their country in occupied territory. Tu finances a good part of Shanghai's resistance against Japan; Chu is still his first lieutenant and in touch with every phase of it.

Of course, it is not all his doing. The Government, the Communists, the press and patriotic organizations keep close contact with Shanghailanders; it often happens that Chungking broadcasts the news of an act of sabotage or the execution of a traitor there before the Japanese authorities have time to learn about it. China can still get indispensable supplies from and through Shanghai, and loyal Chinese may travel forth and back unimpeded. Japanese vigilance and bestiality are ineffective where a whole population stands by the Government, unbeatable in spirit and irreducible in its tenacity.

Shortly after my interview with Tu, I left for Nanking. I had an invitation to stay with John and Faith Magee, but preferred to stop at the Nanking Hotel. I was afraid of getting into another saintly environment. I called on them, however, and found them a most charming, easy-going couple. John wore a light gray gabardine suit, and not the black minister's dress that would have paralyzed me. We laughed and joked. Piousness was certainly not at home in the Hsiakwan American Church Mission, and their two younger sons, Christopher, nine, and Hugh, three, were refreshingly unruly kids.

After tea, John said casually, with a merry twinkle: "And now that you have looked the Magees over and found that they are not a bunch of stuck-up missionaries, I suggest that we hop into a ricksha and fetch your belongings. Your room upstairs is ready." I said "yes" with real joy.

But I did not stay very long, then. A painful neuritis in my shoulder which had tormented me more than three months drove me back to Shanghai.

I finally decided to get a thorough medical examination, and chose the Chinese Red Cross Hospital. None of the renowned foreign hospitals appealed to me. I had to have a Chinese one. What tempted me in particular was the fact that the head of the Red Cross Hospital was Tu Yueh-sen's intimate friend and fellow member on various opium committees, Dr. F. C. Yen.

I wanted to see his hospital from the inside. Dick said it was sheer insanity on my part to insist on placing myself in the gang's hands.

The receptionist at the C.R.C. told me there were some flowers waiting for me. I contemplated them with some uneasiness: a huge basket of white carnations forming a base and a wreath — exactly like a tombstone. I thought of the caskets Tu Yueh-sen used to send to people who had thwarted him, and my hands were moist and trembled as I tore open the little envelope. . . . Dick's visiting card with best wishes for a speedy recovery. It came out later that he had ordered a simple bunch of carnations, but artistic feeling had prompted the florist to improve upon this coarse taste. Dick had not seen the arrangement and laughed heartily when I told him of my shock.

The medical staff and treatment at the hospital were excellent. I was under the special care of the first and only neurologist in China — a red-haired girl from Austria, Dr. Halpern.

She had taken up a single-handed battle against public opinion and superstition and had persuaded the Government to build the first insane asylum in China. Until then the insane had been either considered possessed by spirits or kept in chains like wild beasts. At my bedside, Dr. Halpern gave a brief lecture on my case to half a dozen young Chinese interns. Neuritis or neuralgia. Cause unknown. The source of the evil had to be found. She distributed the various tasks among them. The young men set out to work with a zeal, an efficiency and a devotion that I had never encountered in any first-class clinic in the world. They made all up-to-date tests known to medical science. Each reported his findings every day in my presence. After a week's time my physical being held no more secrets for them. They knew the density of my skin, the composition of my blood, my nervous reflexes, the behavior of every gland; they had X-rayed every tooth and all the rest. There was no inflammation anywhere, no organic reason for the pains. Dr. Halpern tried a new vaccine. For months, other doctors had made me swallow all kinds of remedies. Nothing seemed to touch the spot. Here, after the third vaccination, came a marked relief.

The rest of the hospital service presented a glaring contrast. Most of our wards were badly lighted and primitive. I had a private room — the best in the house, I was told — at the end of a long gallery, usually crowded with convalescents. My room was like a sun parlor or an observation tower; nothing but windows, with a glass door to the gallery. There were voile curtains at the glass door, but they were fixed on the outside, so that whoever felt like taking a peep at me could do so at any time of the day or the night. Patients, visitors and nurses made abundant use of this diversion.

December nights in the unheated room were biting cold, but — tips or no tips — I never got the miniature electric heater except a few minutes before a doctor's visit. I did not like to complain to Dr. Halpern. Besides, no nurse took her seriously. She was considered something of a lunatic. Chinese medical tradition knew nothing of nerves or nervous diseases; consequently she and any person treated by her must be "cracked." They replied yes-yes to everything I said, for fear I might become violent. The 6 A.M. nurse did not bother to take the tray with the sterilized thermometers. She took one thermometer and made her round, sticking it into one patient's mouth after another's. I objected. She stroked my forehead soothingly and showed me a dirty little dab of cotton which smelled of alcohol — explaining that she wiped the thermometer each time with it before giving it to the next patient, so it was clean! The tepid greasy food was served on oil-smudged enamel trays in sticky, chipped-off enamel bowls. Besides rice and vegetables it contained whatever had fallen into the pots and pans. At one meal, I made a collection: some chicken feathers, a match, a hair, a piece of whisk-broom. The nurse was unimpressed. This should not worry me, she said — whatever was in the food was boiled, so there were no microbes.

Dr. F. C. Yen was getting handsome sums each year for his hospital, but there were only twenty-nine bedpans for 300 patients. The thirtieth had been stolen. In view of such dishonesty among the patients, the bedpan lady, who was in charge of these precious requisites, never left you alone with one. She had the lot under lock and key, and during her afternoons off we had to wait many a trying hour. . . .

Were there any foreigners in the hospital? I wanted to know. Yes, one Englishman. I did not believe my ears. . . . The English were the most exclusive of all diehards. What was the matter with him? Dementia praecox. The police had brought him in. Third class. Dr. Halpern was taking care of him.

That made me think. . . . One had to be a madman or Ralf Sues to stay at the C.R.C. . . . When, an hour later, one of the little pink-cheeked nurses snorted in my room, looked round for the spittoon, which had been removed because foreigners don't use them, and then spat into my wastepaper basket, I saw red. Never mind their using my comb and lipstick — but this was too much. I dressed in a jiffy and beat it. I would continue my treatment as outpatient.

Dr. F. C. Yen had never learned of my presence in his hospital.

On December 13, 1936, the news broke like a bombshell that Young Marshal Chang Hsueh-liang had captured the Generalissimo in Sian. China and the rest of the world went frantic over this incident which Nanking presented as a *"coup d'état,"* "kidnaping for ransom," and worse.

I was still in Shanghai when the Young Marshal's telegram to Madame Chiang Kai-shek, assuring her that he was vouching with his life for Generalissimo's safety, appeared in the press. After what Donald had told me about the man, I believed him. And I was in Nanking on December 25, when Generalissimo and his "captor" arrived by plane and were given a rousing welcome by the entire people of China.

The details of what had happened in the meantime have been recounted many times and in many different ways. One fact only has gone down in history and cannot be distorted: It was during those two hectic weeks in Sian that China's United Anti-Japanese Front was born. Without Sian, China would today probably not be one of the foremost United Nations.

The gist of the affair was that the majority of the thinking Chinese people — many groups of intellectuals, students, and national organizations — wanted the Government to stop the ten-year-old civil war with the Chinese Communists, and to resist Japan, which had been allowed to take Manchuria and Northern China with impunity, "while Chinese brothers were fighting." This fact was kept from the Generalissimo, who was surrounded, and practically isolated from his people, by an iron ring of the most reactionary and pro-Japanese cabinet China had ever seen.

The outstanding light in this cabinet was Minister of War

Ho Ying-ch'in, who, among other unsavory acts, had signed the Ho-Umetsu Agreement virtually abandoning the Northern Provinces to Japan.

Inside this iron ring, there were only two stormy petrels who, according to this cabinet, "poisoned the Generalissimo's mind with foreign, democratic ideas," namely Madame Chiang Kai-shek and W. H. Donald. They worked for war with Japan and collaboration with the United States, Great Britain, and — if need be — with Soviet Russia.

There was yet another face to this problem, the question who would, someday, succeed the Generalissimo. The reactionaries and the army officers owing their appointment to the Minister of War stood firmly behind Ho Ying-ch'in. The rest of anti-Japanese, democratic China, including the Madame and Donald, referred to the Young Marshal as "China's Number Two."

The Young Marshal did not "capture" the Generalissimo. He detained him in Sian long enough to acquaint him with the attitude of extragovernmental China, and to persuade him that the great majority of the Chinese people, including the Communists, were ready to rise under his leadership like one man and resist Japan.

The greatness and the weakness in Generalissimo's character is his open mind; he can be convinced by anyone who keeps on talking long enough. All Chinese politicians are aware of this, and every group maneuvers to have its best talkers nearest to the Generalissimo and to obtain the exclusive rights to the Strong Man's attention.

Nanking realized the danger of having Generalissimo listen to the other side. This alone can explain the extraordinary fact that Ho Ying-ch'in dispatched a punitive army to Sian and ordered the air force to blast the city into smithereens, with Generalissimo, Madame, Donald, T. V. Soong, Chang Hsueh-liang and Yang Hu-cheng inside. They preferred a dead Generalissimo to a Generalissimo getting "independent" and fighting Japan at the head of a whole united people.

"If we hadn't had five days of the most terrible snowstorm, which prevented the bombers from attacking, we would all be dead and forgotten by now," Donald told me later.

When the temperamental young officers in Sian got out of hand, Chang Hsueh-liang kept his promise and protected the Generalissimo. When the foundations for a United Anti-Japanese Front had been laid, the chivalrous Young Marshal accompanied his Chief to Nanking, "to ask for punishment for his insubordination."

Royal Leonard, the pilot who flew that historic Boeing back to Nanking, gave an illuminating glimpse of the moods of his five illustrious passengers: —

Five minutes after we had taken off, the Young Marshal turned a drawn, strained face to me. He pointed over his shoulder. I looked back, and there, to my amazement, I saw the slight figure of the Generalissimo, eyes closed and face haggard, sleeping on the single lounge of the Boeing. . . . Madame was looking out of a window, a faint smile of happiness on her face. Donald was chuckling to himself. T. V. Soong occasionally looked at some papers but spent most of the time resting, with his eyes closed.*

Chang Hsueh-liang was "sentenced" by the National Government, and "pardoned" by the Generalissimo twenty-four hours later, but was never released.

Ho Ying-ch'in, who ordered the Generalissimo bombed out of existence, is still Minister of War, Chief of the General Staff, and today more powerful than ever.

Young Marshal Chang Hsueh-liang, whom China and the world have to thank for China's United Anti-Japanese Front, and who saved Generalissimo's life, is still kept incommunicado (the eighth year!) in a temple somewhere in Szechuen.

Incomprehensible? Not by a long shot. Donald had the explanation for situations of this kind. "This is China."

* Leonard: *I Flew for China* (Doubleday Doran, 1942).

V

Nanking

THE AIR, the atmosphere, the people — everything was different in Nanking. Here the Chinese were at home, with no foreign Concession to remind them of the "superiority" of the white race. And the mentality of most of the foreigners was different too; they belonged to another species — professors, missionaries, the diplomatic corps, who mixed easily and gracefully with Chinese society, intellectuals, and officials. The exclusive and rapacious preferred Shanghai and lived there.

The capital was in the process of growing into a metropolis. The Government, the municipality, concerns and private individuals vied with each other in their zeal for lending it Oriental glamor and modern grandeur.

But Nanking was not a city yet: it was a huge terrain surrounded by a strong, high, beautiful wall with well-kept, picturesque gates and deep moats. The interior of the city had been burned during the Taiping Rebellion, and most of it was still wasteland, ponds, and even cultivated fields. There were some populous sections, mostly huddling round the gates: hundreds of old-fashioned houses, dark, narrow lanes, temples, theaters, teahouses — reminding one of medieval towns, so crowded there seemed to be hardly any space to step, hardly any air to breathe.

There were a few magnificent wide surfaced roads recently built by the Government — future avenues, waiting for the modern buildings that will line them someday.

Along the 16 kilometers of Chungshan Road stood Nanking's most important edifices: the big, up-to-date, luxurious, aye, even air-conditioned, Metropolitan Hotel; the magnificent buildings of the Ministry of Railways and, facing it, the Ministry of Communications; the Ministry of Foreign Affairs, a hideous dark brick building that could be a Shanghai textile factory; the Drum Tower American Hospital and School; a couple of large, gaudy, brand-new Motion Picture Palaces; the Officers' Moral Endeavor Association — an exquisitely charming success of ancient and modern Chinese architecture; and the Medical Center, magnificent and imposing series of sober, rectilinear buildings.

Taiping Road was the only fashionable shopping center, and resembled a street. All other houses stood so far apart that one had to take a ricksha from one to another. Looking down from the window of the Ministry of Foreign Affairs, one could watch water buffaloes bathing in a large pool of water, or grazing peacefully.

The welcome the Magees gave me on my return, with Christopher setting off heaps of firecrackers and the Christmas tree waiting for him and me to trim it, made me feel like one of the family. Our warm friendship never ceased; it is one of the finest things I brought back from China. Others collect jade, porcelain, rugs, or curios. I collect only human gems; and a pair of rare, flawless, beautiful gems like Faith and John are worth more to me than Madame Wellington Koo's priceless collection of jade.

It is a difficult thing to be a missionary without slipping into the pitfall of piousness, or doing violence to one's impulses behind a painful façade of apostolic perfection. The Magees did not strain to be saints. They were profoundly human with that simple, direct, intelligent approach to the joys and sorrows, and problems and madnesses, of life in our time. Religion to them was not a corset but a way of living. Their faith was as deep and natural as that of the first Christians when Jesus still walked on earth; they did not preach it, they lived it.

I helped John with his mail, and Christopher with his schoolwork, and I studied Chinese with a fine old Peiping professor, when I did not roam round the country looking into the various reconstruction projects. The Ministries of Industry, and of Education, and the National Health Administration, were particularly helpful.

There was feverish activity in every domain of national life — fifty revolutions started simultaneously, with the co-operation of the League of Nations and foreign experts, to make a modern country out of China. Western medicine, agricultural methods, machinery, manufacturing processes and educational programs were introduced, tested, rejected, promulgated.

In the absence of a uniform plan, of a fundamental social-economic idea, reconstruction was a free-for-all scramble for power, for wealth, or for public-spirited effort. It depended on the individual who put up the money, on the politician who pulled the wires. I have seen stunning progress in projects where the right people happened to be in the right place, even with limited funds, but free from political interference. One of China's national characteristics is the innate driving power of the young towards progress and perfection, and their boundless devotion to the task in which they believe. I have seen other projects where corruption, mismanagement, political intrigues were responsible for millions of capital wasted, and for the ruin of entire districts.

Out of the many nameless men and women whose splendid pioneer work I have admired in many parts of the country, I have selected Dr. Huang Tse-fang as the typical example of a young Chinese giving his life to build a new, a better China. I had grown fond of the Huangs in Geneva, where Tse-fang was for three years member of the League's Health Section. He had studied in the United States and married a co-ed — redheaded

Blanche, from Albany, New York. I cannot think of any couple more harmoniously matched than these two. They were both of middle stature, svelte, refined, quick and energetic in motion. They even had the same fine skin texture, except that Tse-fang's pale, oval face was almost transparent, and his black eyes looked at mankind with meditative skepticism, whereas Blanche's delicate complexion was rosily transparent and her large brown eyes seemed to challenge the world. Two of that rare species of intellectuals who had escaped fossilization and remained human, they combined the best that America and China could offer. They had two charming, bright sons, Paul and Jay.

Dr. Huang had been one of the most assiduous workers in the Health Section at Geneva. But it was in China that I realized the whole import of Tse-fang's work. He lived part of the week in Shanghai and part in Nanking, organizing the health service for the Ministry of Railways.

He was not with the Health Administration.

"I won't stand for political crooks using public health as their playball," he explained to me with usual candor. "I would stifle in that atmosphere of corruption, intrigue and servility. I have studied medicine and public health, not opportunism, and I am going to stick to my profession or burst in the attempt."

It was my first visit to their Shanghai home. I had not seen them for three years. It felt good to be back among friends who saw clearly, talked straight, and acted decently. I was interested in Tse-fang's work.

"Drop in at my hospital tomorrow," he said, "and you will see a new thing started. The building is an old shack, but it is our first railway hospital, and the beginning of medical care for railway workers."

"Under Chang Kia-ngau, the pro-Japanese Railway Minister?" I asked, unguardedly.

Tse-fang raised his eyebrows ironically: "Aren't you yet fed up with politics, after so many years in Geneva? I am. I have never gone into Chang Kia-ngau's political credo. What counts is the man and his work — in his case both are O.K. Our railways today compare favorably with those in any country. He has increased the rolling stock, set up well-equipped repair shops. The trains are clean and keep to the schedule — a thing they never did before. He is building new railroads at an American speed. He has done away with corruption and, what I am most interested in, he takes care of the personnel."

The three-story building was really a bit old. For lack of a waiting room, the entrance hall was full of poorly clad people. A handful of doctors and nurses attended to the outpatients on the floor above. They were snappy and cheerful. Tse-fang showed me around. Beds were few as yet. Only serious accident "cases" could be taken care of. But what struck me was how the faces brightened up wherever Dr. Huang appeared. He had a friendly word for all, knew their names and family conditions. The dark hall downstairs fairly brightened up with teethy grins. Free pamphlets were stacked up on a table dealing with such subjects as accident prevention, first aid, hygiene, child care. They were written in the simplest, most accessible form, and thousands were already in circulation among the workers.

Tse-fang's statistical tables and reports were as meticulous here as they had been in Geneva. They showed an appreciable decrease in accidents and a considerable reduction of absenteeism due to illness. Where workers used to be fired before, when they did not report for work, they were now examined by a physician or a visiting nurse. Preventive medicine was introduced all along the line, with vaccination of personnel and their families, free consultations, dispensaries, health lectures. Environmental and nutrition conditions were studied and remedied wherever possible. Chang Kia-ngau was broadminded enough to make fair budget provisions, and Dr. Huang and his colleagues proved that proper care and treatment of the workers increased efficiency, conscientiousness and loyalty. In China, where labor legislation is nonexistent and where the vast majority of the

Government and employers maintain the attitude that there is enough man power in the country to replace any sick or dead "coolies," this was a daring experiment and formidable progress.

I soon found out that this was only one of Tse-fang's jobs. He took a very active part in the Chinese Medical Association; he was the editor of the Chinese medical *Journal;* a member of the Committee on Nutrition as well as that on Venereal Diseases, and of others. I saw a number of his reports, concerning every vital phase of China's health problems: studies of the appalling conditions, followed up by up-to-date constructive suggestions. He traveled a lot to investigate things for himself, and placed reliable men in key positions. Sloppiness simply did not exist in the services where he had anything to say.

"A fellow's got to know his work and to have his heart in it," he used to say. And on this basis he appointed his subordinates. He himself worked passionately, forgetting his own delicate health and seeing very little of his family.

One day we drove out in Huang's old-fashioned limousine to see his pet project — an experimental rural center a few kilometers west of Shanghai. On the way he explained that the Rockefeller Foundation and the Chinese Medical Association were financing the work, that the Government had nothing to say there, that politics and the New Life Movement were taboo, and that the place was neither a "model district" nor a "show place." He despised exhibitionism in any form.

The countryside round Shanghai was poorer than ever after the 1932 battles. The villages were despicably filthy, the people destitute, sickly and neglected. The ponds where the inhabitants dumped refuse, washed their clothes, rinsed their vegetables, and got their water for cooking, were ideal breeding places for mosquitoes and carriers of cholera, typhoid and other germs. The undernourished population was an easy victim to epidemics. In case of an epidemic it was quite common for a few villages to die out completely. No one wondered and no one cared.

In front of each hut stood an oversized bucket containing the family manure, carefully collected and preciously guarded as the only available fertilizer. The buckets were open and surrounded by millions of flies. An unbearable fetor filled the air.

Dr. Huang and his collaborators had picked three such villages for their experiment. We stopped just outside the largest, Tachang. Right at the entrance stood a wooden pole with a blue signboard — vital statistics of the year. Tse-fang indicated the columns: number of families, number of adults, number of children at the beginning of the year; number of literate persons. Then, month by month, neatly registered in white on blue: number of births, number of persons vaccinated, *idem* inoculated; cases of illness, number of deaths. Adult class attendance, children's school attendance . . . Number of lectures and attendance . . .

I laughed, amused: "Have you ever met anyone quite as pedantic as yourself?"

He smiled indulgently. "I'll give you just one example of the usefulness of this table," he said. "A few months ago we had one of the most severe smallpox epidemics. Tens of thousands in this district alone were stricken, and some eighty per cent died. Our villages were spared. We had ten cases, of which three were in Tachang, and not one of them was fatal. Every person here had been vaccinated. The moral effect was colossal. Now they have an absolute confidence in us and we get a hundred per cent collaboration. Besides, other towns and villages invite us to open health centers and ask that we vaccinate their population to ward off the evil spirits of disease. The Tachang people take great pride in these tables because every passer-by can see at a glance just how progressive the community is."

We walked up the main street; it looked as clean as a toy village at Macy's. Each little house and hut had a white number on a little blue plaque. That was quite a new thing, and so were the names of the streets, chosen by the village meetings: Cleanliness Street, Thrift Lane, Co-operative Road, Health Lane, Crop Selection Street, and the like. Harvest was in, and most people were working outdoors, carding cotton with most primitive hand tools and sifting rice. All had an air of quiet contentment which I had never seen anywhere before. That in itself was wonderful. And suddenly I became aware that the air was filled with the fragrance of hay.

"One of our first campaigns here was the anti-fly campaign," Dr. Huang explained. "Look around: all manure buckets have tight lids. Over there, the grocery store — can you see? All food-stuffs have screen covers. At first the peasants laughed at us when we said that flies are dirty and carry disease. But the micro-scope did wonders: we put it up in the market place and asked a kid to catch a fly and give us one of its legs. Then everybody in turn could look at it through the magnifying 'health cannon.' You should have heard the 'Ai-yahs' and the discussions. The battle was won; they listened readily. We shared expenses fifty-fifty. The same method was used to convince them that the ponds were polluted. We dug a well at our expense and made them compare a drop of water from the pond with a drop from the well. They were disgusted at the sight of the swarm of hor-rible bacteria they had been drinking. That gave us a chance to display our educational charts and explain the diseases carried by the different monsters, the symptoms and prevention. The Chinese peasant has got to see a thing before he believes it, but once he is convinced, you can find no better collaborator in the world. They all turned to the well. And as one well was not sufficient, the village elders asked us if we would drill some more; they were ready to put up the usual fifty per cent. We spray the pond regularly for mosquitoes. The women do their laundering in it. Refuse is burned, not dumped into the water."

We were stopped frequently on our way by villagers who wanted to exchange a few words with Tse-fang. The seeds the Committee had distributed, which at first were accepted rather skeptically, had yielded more and better rice and superior cotton, they said.

We visited the trim little hut of the proud winner of the

"Cleanliness Contest"; the prize was a little wooden tablet, with flowers and text painted in lively colors. It hung in a place of high honor, right over the table with the ancestral tablets.

The white schoolhouse had two rooms — a classroom, and a recreation room with books and ping-pong table. It was never empty, as kindergarten, grammar school, women's sewing and knitting classes, and lectures on agricultural, social, and health questions were succeeding each other from dawn to sunset.

Young Dr. Shih, the permanent physician of Tachang, was one of the four people selected by Tse-fang who had accomplished the work under his guidance. The others were a trained nurse, a teacher, and an agronomist who was at the same time conducting the necessary sanitary engineering.

In 1937, during the Shanghai war, Dr. Huang was called upon to organize a huge experimental center in Kaochiao, taking care of thousands of refugees. Dr. Huang was very ill and conducted the work from his bed. The enterprise had just begun to show results when the pressure of the Japanese forced its transfer to Soochow. He went to organize the work there, despite the advice of his doctors, who had found that he suffered from stomach ulcers. After a hemorrhage, he was brought back to Shanghai and spent months in bed; his room was the meeting place for most of the Chinese Medical Association's committee meetings, and he never stopped editing the Chinese medical *Journal*. So long as he could do constructive work, he ignored pains and illness, they were just secondary matters.

No sooner did he get up than the National Medical College was moved to the interior, and he was asked to organize another health demonstration center in Yunnan Province. He selected the locality, conducted a survey, laid the first foundations. This taxed his delicate health to the utmost. An epidemic broke out and Tse-fang came down with typhus. He recovered, asked for a month's vacation and set out for Shanghai, to see Blanche and the boys. He got as far as Hong Kong, where he had to be admitted to a hospital. He asked for paper and started his report on the work accomplished in the new center. I have these penciled notes before me; here are some extracts: —

Following consultations with the local health authorities, the choice of the location for the health center fell on Kutsing, Yunnan, a *hsien* of about 150,000 population. . . . The points thought to be in favor of the location are several: Kutsing is a typical small area with resources below the average. It is a strategic wartime center of communication. It is on the line of entry of cholera and other epidemics from the Central Provinces into Yunnan. It is not near to any important government center, which may be an advantage from the standpoint of freedom from political interference. . . .

Surveys of the population have been made and a house-to-house census was taken in February, 1940. In connection with the census, the irregular house numbers throughout the town were rearranged and put on a uniform basis. The total number of families in the town and its small suburbs outside the four city gates was found to be 2,465, and the population, 10,947; an average of 4.44 persons per family. In the preliminary surveys made in October, 1939, of a population of 7,521 studied, the number of births in 1938 was reported to have been 294, the number of deaths, 99, and infant death, 53 — giving a crude birth rate of 39.1; crude death rate, 13.2; and infant mortality 180. In the recent census, of a population of 10,947, the following statistics were reported for 1939: 439 births, a birth rate of 40.1; 207 deaths, or a death rate of 18.9. Other population data collected in this census are being analyzed. . . .

The report broke off abruptly. Huang Tse-fang had closed his eyes forever.

In his last will he asked that he be cremated and that his ashes be placed for a few days at the National Medical Association, among the books he loved, and where his life's work lay.

I visited the Schools of the Children of the Heroes of the Revolution several times: two beautiful large campuses facing each other outside Chungshan Men gate, between Dr. Sun Yat-sen's Mausoleum and the Ming Tombs, at the foot of Purple Mountain. They were expertly planned. The brand-new buildings were the last word in modern college architecture, airy, spacious, well-furnished. There were playgrounds, a swimming pool, a covered court for rainy weather, model classrooms, gymnasium, dormitories — in short, an up-to-date American college for the upper ten thousand, right in the heart of China. The idea of affording free education to the children of soldiers who had died in the defense of the Revolution had originally come from Madame Sun Yat-sen and Tsai Yuan-pei, but Madame Chiang Kai-shek and the Generalissimo had adopted the schools as their own, and most of the students were orphans or younger brothers and sisters of soldiers who had fallen during the civil war. Generalissimo and Madame raised most of the funds. The buildings were estimated at NC $500,000. A like sum was contributed from various sources as an endowment. The Ministry of Finance contributed NC $12,000 per annum, the Ministry of Education and other sources also co-operated.

Madame desired the two schools to be the model schools for China. She had chosen the site for its scenic beauty. "The children who are privileged to study in the Institute," she said, "will certainly enjoy the esthetic influence of nature, which, coupled with the guidance of their teachers, will tend favorably to the development of their talents and characters."

Only healthy children were enrolled. This was a guarantee of their future services to the nation. Madame herself chose the teachers for their ability and qualifications. She rejected many a candidate recommended by Kuomintang and government leaders, saying that she was "opposed to mixing up education with politics." The Party resented this. But the children led a wonderful life. They had the best food and the best clothes money could buy, and special beautiful outfits for every sport. They had an excellent well-balanced curriculum and — from the fourth and fifth grade upward — practical training. There were 1000 acres of land on which the boys could try their hand at gardening and agriculture. They grew flowers and vegetables and sold them in their own shops. But their pride was their dairy. Madame had imported ten cows from the United States and ten were bought locally. Their milk and butter beat all the professional dairies, and all Nanking foreigners were eager to secure them. The demand exceeded production. The first time I went to I Tzu Hsueh Hsiao to take pictures of the kids at play and at work, they fidgeted until I let myself be dragged to those splendid specimens of white and black cows. I had to snap them in many poses. Then the boys had a special surprise for me — they were quite excited about it. They brought out two newborn calves that had hardly learned to walk. "We have made these ourselves," one of the youngsters in a Boy Scout uniform announced proudly. Such an attitude was a hopeful, novel thing to me. First, because dairies are quite a non-Chinese proposition. It is beneath human dignity to drink animal milk, except when prescribed as a medicine; butter is looked down upon and called *niou-you* — "cow oil" — and cheese is nothing but spoiled milk. Second, because the average Chinese has no sympathy for animals and is stupidly cruel to them.

The girls were trained in all household work, sewing, hosiery, embroidery, weaving, making artificial flowers, toys and rattan work. They supplied the stockings and socks for both schools and sold their other products.

The younger children were washed and kept tidy by amahs or by the older students. The bigger boys and girls did their own washing and mending and kept their quarters clean. There were some 200 girls and 500 boys, raised like brothers and sisters of one big well-to-do family. The teachers acted as tutors, conducting daily morning meetings on cleanliness, watching over the behavior in classrooms, bedrooms, playgrounds, and instructing the kids in proper table manners at mealtime. They were amazingly well-behaved and conscious of the part they were to play in the future as the "pillars and reformers of Chinese society." And they adored Madame and the Generalissimo.

Hygiene, discipline and physical training were unequaled any-where else. Girls and boys gave teachers the military salute. They wore becoming uniforms or Boy and Girl Scout outfits.

On Commencement Day — June 1937, the last before the war — the whole campus was decorated with flags and flowers and lanterns. There was a big athletic show, folk-dancing by the little ones, competitive theatricals by every grade, speeches, music, distribution of prizes and honors. The teachers had made all the costumes out of paper — and the performance of "The Wolf and the Little Goats" was an outstanding success.

I sat in a refreshment tent with a group of teachers and asked where they would spend their vacation. At the campus, they said. All children were confined to the campus from the day of enrollment to the day of graduation. They were not allowed to visit their homes except when the funeral of an elder required their presence. Madame feared that poor surroundings and bad manners might be detrimental to their characters. Relatives were allowed to visit the children once, on Commencement Day; however, as they lived in distant provinces, most of them could not afford the traveling expenses. Only a very few were present.

My heart grew heavy. Poor kids, poor teachers, poor China. How would these "pillars of society" ever be able to under-stand the heart of the poor, downtrodden people? Oh, said the teachers, the children are brought up in the principles of charity — after each meal the leftovers are collected in big pails and the children themselves distribute it among the poor villagers waiting outside the walls.

I saw them sitting, bowl in hand, on the dusty roadside, those children of the good earth — hollow-cheeked men, women and babes — long before dinnertime, waiting for the privileged chil-dren's charity.

On my way home, I pondered. The school as such was a fine thing, but what was the motive behind it? Was it a para-military institute, the nucleus of a future Chiang Youth? There were

War Area Service Corps: George Fitch (*second*)
and Col. J. L. Huang (*right*)

School of the Children of the Revolution

unmistakable resemblances to Mussolini's Fascist Youth and to the Hitler *Jugend* — severing the children from their families, and grouping them round one leader. On the other hand, charity was not a part of Fascist or Nazi doctrine. Madame might consider it a Christian virtue; but as it was applied here, it looked more like a remnant of Western feudalism. Rich or poor, the Chinese are a proud people. Here human dignity was trampled on, poverty was turned into pauperism. Charity is neither a Chinese virtue nor a Chinese vice, it is essentially un-Chinese. The nationwide custom is that poor relatives — even of the remotest branch, even those one does not know personally — can come to the house of the better-off members of the family, eat there, live there, and get help in securing work. And those who have no family or are far from home are given the same hospitality by strangers who are natives of their province. It is not almsgiving but sharing. It is not charity but the deep-rooted feeling of common decency, so common that no Chinese would ever think of playing it up as a virtue.

Could those youngsters, pampered like princes, brought up in the idea that they belonged to the privileged few, that they were the pillars of society, grow up to be anything else than the former imperial mandarins, or the present-day magistrates lording it over the common people? I failed to see any relationship between this spirit and Madame's repeated assertions that China was on the road to democracy. . . . After all, in a democracy education is not a privilege of the few, but the basic right of all citizens. I was very much puzzled. . . .

Extracts from my letter to W. H. Donald, July 9, 1937

Iltis Huk, Tsingtao.

. . . You know my own views in the matter of opium monopolies: I still believe that government-stamped opium is as efficacious a poison to the nation as is the smuggler's own brand. . . .

. . . Have you ever seen a public burning of opium? I have,

on the nation-wide Opium Suppression Day — June 3 — in Nanking. The municipality must have raided some garbage bins in the Futze-miao district to get all the rubbish together — any old thing, from bamboo sticks and rusty saucepans, tins, newspaper, to a few opium pipes and even a lonely opium lamp. There wasn't a sign or smell of dope. A dozen busy firemen had to stir and fan the flame to keep it alive, so that the official photographer with his giant camera could take an impressive picture. A poor, bashful little *auto-da-fé* and — a few yards off the tiny heap — in cheerful contrast to it, the biggest fire engine I ever set eyes upon, brand-new, sparkling red and gold, ready to protect the capital from the terrific blaze!

Hundreds of spectators, mostly coolies, grinning their heads off, wide awake to the grotesqueness of the situation . . .

A government narcotic commissioner explained to me, some time later, that opium was too expensive to be burned, but that — to prove its seriousness in the matter — the Government had executed that day at Nanking three narcotic offenders. As a matter of fact, I had seen these poor blighters when soldiers paraded them, on a motor truck, through the streets of Nanking, towards the Arsenal. Of course, bullets are cheaper than opium, but on an occasion like this nation-wide festival, the authorities could have made *le grand geste* and sacrificed a ton of opium, if only for the sake of the reek and to carry off the bluff in a more convincing manner.

I remember what you told me at Shanghai, one day: "The manliest man in China, the most energetic and active man in China, the man who is loyal and stands by the people and wants to do the best for it — is Madame Chiang Kai-shek." This is a job for the manliest man in China — can't Madame take it up and make a success of it, as she does with everything else she tackles? I think she would make a perfect Secretary General of Opium Suppression. I have an implicit faith in her earnestness of purpose, in her intelligence, in her wisdom, in her heart, in her judgment of people and in her courage. And as it is she who found W. H. D. for a friendly adviser, she can't go wrong in picking the right man to advise her on opium matters — a man who would sail clear of any blood-brotherhood or schoolmateship or other dainty ties, and would combine integrity with thorough knowledge of the game and with the guts to call a spade a bloody shovel. . . .

As this happens to be an opium letter, I will comply with the best traditions of the Opium Suppression Commission and wind up with some slogans: —

Self-protection demands the withdrawal of extrality rights from every individual engaged in illicit manufacture, sale or distribution of opium and manufactured narcotics.

The welfare of the Nation demands the capital punishment of twelve of the most influential citizens of the Republic notoriously engaged in promoting the narcotic trade.

(Lots could be drawn to determine the first dozen, with the promise that other executions will follow *ad libitum*.)

This may sound radical, but I see no better solution as far as morphine and heroin are concerned. It may be premature — I don't know just how far Generalissimo can go at present — but I believe that, in the not too distant future, he will be powerful enough to go to the limit.

I won't apologize for this lengthy letter — I am too glad to have got it off my chest. There are so darned few people to whom I can write as frankly as I can to you. And although you may cuss me out for it — (I can almost hear your peculiarly expressive "damn") — I know that you will use whatever is useful in the best interest of China. And that is all I want.

More power to you and your fine work, and three cheers for the Triumvirate.

Extracts from W. H. Donald's reply, July 16, 1937

Kuling.

So you got out of the wrong side of the bed on July 9th. What is the idea of your disturbing the tranquility of Iltis Huk, and causing a similar reaction at Kuling, by a double-fisted attack upon me? Do you not know I am quite an innocent fellow about opium? How the devil I got the reputation of being an anti-opium crusader I don't know. Did you not read the issue of *Time* which had a character sketch of me and suggested between the lines that I was a dealer in opium myself? Or, have you found out that I am in that great game? . . .

You say that I am undoubtedly aware of the racket going on in Shanghai and Hankow, etc. Dash my boots, I am not aware of anything! You tell me things I never even heard of, but I think you must be right when you write "they do not leave a stone unturned to frustrate the Generalissimo's efforts." There are lots of them at the same game — not only the opium racketeers. Did you ever hear of the Sian incident? Did you ever hear that an open attack was made upon this innocent child to get him kicked out of China? Do you realize who they were, and why they did it? Have you read a short story by Madame Chiang Kai-shek on her experiences in the Sian business? Can you read between the lines, or are you myopic?

My trouble is that no one tells me anything *that is backed up with irrefutable proof that I can act upon*. This letter of yours, the product, no doubt, of a late night, or an early morning urge for reform, says a lot of things, but can you give me the proof?

You ask me if I have ever seen a public burning of opium. Fie, fie! I am Scotch and if I saw a waste of good product it would seriously affect my commercial instincts, but if ever I hear of one which is to take place I am going, as your description attracts me tremendously.

You make an accusation against me which I must oppose, resist, or do whatever should be done about such a thing. Here am I in the environment of missionaries, surrounded by perambulating Bibles, smothered by prayer, and you say I call a spade a "bloody shovel." I am really shocked that you should make such an allegation about me in cold type. *Time* said I was a lot of things, but they did not go so far as that.

But this shows I have read through the letter and I have even got down to the slogan part of it. I do not understand why they should have a slogan that individuals engaged in illicit manufacture should have extrality rights withdrawn from them. Do you not realize that the bright and intelligent fraternity of nationalists want to withdraw extrality rights from me, to say nothing of the praying missionaries and other harmless people? If I start them out by saying that they should only withdraw extrality rights from people engaged in opium, I would take the thunder out of their talking.

Ah, now I get to it. You want to have twelve of the most influential citizens of the Republic shot. I hope I don't get into this class. But I agree with you. It would be a lot of fun to line up a lot of people we don't like and then you and I draw lots to see which of them should be massacred.

And you say "This may sound radical." Bless you, they shoot people for far less. . . .

Now to be serious, what the devil do you think I am going to do with all this stuff? To whom do you think I am going to give it? How can I give stuff written in English to anyone who only reads Chinese? Who will translate it? Who will pay for the translation? Do you think those who want to sustain the semi-official opium den, or whatever it is, will want to translate it? But having asked you all these questions, I will answer them myself. I think I will have to give it to — well, never mind, I won't tell you. But I will give it to somebody.

. . . After all, you must remember that everyone picks on me. My mail is one mass of stuff asking me to do something or other, or to buy something or other — but strange to relate no one ever writes me to tell me how much they love me. I do try to survive, but I must confess life is hard and sad. Nevertheless, you being a nice person, the next time you get up early in the morning with the feeling of indigestion, or whatever it is, please, spare me. Yet, if you want to tell me how blue the sea is at Tsingtao, or how nice is the air blowing through the serrated rocks, or round the beetling cliffs, then you can write.

I am supposed to have four jobs at Tsingtao. If you do not believe me, ask the Mayor. I am supposed to be the Inspector of the Beaches, so that I can line up all the bathing beauties to see if they are properly dressed; I am supposed to be Head of the Fishing Department so that I can get the best fishing place; I am supposed to be Supervisor of the Golf Course so that I can have the course to myself when I want it, and I am supposed to be the Oppressor of Smugglers so that I can get a steam launch to collect all the beauties off the beach to go fishing in the places where the fish are most likely to bite. One of these days I am going to go to Tsingtao and take up this collection of jobs and give up forever and ever trying to stop people from smoking opium when they really want to smoke it. Have you not yet found out that I am one person whose one belief is that the charm of life is that everyone should be allowed to do just as they damn well like?

Au revoir. Take a dive for me and good luck to you.

Very sincerely,

W. H. DONALD

I toured the interior of Shantung Province alone during a few weeks, and joined the Magee family at their lovely summer home in Iltis Huk, suburb of Tsingtao, shortly before July 7, 1937, the day of the Lukochiao (Marco Polo Bridge) incident, when the Japanese set out upon new conquest of Chinese territory.

On September 1, the 16,000 Japanese residents of Tsingtao received orders from their government to leave for Japan. Boats lay ready in the harbor. Three days later there was not a single Japanese in the city. All of them had turned over the keys of their factories, shops, and residences to Mayor Shen, and asked him to take good care of their property until they returned.

On September 13, the Japanese Navy attacked Shanghai and Generalissimo's troops resisted. The people in Tsingtao heard the news with mixed feelings, anything from rousing patriotism to panic. For one thing, all trains and main roads were chock-full: those who were in Tsingtao fled to the interior, and those from the interior fled to Tsingtao. All boats were crowded, too. Mayor Shen placed Chinese sentries in front of every Japanese factory and important building, to protect the property entrusted to him from possible sabotage by the Chinese populace. He did so under orders from Han Fu-ch'ü, Governor of Shantung Province, who was sitting on the fence; no one knew for sure whether his well-equipped and well-trained troops would fight the Japanese or the National Government. As it happened, his army avoided meeting the Japanese for a long time. Finally he was convicted of treason by court-martial in Kaifeng and shot at Wuchang in 1938.

The immediate reaction of the common people to the war was fear of being drafted. No villager dared bring his vegetables or other produce to the town market. All men of draft age fled into the mountains — including the Tsingtao streetcleaners and sanitary squad, who disappeared leaving their uniforms in a heap in the middle of their courtyard. I was shocked at this attitude, but when I saw the first recruits, I quite understood it. There was no draft law. Peasants and workers ("no decent people") were taken by force, regardless of age or family, roped together by their wrists, and led to the barracks in long Indian file. They were kicked and beaten en route by the escorting military.

Shortly afterwards the American Consulate in Tsingtao sent out instructions to all American families, advising all those whose presence in China was not essential, but particularly all women with children, to pack their suitcases and be ready to embark at a moment's notice. Faith and the boys were getting ready. John came up from Nanking to bid them farewell. He had decided to stay on in the capital, no matter what happened. The foreigners there were establishing a safety zone for the poor Chinese who would not be able to evacuate in case the Japanese took Nanking.

I had no idea what I should do, but as soon as Generalissimo released the seven National Salvation people who had been kept in jail for anti-Japanese and democratic activities, I said to myself, "Hurrah, this is the first proof that the Old Man means business. The United Front begins to work." I wired J. Heng Liu, offering my services as nurse at the front, and I wrote John Magee saying I was ready to work for the Government. Dr. Liu never replied; he told me later personally that he "wouldn't take any chances" with me. The two of us always had friendly skirmishes; probably because we knew each other's positions on the opium field.

Hardly had John arrived in Tsingtao when he got a cable from Y. T. Tsur, Vice Minister of Industries, in reference to my offer and asking him to "bring Miss Sues to Nanking" with him. Dr. Tsur was one of those very few government officials who placed the country's and the people's interests above private affairs. He took no part in politics, worked hard, and was a man above reproach. I was glad to be called by him and wondered what would be my assignment.

I cannot think of anything more touching and beautiful than the moment when Faith and John said good-by to each other. Faith and the boys were going to her family in England, where their two elder sons — John, Jr., and David — were in school. John was going to face the worst in Nanking. The hearts of those two fine people who loved each other so dearly were at breaking point. But the call of duty to God and to China was stronger. They kept a courageous, pathetic little smile on their faces and Faith and the boys stood in front of the house waving their hands until our cab turned the corner.

Nanking had had its bombings and had put on its war garb. The city was strewn with dugouts for the population and private shelters. At every few steps there were arrows pointing to the nearest place of refuge, in English and Chinese. Most houses were painted black, to prevent glare during raids. The formerly light blue street-buses now wore a coat of drab olive.

Most foreign women had left. John and some other men lived

in the Magees' house, while I stayed with the girl teachers on the compound. Guei-Guei was glad to be back in Nanking and had the run of both houses and the garden.

The school had become a hospital; it was filling with civilian victims of bombings. Our terrace was tightly filled with baskets full of sand; this was to protect the cellar, which served as shelter for the whole compound, against direct hits.

The Japanese raided the city practically every day. At the first sound of the sirens, the population would hurry to the shelters, but never have I seen any sign of panic. The usually so noisy Chinese talked in whispers. Somebody had circulated the rumor that the Japanese had such fine sound detectors in their planes that they could hear even a whisper. This absolute silence had something ominous in the dark shelters. I went there only once or twice, when John insisted that we had to comply with government orders. Otherwise I would watch the planes, horrified and fascinated.

Guei-Guei soon became air-raid-conscious. He would prick up his ears at the first signal, a slow, warbling sound "Alarm," but would continue to go about his business quietly, knowing that he had at least twenty minutes before the second, the frantically fast warbling "Hoo-aa-hoo-aa-hoo-aa," would fill skies and hearts with tremor. When he heard this signal the Japs were practically overhead. Guei-Guei did not like the noise of exploding bombs; he dashed to his shelter under the bed, and no force could get him out of there before the All Clear sounded. Then he would come out, pretending, like any of us, that he had not been scared at all, and stalk about with an air of superior indifference. Even today in New York he looks up at every plane and ducks instinctively when it passes overhead. But he does not hide any more.

Back in Nanking, on September 29, 1937, I immediately phoned Donald at Headquarters, to tell him that I had volunteered to work for the Government.

"Don't ask *me* for any job," he interrupted me, on the defensive. "I have my hands full refusing foreigners. Everybody expects *me* to give him a job."

"I'm not asking you for a job. All I want you to do is tell me whether Y. T. Tsur is O. K. He wired me to come down; I am to do some publicity work."

A moment's silence, then the voice came back — calm, businesslike: —

"Y. T. Tsur is O. K. . . . Publicity? To whom are you to report?"

"No idea. Probably to the Foreign Office, to T. T. Li. You know what we think of his propaganda in Geneva!"

"N-n-no," said Donald reflectively, "they'll probably have you work for Cheng Kung-po."

"Who is he?"

"Propaganda Minister."

"What kind of a man?"

"Find out yourself."

"Thank you. That's all. Good-by."

"Wait a moment — let me know any further developments, will you?"

"Yes, Mr. Donald."

Mr. Tsur sent me to T. T. Li, a short, slight, smooth little bureaucrat who held the important position of Chief of Press at the *Waichiaopu*, the Foreign Office, and whose main characteristic was his extreme caution. He was so careful not to commit himself or his government that, during the time the Sino-Japanese conflict was before the League of Nations and the Japanese had an army of alert propaganda agents swamping Geneva with expertly prepared official and unofficial material, the Chinese delegation had been left high and dry without any information from Nanking. The culminating point of this discretion came when Brazil and China were competing for a vacancy on the League's Council. Japan was permanently represented. It was only just and reasonable that the victim of her aggression should obtain the semi-permanent seat. The gallant little Chinese delegation fought tooth and nail to ensure a majority vote for China. Most of the International Press was sympathetic. But everybody waited for a declaration from Nanking — a peg to hang a story on, a statement to boost. Days passed; diplomats and journalists grew impatient. Finally, a day or two before the election, the Chinese Press Agency brought out a four-page stenciled statement — 200 correspondents grabbed it, hungry for a last-minute story, and stood aghast. All the four pages contained was a concise history of the life of Confucius!

Smooth people are most enervating. Five minutes after I had met dapper T. T. Li, I could not help bringing up this story. I told him he should have been present at the League's lobby to hear the pressmen curse China and its propaganda chief in unison. So polite was the little diplomat, he did not even lose his temper. We exchanged views concerning foreign propaganda, and neither convinced the other.

However, it was not the *Waichiaopu* I was to work for; would I please see Mr. Cheng Kung-po, Propaganda Minister?

I rang up Francis to find out what my prospective chief was like, but my friend was singularly uninformative. All I could get out of him was that Cheng Kung-po had been a member of the Hankow Revolutionary Government in 1927, but had changed since.

"Well, what kind of a man is he?"

"Find out yourself."

Same reply as Donald's. Some enigmatic personality, I thought.

Just before my appointment with Cheng Kung-po, George Fitch took me to a luncheon given by Hubert Liang to the foreign press correspondents. Hubert Liang is one of those people with ever-present charming smiles who never have anything to say, but say it beautifully. He was friendly with everybody, and the Government had told him to get from foreign journalists suggestions and criticism which would make China's propaganda more effective abroad. He got an earful from the boys. There were sixteen of them.

Never was a more vivid picture painted of the absolute impossibility of obtaining information on what was going on at the front. Instead of one official information center, the capital had four: the Foreign Office Press Bureau under T. T. Li, the Kuomintang Publicity Office under Chiang Kang-li, the newly established Propaganda Ministry or Fifth Department under Cheng Kung-po, and the Military Intelligence Bureau under General Yang. The latter the boys knew only from hearsay, as it was outside the city walls, concealed at a strategic point on Purple Mountain. With the other three they had daily dealings. The routine was invariably the same. T. T. Li had no information and would send them to Chiang Kang-li, a mere eight miles away, who would send them to Cheng Kung-po, some ten miles away, who again would send them back to Mr. T. T. Li. . . . By that time it would be mid-afternoon, and they would not have been able to satisfy their agencies, who would be sending cable after cable demanding reports. If there were no air raids over Nanking, which they watched at close quarters, they might just as well close shop.

Cheng Kung-po was a man of middle stature, square-shouldered, short-necked, with a head somewhat too big and a pale face which bore traces of former handsomeness and energy. Yet I had never encountered anyone as worn-down by life and as weary-looking. A pitifully stooping figure . . . all the muscles under his dark Chungshan uniform seemed flabby. Most striking was the dejected, disillusioned look in his deepset black eyes. There was fatigue in every gesture, in the low, melodious voice.

He, too, wanted to know what people abroad thought of China's propaganda, and I made a quick survey for him. He nodded wearily and went into a long series of complaints. No-body knew what obstacles he had to face, he said. Generalissimo and Madame showed no interest in publicity. The Kuomintang pulled in one direction, and the *Waichiaopu* in another. War news was unobtainable because it was a military secret. Civilian defense news was unavailable because it was a Party secret. Each of the four propaganda organs claimed autonomy and priority. The four chiefs were to meet three times a week to co-ordinate activities, but they seldom met — the distances were too great. And when they met, they never agreed. Oh, propaganda was a very difficult, delicate problem to solve.

One could hardly imagine anyone more helpless: I felt very sorry for him and tried to pep him up. Why not ask Generalis-simo to clamp down on all the others and give full powers to the Propaganda Ministry? Headquarters realized the importance of publicity, and with Generalissimo's backing he could set up a model organization in no time. . . .

Cheng Kung-po stared at me as though I had fallen from an-other planet, shook his head gloomily, and changed the subject. Would I draft a scheme showing how China's propaganda should be handled abroad? I replied that I was no publicity ex-pert, but that I would do my best. He had not said a word about appointing me, but I looked upon the thing as some sort of examination paper.

It was not very difficult to write down a few suggestions in a country where foreign publicity was, so to speak, nonexistent. All I had to do was recall the functioning of any one of the more successful government press agencies and give a rough outline of the cheapest and most direct approach to public opinion in Europe and America.

I started out with a concise criticism and then suggested the establishment of one well-equipped center of information, the appointment of a score of hand-picked journalists familiar with the Western mentality, the issuing of daily press releases fea-turing news and human interest stories, the holding of press

conferences, also facilities for and closest collaboration with
foreign correspondents, broadcasts, photo service and so on.
Briefly, the A B C of publicity. The fact that probably any
clerk in any American advertising agency would have done a
better job did not bother me. I had done my best. China's situation was too serious to play around with niceties. Drastic changes
had to be made. I did not pull my punches. This was my con-
tribution to China's war chest. But China is China. I realized
that here my "rough notes" were dynamite and would scare the
wits out of a fellow like Cheng Kung-po.

I addressed the original with a polite note to him, and sent a
copy to Donald, for information, suggesting that the Triumvirate
— Generalissimo, Madame and Donald — would have to step on
the publicity people personally, if they wanted to achieve anything.

As far as I was concerned, the matter was closed. The gloomy
minister would not touch a person with such radical ideas, and
if Donald read the stuff at all, he would shrug his shoulders and
laugh at the simpleton. I would try again to go to the front as
a nurse.

Francis and I spent next morning tramping round the grounds
of Nanking's imposing Medical Center, which the Japanese had
chosen as their target. That's where they tried out the effective-
ness of their first two 1000-pound bombs. The result was fortunately enough only two enormous craters in the red mud. Part
of the auditorium was smashed and all buildings were pock-
marked with shrapnel and machine gun bullets. By sheer miracle
not one of the hundreds of wounded and doctors and nurses was
hurt. Nanking's pride — the beautiful concrete buildings — had
shielded them. The only two casualties were two electricians
who happened to be out on the compound. But the beastliness
of singling out a hospital for a major attack made one furious
and sick at heart.

The moment my ricksha turned into the gates of the Sheng

Kung Hwei, John Magee came out to meet me. He did not walk, he ran, gesticulating excitedly with his long arms.

"Hurry up, Ralf — Mr. Donald called up twice — you are to give him a ring at once."

I rushed to the phone. There was Donald, chiding me with superb mockery: —

"So that's what you're up to now? Writing memos to teach the Chinese how to run their affairs? You know it all, don't you? Dammit, I have written so many memos in my life, you could cover the entire globe with them. 'Tis easy to make suggestions. . . ."

I felt hot and embarrassed and retorted meekly that I had drafted my notes only because Cheng Kung-po had asked me to, that I had sent a copy to Donald to keep him posted, that I realized how inadequate my attempt was, but that I had not expected so immediate and so violent a reaction. . . .

Donald laughed: "You've done a damn good job. I like your memo. I want to talk it over with you, right away. I am sending you a car."

I was so puzzled I could hardly catch my breath.

"But, Mr. Donald . . . my luggage hasn't yet come down from Tsingtao . . . I've no change of clothes . . . I am filthy, covered with mud from head to toe. . . ."

"I never expected any better of you. . . . Where do you hang out?"

"*Hsiakwan Sheng Kung Hwei* . . ."

"Don't swear at me in Chinese. Hey, boy," he yelled in the other direction, "take this address."

The car speeded the sixteen kilometers across the city, passed the Chungshan Men gate at the opposite end, rolled on toward Purple Mountain. I had no idea where Donald lived. We came to a little palace with round turrets and gabled roofs, all painted in black. A Hollywood reproduction of a German medieval castle . . . Soldiers at the gate, presenting arms, shouting "*Chin lee!*" . . . Soldiers at the entrance, shouting "*Chin lee!*"

The interior was quite European: a long tiled hall, a large salon with a beautiful waxed parquet which made me feel less presentable than before. I looked round trying to guess where I was, but the furnishings were noncommittal. A very few armchairs, one or two precious vases, and, above the mantelpiece, a large portrait of Dr. Sun Yat-sen. No picture of Generalissimo, no picture of Madame — so it was not Donald's house, I decided. Besides, it was too stiff, too conventional and too well guarded. . . .

Donald came in. Before I could say a word, he crushed me in his arms — my ribs seemed to crack. "Attaboy, Attaboy," he cried exuberantly, patting me on both shoulders with such force that I felt like a punching bag. "Attaboy . . . you don't know how good your memo is . . . just the radical stuff we've been waiting for . . . Madame was delighted with it . . . Sit down . . ." He released his grip, and I staggered into the nearest chair. . . . "Did you get a reply from Cheng Kung-po?"

"Not yet. It will probably take some time — "

"That's what I thought. That bastard hasn't got enough sense to reply. . . . What do you think of him?"

"A poor fish . . . the last man I would have appointed Propaganda Minister. But a likeable fellow . . ."

" 'A likeable fellow'!" Donald snapped furiously — "That scoundrel? He is Wang Ching-wei's man."

"What's wrong with that? Wang Ching-wei is President of the Executive *Yuan* . . ."

"And Chiang Kai-shek's most bitter rival. He is just waiting for a chance to sell out to the Japanese."

"You mean to say that Cheng Kung-po's defeatism is intentional?"

"I mean to say that he is a God-damn . . . Do you mind my swearing?"

"Not at all. It clears the atmosphere and puts me at ease." I fumbled in my bag, craving a cigarette. "Would you mind telling me what weird place this is — I haven't seen an ash tray around."

"You may throw the ashes on the floor. It is H. H. Kung's house. . . . Listen, Madame's going to reorganize publicity. What do you think we should do with your 'likeable fellow'?"

"I suppose the traditional course would be to send him abroad on a study tour?"

Donald grinned. They must have been planning this right along. We talked for a while. Then he looked at his wrist watch, and said solemnly: —

"Miss Sues, it is seven minutes to five, October 7, 1937. Remember this moment: you are hereby engaged by Madame Chiang Kai-shek to help reorganize publicity in accordance with your memorandum."

"What?" The shock was too unexpected. I felt as though the world were crumbling round me. I stretched out my hand: —

"Mr. Donald . . . pinch me . . . I must be dreaming . . ."

He bit my wrist. I suppressed a scream.

"Do you believe it now? Are you happy?"

"Happy? I am scared stiff at the idea. . . . I don't want the job. I don't know how to organize a damn thing. Let me go home."

"Sit down and don't be an idiot. You have a program, and a damn good one. Have you got the guts to defend it? Yes or no?"

"Yes." After all, I was not a quitter.

"That's better. I am not appointing you Propaganda Minister. All you have to do is stick to your guns. You will be the expert on foreign publicity — unofficial adviser, with no executive power. Madame and I will back you. At first, you will work in my office, to get the right training. T. V. Soong and Harry Timperley are handling our foreign publicity in Shanghai. You'll turn out an article a day; they'll place it. It will be some job kicking Cheng Kung-po and his gang out of office, but we'll do it. Then we'll set up a decent publicity board with Hollington Tong in charge. . . . Madame has wired him to come down from Shanghai. . . . You will get along all right. . . . Feeling better now?"

"Somewhat . . ."

"Then let's get down to brass tacks. What salary do you expect?"

"Three hundred dollars, Chinese."

"You *are* crazy."

"John Magee said this is the minimum a foreigner can live on. Personally I think it is rather high, I can live much cheaper, on Chinese food. I should hate the idea of robbing the Government. Just pay me whatever you consider right."

Donald shook his head in a way that made me feel hopelessly stupid.

"You'll get five hundred plus household expenses. We will find you a house near Headquarters, a car and a reliable chauffeur. J. L. Huang will help you find a cook, a boy and a coolie and anything else you may need."

Both schools for the Children of the Heroes of the Revolution had been disbanded; the children were sent back home with the exception of a small number of the older ones who remained and cared for the wounded. Most of the buildings were turned into hospital wards, packed with wounded soldiers.

Madame played fairy godmother to Cinderella. Donald took me round to George Shepherd's bungalow, a charming little place all painted black on account of air raids, and lost in a remote corner of the campus among the lovely unkempt trees and bushes. "Would you like to live here?" asked W. H. D. And when I said it would simply be a dream, he ordered Colonel J. L. Huang to have the house cleared, and me and my bags moved in.

Huge J. L., with his round, smiling face and Boy Scout mentality, was the Chiangs' number-one office boy. American-educated, with a four-years training at Ford's, then Secretary General of the Chinese Y.M.C.A., he was now the soul of the New

Life Movement and of the Officers' Moral Endeavor Association. Headquarters could not do without him any more than China could do without bamboo. Dependable, loyal, totally unimaginative, he carried out every order to the iota, smiling, panting a little, risking his life if need be. If everything went smoothly at H.Q. it was certainly largely J. L.'s merit, though nobody bothered to pat him on the shoulder. But let anything go wrong anywhere in the world — J. L. was always the one who got hell. He would shrug his powerful shoulders wistfully, leave the room on tiptoe, console himself with a hearty meal, and be back on duty with the same good-natured stolidity an hour later.

My house was ready in twenty-four hours, and J. L. had thrown in a courtyard-full of blue-black A-1 anthracite, otherwise unobtainable, and had decorated all rooms with flowers as for a bridal reception. Pretty young May Chan, Donald's secretary, was to live with me there.

J. L. and one of his assistants were there to welcome us upon arrival. They had done a marvelous job; nothing was missing in this cozy, thoughtfully equipped home — nothing except carpets. But Donald came in, looked at the floor, frowned. Next day coolies covered the huge parlor and the smaller rooms with priceless, heavy rugs. "Where did you get these?" "Oh," Donald laughed, "I raided H. H. Kung's attic."

The War Area Service Corps had a hostel downtown — a high-class American-style bachelors' club. J. L. and George Fitch and most of the young American-trained officers lived there. J. L. loved good food. It was the only thing in which he really indulged himself. Oh, he could do with a bowl of rice and a handful of salt turnip when he was somewhere in the interior, on a perilous mission. Service to the Generalissimo came first and foremost in his life. He was ready to starve and die for Generalissimo. But when he had a chance — and he had a chance in Nanking — only the choicest and daintiest food was placed on his table.

The club's cook was the greatest artist in Nanking, his cuisine and epicurean dream. And to watch gourmet J. L. enjoy his meal was a treat in itself. The most acrimonious old dyspeptic would be converted to the pleasures of the palate! I had never tasted anything more excitingly refined, more voluptuously spiced, more exquisitely perfumed than a dinner we were served there one evening.

"There is only one more thing I should like to have, to make life perfect," I said to J. L. "Your cook."

I meant it as a compliment, but J. L. took everything seriously. He turned pale. Donald had ordered him to comply with my wishes. . . . Would I rob him of the most precious thing he possessed? He refused. I am sure it was the only order he ever refused to execute, and I liked him even better for it — it was so darn human. The club could not do without Ta She-fu, he said, but Ta She-fu had a younger brother, almost as good as himself. . . . So I got the second-best cook in Nanking.

Francis found me a Peiping boy — they are the best *stylé* in the world, just as Cantonese cooks are the last word in perfection.

A good cook is a gift of heaven, a pet to be spoiled, a despot whose whims are law. In China he is called Ta She-fu, the Big Servant. My Big Servant was four feet six tall, a handsome, slim lad of about twenty-three, but he had the calm composure of an old one. And he had his principles.

His dignity forbade his preparing my breakfast coffee, toast and eggs — the only foreign meal I would not miss. The boy was good enough to be trained in such barbarian methods.

Cook would not sleep in the house. I had to ask J. L. to get a bicycle for him. Half an hour after dinner he was all dolled up like a little gentleman and pedaled off to spend the night with his sweetheart in the city.

We had an American stove, a huge iron-and-nickel affair

that occupied one third of the very large kitchen and heated the water in the bathroom. It would have been the pride of any Western housewife. Cook gave it one look, then he looked at the mountain of anthracite, then he went out and came back with two one-hole portable charcoal stoves and a paper bag full of charcoal. He and the coolie would take these out into the courtyard every morning, clean them, start the fire, and fan them with a big fan until all smoke was gone and the coal was red hot. Then the stoves would be brought into the kitchen and Ta She-fu would cook all the meals on them.

The range remained cold, and so did the water in the bathroom. Cook listened respectfully to my daily explanations and orders and did not touch it. He said there was not enough draft in the pipes. Exasperated, I called in Donald's boy, a shiny-eyed live wire of eighteen, whom his master had brought up and trained to perfection. He lit the stove in a jiffy, explained everything to Cook. The fire crackled merrily, I had a hot bath; but dinner was cooked on the charcoal stoves! Ta She-fu declared that the foreign fire was too cool to cook a decent meal. My bathroom water regained its frigidaire temperature. I would have fired anyone else for such dastardly stubbornness, but that little devil knew my soft spot; he knew I would rather catch pneumonia than forgo the daily culinary treat.

One day, however, after an icy shower on a bitter cold October morning, I decided upon drastic action before lunch — in other words before my heart was softened by a luscious repast. I told him that if the stove did not work and if there was no hot water in the bathroom within the next twenty-four hours, I would have to face the deep sorrow of parting company with my cook, whose great qualities I sincerely appreciated and admired. May interpreted, as the little fellow understood nothing but Cantonese. He nodded with the same respectful air.

When I came back a few hours later, there were workmen round the house, in the kitchen, on the roof, hammering like mad against the chimney. My first thought was that a fire had broken out. But Cook went quietly about his work, deaf to the rumpus. The boy explained that Cook had summoned the workmen from Nanking to repair the stove. The foreman said that it was a very unusual model, that they would have to take off part of the roof and open the chimney all the way down to see why the fire would not get hot. A man on the roof brandished two shingles.

I made him replace the shingles and ordered them to stop and go home. The house did not belong to me, and I had no right to have it dismantled.

They obeyed grinning, and just a trifle too quickly, and they said I did not owe them anything. I had to force a couple of dollars on them, and they left.

Curious, I thought; a dozen workmen, a terrific noise, and only two little shingles removed? I understood: Cook's friends had come as a living proof that something *was* wrong with the stove. Cook had shown his best intentions to remedy the evil. I had reacted exactly as they had expected me to react. By preventing repairs, I had shifted the burden of responsibility onto my shoulders. Cook's face was saved.

There was boiling hot water in the bathroom that night: two enormous tin jugs full. It could be bought at the hot water peddler's round the corner, the boy said, at the cost of a few coppers. Cook had scored again. Could there be a more flawless demonstration of the utter superfluousness of that despicable shiny iron monster in the kitchen?

The little path leading up to the house was too narrow for any full-grown car, so Donald retrieved George Shepherd's baby Ford, which fitted perfectly into the landscape.

I asked J. L. to choose a childless chauffeur, so I need not worry about his driving round during air raids. "Every man over twenty is married and has plenty children," was his reply, "and in wartime the first duty of a Chinese is to die for his country. We must not be sentimental. The fellow I picked for you is twenty-six, father of four children. He comes from Szechuen, and has been with us for years."

He was a nice bright boy, just the right size for my peanut car, and his uniform and deportment did honor to the War Area Service Corps. I acquainted him with Donald's orders: at the first sound of the siren we were to drive up on a hill, park the car under a tree, and watch the planes. We had to get air-minded.

An hour later, we had an air-raid alarm. I sat beside him, repeated the order, and we raced through the deserted fields. But instead of going uphill we went downhill. We came to a bridge. He parked the car alongside other cars. There were so many trees one could not see the sky. A few men stood around; I recognized the blue enamel badges of the Kuomintang. The bridge was one of those huge solid stone structures, ten feet deep, which no bomb could possibly destroy. The chauffeur insisted we should take shelter under it. He turned a deaf ear to my angry order to proceed to a place where we could see the raiders. There was nothing else to do but look underneath that bridge. A number of long heavy logs were placed across the narrow strip of water, and on them sat some fifty Kuomintang officials with wide-open eyes, listening to the planes droning overhead. I was disgusted and went back to the car, but my chauffeur remained in hiding long after the planes had gone. I gave him a good scolding on the way back, and Donald gave me a good scolding for not having seen the dogfight.

Next day the same thing happened, only the bridge was a different bridge. "Also a very safe Kuomintang shelter," the chauffeur assured me.

"How did you like the raid?" asked Donald.

"This damn chauffeur of mine won't go uphill," I wailed, "all he knows is Kuomintang hideouts."

Donald hollered for ten minutes and made it quite clear what he thought of my lack of authority, of the Party, and of the chauffeur. Finally I got him to name a hill — maybe a precise destination would be more effective than a rather vague "go uphill."

"Go up to the Golf Course," said Donald, "and tell the fellow he'll get court-martialed for disobedience."

As I did not know the Chinese words for Golf Club or court-martial, I asked J. L. up to the house, to convey Donald's message, and he made a thorough job of it. Donald could not have shouted louder. My chauffeur stood at attention, and his face was very pale.

The following air raid found us on the road speeding uphill. I had not known the Golf Course was so far away. We heard the droning of nearing Japanese bombers. "Step on her!" I ordered nervously. He obeyed, but the peanut car's top speed was seventy miles downhill, and we were going uphill. The first three planes caught up with us and dropped a load near enough to cover our car with lumps of dirt and dust. The explosion was terrific. The car nearly landed in the ditch. The lad slowed her up. He turned to me. His face was green with fear, and I felt mine was the same color.

"What shall we do?" he asked.

"Follow instructions," I said huskily.

He stepped on the accelerator. We still heard the sound of the disappearing planes, then we saw someone coming up the road. It was a little old peasant woman in black silk pants and blouse. She walked very erect, balancing a new mattress on her head, which she probably had to deliver somewhere in town. There was the same stoic serenity in her as in the sky and the trees and the grass around us. War, Japs, bombs were passing phenomena, too unimportant to change the pace of life. . . .

The boy and I looked at each other. We had the same thought.

"The little old mother is not afraid," I said; "we two were terribly scared."

We both smiled, a little ashamed.

He did not hide, as usual, under the trees, but walked up the soft, velvety green slope leading to the Club, a little distance from me, and stood beside the Chinese sentry.

I introduced myself to a group of four or five American volunteer aviators.

"Here they come again," somebody shouted. The nine bombers were returning. "And here come our boys, hurrah!" Six Chinese pursuit planes came out of the blue sky, swooped down. There was a short dogfight — oh, minutes only — we held our breath. Two bombers came down — one very swiftly — it crashed out of sight, we heard a faint explosion. The other one stood on its nose in the air and came down in flames, very slowly, like a torch, leaving a thick smudge of black smoke against the pale blue background.

Only then did I notice an officer who must have come up behind us from the clubhouse. He walked slowly past us. The boys saluted. He touched his Mongolian fur cap with his slim white hand. The contrast of this white aristocratic hand to the sun-tanned lean face attracted my attention. He stopped a few steps farther on, scrutinizing the sky. I admired the fine sharp profile and the svelte silhouette.

"The Colonel," whispered the boy next to me affectionately. "He is a prince."

Colonel Chennault, the man whose name was never pronounced, the man who was referred to in subdued whispers as "The Colonel," the legendary leader of the International Squadron. . . . His and his boys' identity had to be kept secret lest the United States Government withdraw their passports and their nationality.

I debated with myself whether I should introduce myself or whether it would be tactless to interrupt his meditation, when a long-drawn-out sound came up from the valley below — it was something between an animal cry and a small stifled siren. The aviators laughed. The Colonel joined in the chorus, turned on his heel and walked swiftly back to the Club.

"All clear," explained one of the boys. "There is a mule down there in the grove where the army hides its horses during the air raids. He keeps mum during the raid, no matter how long it lasts, but half a minute before the All Clear sounds, he gives the signal. That mule has never made a mistake yet. We can't tell whether it's instinct, premonition, or inside information. . . . Here go the sirens."

On our way home my chauffeur and I discussed the dogfight. We were both thrilled and, from that day on, we were both air raid fans.

I was sure the Colonel had not even noticed my presence, but when we got to H.Q., Donald said that Chennault had just telephoned to make sure I really worked for Madame. "And by the way," he had told Donald, "I'd rather not have any women hanging around the Golf Club; the boys are talkative and might let some information slip out."

From then on I watched the air raids with Donald from a hill at the foot of Purple Mountain.

Donald dropped in occasionally for tea and a chat. One day he told me of six new fliers who had just arrived. "Tough chaps, every one of them an ace, simply looking for trouble. They had offered their services to Franco; he turned them down. So they flew for the Loyalists. And whenever they shot down a rebel plane, they would photograph it and send the snapshot to Franco with a note on the back 'Aren't you sorry you didn't accept us?'"

Nothing pleased Donald more than sense of humor.

"Wait a minute," I interrupted our laughter, "this sounds almost like Vincent Schmidt — is he among them?"

"How do you happen to know him? He is the squadron leader."

"Met him at the *Café du Dome* in Paris. Charming fellow, romantic as hell; he introduced himself as 'soldier of fortune.' Wallenstein, the greatest mercenary soldier of the Thirty

Years' War, is his preferred hero. He had just come back from fighting the Italians in Ethiopia and was trying his darndest to get into the Spanish war, his sixth war! Where does he hang out?"

"At the Metropolitan, but have him come up here. The hotel is full of spies, you might warn him too."

Then Donald spoke about Chinese caught spying for Japan. Luminous arrows had been found in the fields, pointing to the airdrome! Japan had had ample time to organize the service. Most of the traitors, from every walk of life, were drug addicts; they were now paid in drugs and money.

Next day I sent my peanut car for Smitty. He was a big, husky bombardier, awkward in his movements and gentle in his approach. He had short-cropped fair hair, kindly gray eyes, a stubborn, dreamy mouth and a captivating boyish smile. Fearless, cool-headed, with war his only passion, this American ace became China's most reliable raider and instructor. He led the squadron in the one and only bombing raid over Formosa early in 1938. Cook served us a particularly dainty tiffin, and Smitty aired his philosophy. Wars should be fought only by mercenary armies, he maintained, then fighting would be an honest affair, a clean sport. There should be no compulsory military service, no national armies where young men are taught to hate. Hatred was the basest of all feelings, the source of all evil and unhappiness.

"Do you mean to say that you've fought in six wars and never hated your adversaries, Smitty?"

"Never," he retorted calmly. "And if I ever should have a feeling of hate, I would be so ashamed of myself, I would quit. Soldier of Fortune means fair play."

During the first week, I got no glimpse of Madame, though she and Generalissimo lived across the road in Donald's tiny bungalow, which was heavily camouflaged for the purpose. Donald had moved to a bigger and more exposed place. Madame's two Chinese male secretaries occupied the rear of the house, May and I worked together in a room adjoining Donald's office. Donald himself had no privacy whatsoever: everybody had to pass through his dining-living room, and he had even placed his bedroom at our disposal; May could take a nap there whenever she felt sleepy, and we could both listen to his radio. I often wondered where he had found that museum piece of a radio — it looked like an attic full of dusty, rusty scrap iron, but it was the most powerful short-wave radio I ever saw in China. We could hear the whole world. Donald kept his finger on the pulse of international affairs, jotting down the high lights of the news, of speeches and international developments, and interpreting them to the Chiangs. It was like a game of bridge: Generalissimo and Madame held the cards, but Donald advised them when and what to bid and which card to play. They did not fare badly.

Even a casual observer glancing through Chiang's history would notice the abrupt change in China's international approach in 1934. She adjusted her relationship with the League of Nations with great skill. The League agreed not only to reduce the amount of China's overdue contributions, but also to use such arrears for the economic development and for the improvement of health conditions in China, in close collaboration with the League's technical organs, who sent a number of high-ranking experts to Nanking.

The painfully introvert Chinese diplomacy made room for a keenly alert extrovert policy. China's voice rang out audibly on the international platform. Her interventions became timely, eminently well prepared and presented. The myth of China, "the backward country of dragons, curios and laundrymen," was exploded. She moved into the foreground as a member of the international community. Her ambassadors to Geneva and to the capitals that count — men like Dr. W. W. Yen, Dr. Wellington Koo — ranked among the most outstanding diplomats of the Western Powers and enhanced China's prestige enormously.

Few people realize to what extent Donald was responsible for this reorientation. He loved the game and shunned the spotlight.

Donald practically lived at the Chiangs'; he took at least one meal with them, and often two; he was served foreign food, of course. Eight in the morning would find him working at his desk or on the porch, in shirt sleeves: "I am a wild Australian, don't you know? Whenever the sun shines I feel like stripping." Till ten he would work with May and me, dictating with the rapidity and profusion of Niagara Falls. He took care of the most important part of Madame's correspondence. I had to handle the missionaries: "They pray and pray and pray like the devil. . . . Tell them to do more constructive work." "Here is a batch from British social workers. . . . Hell, I wish they'd send us guns instead of good wishes." "Here — some sentimental tommyrot from America . . . Madame's classmates from Wellesley . . . Reply very cordially and dramatically: Madame signs these. . . . Stress the shiploads of oil and scrap the U.S.A. keeps sending to Japan. . . . Emphasize the necessity of boycotting Japanese goods."

Then he would run over to Headquarters, work with Madame — nothing was done without his advice. At 2 P.M. he would come back for a fifteen minutes' nap in his armchair, read the papers and work till 4 P.M. Then to Headquarters again, until Madame was too tired to continue. Back at his desk, he would stretch and say: "Well, this is the time when I can begin to work," and get busy dictating or typing telegrams and memoranda.

No foreigner could see the Chiangs without Donald — not even Colonel Chennault or Commander Malley, an Australian who recruited all stray aviators in the world for service in China while Madame was Chairman of the Aeronautics Commission.

Captain Walther F. N. Stennes, head of Generalissimo's bodyguards, also had to stop at Donald's before going to H.Q.

He was said to have had a quarrel with Hitler and to have escaped from Germany. He was every inch the blond, blue-eyed, toughly elegant, heel-clicking German officer. He wore the best-cut riding breeches in China, high yellow leather boots, and a servile grin when meeting superiors. Chiang Kai-shek used him in many odd jobs, particularly in familiarizing Chinese undercover men with German Secret Service methods. According to reliable information, he is now Chief of the Gestapo in Shanghai!

The most fascinating hours during my employment at Headquarters were watching the air raids with Donald, on a hill at the foot of Purple Mountain. The valley below and the soft contours of the surrounding hills in their rich green, which autumn was slowly splashing with flaming dabs of yellow, red and orange, made a superbly serene setting for the airfield before us and the southern wall of the city to our right. High up behind us, at a distance, cushioned in a velvety carpet, half-up Purple Mountain, the white gleaming Sun Yat-sen Mausoleum with its dark blue roofs . . . To our left, just a little below our hill, the imposing avenue leading up to the portentous Tombs of the Mings, heavy, serene and unadorned: the avenue I had so often admired in pictures, with the huge pairs of animals carved in dazzling white stone, facing each other — two standing elephants, two kneeling elephants, two standing lions, two kneeling lions, two standing camels, two kneeling camels. We could almost stroke their heads from where we sat, waiting for the Japanese raiders. But the animals were not white any longer — they had turned green! Just a coat of paint to camouflage them. . . .

As soon as the first alarm sounded, we would rush up to the hill with our brief cases. Donald would take off his coat. Sometimes we worked there, but mostly he would be swayed by the sunshine and the country around, and would reminisce aloud. Little Jimmie, our sixteen-year-old spotter, who could see the planes before anyone could even hear the sound, lay in the grass somewhere, musing and chewing a grass-blade.

And Donald would blink up into the blue sky and recall a campaign in which he took part, an amusing characteristic of this or that general, a weird intrigue spun twenty years ago which was just blossoming out today, an anecdote about Yuan Shih-kai, Sun Yat-sen, Chiang Kai-shek, the Kungs, the Soongs, and many of the elite who had taken a hand in Chinese politics in the past forty years. I listened spellbound to these unique courses in living history, spiced with Donaldesque humor, punctuated with salvos of laughter. . . .

"You *must* write your memoirs," I once exploded enthusiastically.

"Oh, yes? Wouldn't that be wonderful?" he said mockingly. "I can see myself pulling out the pins from underneath Sun Yat-sen and Chiang Kai-shek! Ha-ha-ha!"

"All this rich experience of yours can't be lost," I insisted. "Come on, W. H. D., you owe it to China and to the world. I can't think of anything more fascinating: forty years of history, told by W. H. Donald, the Richelieu of China . . ."

"Who the hell was he?" asked Donald with a frown. I couldn't quite believe that he had never heard of Richelieu! But I started to explain: "The French cardinal who reigned during the minority . . ."

"Of Lewis Fourteen," Donald interrupted. "Damn your pronunciation — can't you talk English? 'Rich-liew' is the name, 'Rich-liew.' . . . Say," he suddenly turned on me, "I have got nothing to do with that fellow. Put this idea out of your head. And mind you, if you ever make publicity round my name, I'll kick a lung out of you."

I nodded. After a while Donald took up the thread musingly. "Maybe I'll write my memoirs someday. . . . Someday when I am out of here for good . . . when China won't need me any longer. I wish they would kick me out soon; I haven't had a rest for years. I keep telling the Madame: There are twenty-seven roads out of Nanking; just say the word, and I'll go. I'll run so fast my heels will kick up more dust than the Japanese bombs. . . . I have a little yacht waiting for me in Hong Kong. It's brand-new, made to order. I'll go for a cruise, for a long cruise, just anywhere in the world. . . ."

Sometimes an hour or two passed between the first and second air-raid signal. When "Number Two" sounded, Jimmie would jump to his feet and scan the skies with his eagle eyes. Suddenly his high-pitched voice would ring out: —

"Massita, can see tlee . . . six . . . nine . . . many . . ."

Donald's powerful field glasses would follow the direction of the boy's pointing index. The Japs usually came in so high over Nanking that no naked eye but Jimmie's could perceive them.

"All right, I hold them," Donald would say, tensely. "Ready, Sues? What's the time?"

"Twelve–twenty-five and thirty seconds," I would reply, jotting down the notes on my pad.

"Write: Nine planes sighted . . . flying at about 15,000 feet . . . all bombers . . . direction SE. Now, Sues, follow the direction of my glasses. . . ."

Donald could not look down, for fear of losing the tiny dots in the sky. And I could not see the planes.

"Watch out: First three planes releasing their bombs. . . ."

"Yes, sir. . . . One . . . three . . . five explosions in the open field . . . way off to the left of the airfield. . . ."

"Here comes another load. Watch."

"Airfield hit four times. . . . One direct hit on a building . . . I can't see . . . too much smoke — "

"What color smoke?"

"White smoke, light brown dust-columns. Now I can see — the building still stands."

"That's all right. The buildings are empty. White smoke only? that's good — they didn't get the oil tanks."

Donald's eyes were glued to the glasses. He would turn slowly to the right, following the flight: —

"They're releasing a string of bombs. . . . The rascals . . . Indiscriminate bombing . . . Can you see?"

"Yes, sir. Explosions inside the city walls — two, six, eight — Impossible to count them. Dust, bricks, flames, and smoke — "

"They are gone." Donald would lower his field glasses and we would stand watching the billowing smoke expanding skywards and slowly disintegrating into the ether.

When the effects of sudden brutal human interference cleared up, the pale blue sky was just as radiant as before, the velvety hills just as colorful, the whole atmosphere a single great serene beauty. One could not believe that murder had passed there a few minutes before. . . .

A few days after my appointment, we worked late over some dispatches. About 11 P.M. Donald called Hollington K. Tong over. "He is a fine fellow," he told me, "not much of a fighter, but ready to let himself be cut to pieces for the Generalissimo, who was once his pupil. As a matter of fact, he just had an operation; Madame's wire got him out of his sickbed. He is American-educated, was the director of *China Press* and other papers, and is one of China's best newspapermen. He knows everybody, has friends in all quarters, and I am sure he will take care of the foreign correspondents here better than anyone else could. You will like Holly."

I liked the pale, slender, soft-spoken, well-groomed gentleman, with the swaying, apologetic gait, from the very first. The contrast between the two was amusing — the lion and the little white rabbit.

Donald went right down to brass tacks.

"Have you seen Chen Kung-po?"

"Yes, I just came home from his farewell banquet. All official Nanking was present. He is leaving tonight."

"Did you get his statements of account?"

"No. . . . I could not very well ask him . . . "

Donald flew into a temper. For the past two days Holly had been under orders to obtain those statements. Donald insisted that he should telephone Cheng on the spot.

"That would be tactless on my part," said Holly with mellow firmness. "Cheng is my friend, everybody is my friend. I cannot be so indelicate and make enemies."

One sensed that Donald's harsh, boisterous manners were physically painful to him.

There was a moment of silence.

"Do you know what you have come to Nanking for, Holly?" asked Donald evenly.

"To discuss publicity matters, I was told."

"My dear fellah, you are here to replace your friend Cheng as Minister of Propaganda."

Holly stared at him, thunderstruck.

"But he is coming back. . . ." he said faintly, trying to collect his thoughts.

"Who is coming back? Where? Did he tell you so? What does he think we gave him the $50,000 for? To take a joy ride? As a reward for his splendid services? Hell, he is gone, and for good." *

"My God, my God," said Holly in a subdued, desperate voice. He put both elbows on the table and held his forehead. "I cannot be a minister. . . . I don't want to be an official. . . . I am an honest man. . . . I am an independent journalist. . . . I want to remain free. . . . Please let me go home to Shanghai, Mr. Donald."

He was pathetic in his fear of being hurled into the horrors of corrupt officialdom. Donald closed one eye and gave me a quick, roguish grin. History seemed to repeat itself — Holly's reaction to the offer was reminiscent of my own first reaction. And again Donald promised that he and Madame would back the new minister. They wanted an honest man at the head of publicity. He spoke very kindly of Holly's friendship with the Chiangs, of China's great need. Then he depicted with glowing enthusiasm the organization of the new ministry. It

* Cheng Kung-po later joined Wang Ching-wei's puppet government.

would, in reality, be China's first Foreign Relations Department — the most important job in China today. . . . But Holly was totally unnerved, a man on the verge of a collapse; he mopped his forehead and his eyes and kept repeating: "I am an honest man, I can't be an official, let me go home." I was so sorry for him, I nearly wept myself.

Donald must have felt the same, but his reaction was different. He struck the table with his fist and shouted: —

"God damn you, Tong, pull yourself together! China is fighting for her very life. Generalissimo wants it, Madame wants it, so you are damn well going to be a minister."

He leaned forward with blazing eyes, as though he wanted to ban all petty fear from that frail man's heart and breathe some of his own will power into it.

This outbreak had a salutary effect: Holly sat straight as a soldier, very pale, very sad.

Donald got up, put one arm round his shoulder and spoke gently, cordially: "We all like you, old boy, we trust you, we need you. You may just as well get used to the idea that you are indispensable here. I know exactly how you feel, but you will do this for China. Get yourself some rest, take it easy, don't worry. I know you will like the work and do it better than anyone else."

Holly rose slowly. The two shook hands. "I will do my level best," he said sternly.

In Donald's office I had to write an article a day on any subject I chose. My car was there to take me around. A Headquarters sticker on my windshield, the size of a medium frying pan, was my authority to drive even during air raids. I visited schools, hospitals, women's organizations, factories, training camps, and wrote about the war effort behind the front. T. V. Soong and Harry Timperley in Shanghai had substituted themselves for the ineffective Nanking propaganda, and distributed relevant material abroad; our dispatches were incorporated in this material.

Madame had a very good dentist in Shanghai and wished to consult him before the fall of the city. She would then also inspect the front there, and Donald was to accompany her. A day before their departure I was called over to her office, as Donald could not handle all the mail in the rush.

My first impression of Madame was that of a princess confined in a secondhand furniture store. The primitive low-ceilinged dark room, stacked full of chairs, cabinets, couches, with hardly any opening to slip through, was bewildering. Madame must have brought some things she liked with her. Her little desk was tucked away against a wall and littered with papers and magazines. I had to step over a number of objects to get near her.

Donald introduced me and withdrew to his corner to work. She said a few kind words, to which I did not listen because I was too stunned by the cold light she radiated and by her extraordinary beauty, just a trifle overemphasized that day by a too skillful make-up.

Madame wore an exquisite black georgette slack suit with yellow piping, which outlined the graceful slimness of her figure and went well with her vivacious, jerky little movements so reminiscent of happy American college days.

We worked for an hour or so. There were some French and German letters to translate, some notes to take. Her way of thinking, the lightning speed of her decisions, her businesslike approach to matters, her speech, her manners — everything was so utterly American that I had to keep reminding myself that I was in the presence of the First Lady of China.

The telephone rang. I had to jump up to let Madame pass. She got the message: the enemy had downed four Chinese planes. Madame flew into a temper; she evidently considered this a personal insult on the part of the Japanese. She never even mentioned the boys who had lost their lives. They were her boys, she knew them personally . . . I shivered inwardly. One could not conceive of Madame as ever being absent-minded, but she certainly was absent-hearted.

I told Donald that afternoon that I did not want to play secretary either to God Almighty or to Madame Chiang Kai-shek. I was there to do publicity for China. Donald had been telling me of the many people who were dying to work for Madame; he was puzzled and wanted to know the reason.

"Because I am afraid of her. . . . I can't work in sub-zero temperature," I replied.

Donald laughed: "Everybody seems to be afraid of her except myself."

He reassured me by saying that they had asked me to help out because of pressure of work that day, and that he would see to it that it did not become a habit.

I was relieved. What, after all, did it matter that Madame was not the warmhearted woman I had pictured? She had a richness of other qualities: brain, energy, ambition, temperament, charm, sex appeal and beauty. With these she could do and was doing a splendid job which no one else could have attempted.

A tire blew out on their way to Shanghai and Madame had a narrow escape. We lived a few days in anxiety. Then they returned and Donald described the accident to J. L. Huang, to May and to me in his office. The shock had been such that Madame had flown over his head and landed in a mudhole ten yards away, all crumpled up, moaning, unconscious. Donald picked her up — a limp, lifeless little figure. He carried her to a farmer's hut near by. The womenfolk helped. He shook and scolded her, mortally afraid that this was the end. It took two hours before she opened her eyes, but as soon as this happened, Donald was the old tease again. He told her to wash and change, as she looked "like nothing on earth." Bravely Madame obeyed, and bravely she decided to continue her trip, notwithstanding the pain in her side. It turned out later that she had broken a rib. When they sat in the car again, Madame looked so pale and dismal that he feared she might faint anew. He had to say something to buck her up.

"I told her, 'From now on, you'll never be able to say that I didn't pick you up in the gutter!' and she smiled."

We laughed at his impudence then. But I kept thinking of it; Donald never tossed a meaningless phrase into the air. . . . Later the amazing truth dawned upon me: Donald was re-enacting Shaw's *Pygmalion* in China, with the world for a setting, Madame as Eliza, and himself as Professor Higgins. The "gutter" — Shanghai's compradore society . . . This great adventurer and psychologist was creating the masterpiece of his life: the First Lady of China, the First Lady of the World. His knowledge, his soul, his keen sense of humor centered round this daring plan, perfect in its minutest details. . . .

Madame was still confined to her chaise-longue when we had our memorable meeting to discuss the reorganization of the Publicity Board. She was less glamorous, more lovely that day. In the subdued light of a lamp, with practically no make-up, draped in a soft salmon-colored silk deshabille, she looked like a girl in her twenties. And the enthusiasm with which she approached the subject was contagious.

There were Donald, Hollington Tong and myself and, somewhere in a corner, Jeanette Kung, Madame's fifteen-year-old niece, rather bored and trying to concentrate on the contents of her book. Holly looked much better, though still a bit eerie; he sat nervously on the very edge of his chair with trembling knees. I learned later that this was his usual attitude whenever he had to sit down in the presence of Madame or the Generalissimo.

"Cheng Kung-po is out, we have Miss Sues' memo, an excellent outline of our future publicity work, and we are going to organize it immediately," said Madame Chiang buoyantly.

"*You* are going to organize it," chipped in Donald.

"All right, *I* am going to organize it. . . . What do you mean, Don? Don't be silly, you are going to be in it too."

"Oh, am I?" Donald feigned surprise.

"I have eradicated corruption from our air force; I will eradicate corruption from our publicity. There will be no more favoritism, no more nepotism. Don't let anyone dare ask me for a job for his son or nephew or friend. Efficiency and only efficiency is going to count. *I* am going to do the hiring and the firing."

Madame was bewitching in her excitement and with that faint rosy glimmer on her cheeks.

"We will have a Supervisory Body of three: I will be on it. We will take H. H. Kung — he isn't interested and won't interfere. Whom else should we take? Don, how about Wang Ch'ung-hui — do you think he would keep quiet?"

"He won't dare open his mouth with you on the board," assured Donald.

"Fine. Don, you will be our expert and adviser. You, Holly, will be appointed Minister of Publicity — I hate the word Propaganda."

Holly bowed his head.

"You will organize your ministry like a newspaper office. We will see to it that you get the news, the necessary material, adequate funds, and every facility for yourself and the foreign correspondents to travel, investigate, photograph, and broadcast. You will be responsible only to Generalissimo and to the Supervisory Body, that is to myself, and if anyone wants to interfere with your work, just give me a ring. Miss Sues will be your expert and help you and your staff carry out the program in its details."

She gave me a friendly little smile and continued developing the plan. I looked at her admiringly, as she laid down the rules and details of the project tersely, lucidly. This was a revelation; I was thrilled to the depth of my soul. Here was Madame Chiang

Kai-shek off the record, Madame as she really was, pulsating, vibrating, dynamic — not the sentimental Good Samaritan, not the widely publicized pious Bible-quoter, not the bluestocking reformer, but Madame Chiang Kai-shek the Fighter — for a decent government, for an efficient administration, for a modern China: a frail, delicate little lady pitting herself with fiery spirit and unbending will power against an age-old obsolete system, against mildewed tradition, against the almighty monster of corrupt officialdom. A courageous, temperamental little lady with no party to support her, with no foreign power to back her, all alone, trusting in God and challenging the world with her battle cry: "China Will Rise Again."

Suddenly it had become clear to me why Donald was here and why he maintained that Madame was "the manliest man in China." If she wanted to reorganize publicity in this spirit, I was ready to go through hellfire for her.

"Holly," Madame was pursuing her exposé, "we will have to submit proof to the Generalissimo that Cheng Kung-po's outfit is rotten to the core. You and Miss Sues will make an investigation; separate the deadwood from the valuable material; prepare a detailed report on their activities. I want all statements of account — or are you afraid to antagonize anyone?"

"They are all my friends . . . " stammered Holly miserably.

"I understand. Well, then you won't have to say anything. You will just introduce Miss Sues as my special envoy; she will ask all relevant questions. She is a foreigner, she can do all the hollering."

"Sues is afraid of everything," Donald interrupted with a grin; "she is afraid of me, she is afraid of you. . . ."

"I am not afraid of any corrupt Kuomintang official who sabotages publicity," I flared up, "and if I have your authority, Madame, we will submit the report to you within three days."

This sounded so presumptuously heroic that I blushed at my own stupidity and turned to Holly to cover it up with a forced joke: "Don't be afraid, Mr. Minister, I am even ready to protect

you against your friends. You may blame everything on me—
I am a foreign devil without obligations, anyway."

Donald laughed boisterously: "Here comes the hero. . . .
You don't know what you are in for, bless you."

But Madame was delighted. She left everything to me.

"Tell Dr. Tong whom you want to see. He will introduce
you. Try not to embarrass him. You know what we want. You
have my authority to do all the hollering."

For once in my life I was fiery and energetic. I cast aside all
diplomacy and Chinese politeness and headed straight for the
goal. Madame had given me the green light and three days'
time to assemble all data. The miserable Holly sweated blood as
he took me around to the four publicity centers. We were
both aware of the madness of our enterprise. Madame's idea
was excellent, but the tempo which she had set for its execution
was a thing unheard-of in China's history. What are three days
in the flow of millenniums?

The introduction was always the same. Holly, with a morti-
fied look in his eyes and an affable sickly smile on his thin
lips, would present me to each chief in turn with a few apologetic sentences as Madame's special investigator into publicity
matters. At the mention of Madame's name there would be a
visible hostile stiffening. I would abstain from any preliminary
niceties and start asking pertinent questions which, I am sure,
they considered impertinent coming from an outsider so suddenly commissioned to pry into the inner sanctum of official
business. My questions would be straightforward, matter-of-
fact, ruthless. Madame wished to know their budget, the ex-
penditure, the staff employed, the volume of publicity turned
out during the past three months. I asked to look at the files
and books immediately, and insisted upon having all statements
of account not later than within three days.

T. T. Li, of the *Waichiaopu*, was the first and easiest to deal
with. He was ready to withdraw from the interministerial publicity board, as it meant only extra work and worry; the thirty-

dollars monthly addition to his salary was no adequate compensation.

Chiang Kang-li, the publicity chief of the Central Kuomintang, was somewhat sulky and uneasy when Hollington Tong and I called on him. He gave us a very thin folder and handed us over to his bookkeeper. Shirking responsibility just like any League of Nations official. . . .

It came out that he issued information almost exclusively to the official Central News Agency. He saw no reason why he should help the foreign press correspondents; it was their business to ferret out the news for themselves; that's what they were paid for, after all.

Next Holly and I went to the Enemy Propaganda Bureau, where no outsider had ever penetrated. The trip was quite an expedition. Outside the city walls, on our way to the secret camp on a slope of Purple Mountain, we were stopped at least every two minutes by heavily armed soldiers who asked for our credentials.

General Yang was a gaunt, serious officer in his fifties with a thin, long, drooping mustache. His brief, matter-of-fact statement made an excellent impression on us. This man was aware of his responsibilities. He had a staff of eight — thoroughly trained, intelligent and executing their work with military precision. They kept abreast of all Japanese propaganda and countered it, making use of the radio, any available publicity facilities and, more particularly, the channels of the military intelligence service.

On our way back, Hollington Tong and I decided to suggest in our report to Generalissimo that General Yang's department be granted the largest measure of autonomy under the Military Affairs Commission, and that it should not fall under the jurisdiction of either the Propaganda Ministry or any other civilian organ. Though the words were never spoken, we both felt that Kuomintang red tape would be detrimental to any well-organized effort.

*　　*　　*

The hardest nut to crack was the Propaganda Ministry itself. They had practically handed out no propaganda. All told, the three civilian bodies constituting the Publicity Board had issued information amounting to some thirty typewritten pages! The Ministry had spent a few hundred thousand Chinese dollars — which, in itself, would not have been excessive in the three months of its existence, had their business been conducted with any amount of efficiency. I got a most amazing picture of prevailing conditions by questioning first Cheng Kung-po's *alter ego* in charge, and then the treasurer.

The foreign propaganda section, in which we were particularly interested, consisted of some sixty men, none of whom had any knowledge worth mentioning of any foreign language!

There was not a single statement of account. He had a record of the monies received but none of the expenditures. He did not know offhand the monthly amount paid in salaries. In fact, the one and only figure he seemed to be sure of was the rental paid for one of the two office buildings! I asked if they had no bookkeeper, and he replied indignantly that they had eight. They also had three chauffeurs — and only one motor car, which was beyond repair! I spent hours with that stubborn, stalking, evasive treasurer. Holly had to interpret for us, this time, and I was in no mood to make it easy for him. The deeper I went into the subject, the more I wondered whether this chaos was due to incompetence or to sabotage as intimated by Donald. I told the fellow point-blank what I thought of his organization and demanded, in Madame's name, that he submit a detailed statement of account to date within three days. It took us another half hour to beat down his wailing protests. We were ruthless and threatened him with Generalissimo's wrath if he did not comply. When he finally promised it, I felt the irrepressible desire that fellow had to wring my neck.

"If this continues," I told Donald a little later, reporting on the day's work, "I'll make a lot of enemies round here."

"Make enemies?" Donald threw his head back and roared with laughter. "Did you say *make* enemies? My God, girl, you've made more enemies these three days than I have made during my forty years' stay in China. You should hear the reports pouring in about you. It is the natural thing: they hate the Madame, they are furious at you. Don't you realize how many people envy you your position? The whole hell of intrigue is loose, and that means something in Nanking. But never mind it; carry on; to us it is a proof that you are doing the right thing."

Donald, Holly and I discussed our findings and suggestions. Then I wrote the report, or rather two reports: one about the activities of the investigated organizations, and the other about their expenditures. After a lot of heated discussions as to what recommendations were to go into what report, Holly and I signed the first, but no earthly power could make him put his pen to the second. So I signed it alone and Donald rushed both reports over to Madame, who would submit them to Generalissimo at a propitious moment. We had recommended the closing down of the Fifth Board (Cheng Kung-po's Propaganda Ministry), the firing of the whole personnel, and the establishment of a small, efficient, up-to-date publicity board.

While waiting for the reorganization, I continued to work in Headquarters, dividing my time between writing articles, letters and speeches for Madame, and watching air raids with Donald.

Madame had her idiosyncrasies. There were words that were taboo, like, for instance, "propaganda" and "retreat" if applied to Chinese troops. She would fly into a tantrum when anyone used them. We had to say "publicity" and "strategic withdrawal" instead. Garlic was also taboo; its offensive smell was banned in a ten-li radius round Generalissimo's Headquarters. I learned this from Donald who sent me home one day because my Ta She-fu had seasoned my salad with a bit of garlic. But the most important Don't in the catechism of Madame's retinue was that her name should never be pronounced either in public or in private conversation. Nor could her utterances be quoted without express authorization. Why? Probably because "Thou shalt not take the name of Madame, First Lady of China, in vain."

The interesting thing about Madame Chiang Kai-shek was that she was entirely different from the person the Western world pictured her to be. She was no angel of mercy but she was the one and only effective American Ambassador to China. Nelson Johnson was a charming fellow and a connoisseur of Chinese art and history, but pulled no weight politically.

So it was left to Madame and Donald – the only two-man pro-democratic bloc in Generalissimo's entourage – to work for an ever-tighter relationship between the Anglo-Saxon countries and China. With no right of vote and no party behind them, they carried on this tough job with nothing but the weight of personality. Through them, Chiang Kai-shek was constantly in touch with Western thought, Western reactions to anything happening or planned in China. It meant a colossal effort to put over the idea that the Western yardstick should be applied to Chinese affairs, no matter how big or small they were.

The military clique, with war minister Ho Ying-ch'in at the head, hated Madame for her influence upon their leader. They knew that without Donald she would not know how to use it. For years, they tried to have Donald expelled from China, and on several occasions they nearly succeeded.

One day, I remember, my peanut car was in the repair shop, and Donald took me to the air-raid hill in his big roadster. I knocked my elbow against a bulging car-pocket. My investigating hands found a big pistol in it. "Aï-yah," said I, "what do you need a gun for in this model capital where there are no more bandits, according to you?"

"To protect Madame from Ho Ying-ch'in," replied Donald in dead earnest. I remembered the Sian Incident and understood. If he sent bombing planes then to kill the Generalissimo he could well send gunmen to shoot her.

If Madame and Donald had had a solid foundation of democratic principles, if they had collaborated with Madame Sun

Yat-sen and her group and with the Chinese people, who are democratic by nature and by tradition, such a powerful coalition could have swung the whole political machine, and China could have had her constitutional government long ago.

However, Madame Chiang knew as much of democracy as she could see by looking out of the windows of Wellesley College. On her return home, the young graduate had been shocked by the "backwardness" of her countrymen as compared with Western civilization symbolized by flush toilets, clean fingernails, decent table manners and careful grooming. She shrank from the poverty and filth of the Chinese populace then, and she never overcame that feeling.

Now, all three Soong sisters had been educated in America, but when they came back to China, each reacted differently and each married according to her temperament. Ai-ling, the eldest, became the wife of Dr. H. H. Kung, offspring of a landlord and bankers' family, who was then professor at Oberlin College in China, but soon became China's leading capitalist. Ai-ling is unquestionably the greater financier of the two. Ching-ling, the second, married Dr. Sun Yat-sen, founder of the Chinese Republic, a socially minded democrat, who had the following of the Chinese intelligentsia and whose memory is still worshiped by the entire people. May-ling, the youngest, married General Chiang Kai-shek, a military star rising on the horizon.

Those illiterate Chinese masses who have the impudence to judge people by their actions have summed up the three Soong sisters as follows: "One loves money, one loves China, one loves glory." *Vox populi, vox dei.*

Dr. Sun Yat-sen was the father of his people, and during the short period when Ching-ling was China's First Lady, she became the mother of the people. And when he died, in 1925, she carried his life's work on. Changed trends in the Kuomintang Party forced her to do it unofficially. She was watched and persecuted as an incurable revolutionary. For years, she was virtually a prisoner in her little apartment in Shanghai. She never

Photo courtesy China Aid Council

Madame Sun Yat-sen visiting a spinning co-operative

Photo Chuck

Madame Chiang Kai-shek in her garden

lost contact with her friends and with the people. She let slip no occasion to demand the establishment of a constitutional government and a better standard of living for the people. When Shanghai fell in 1937, she went as a voluntary exile to Hong Kong, refusing to take part in a nondemocratic government. I had the privilege of meeting her there. With a small group of friends she was personally conducting the work of the China Defense League which, like the many other relief institutions, collected funds, foodstuffs, medical supplies and clothing for the wounded and the needy. But the difference between the C.D.L. and all the others was that it was not run like a philanthropic affair.

When Madame Chiang, the official First Lady, entered the political scene in 1934, she built her domain on a different level. If Madame Sun is the mother of the people, Madame Chiang is its governess. This explains the New Life Movement better than anything else.

Both sisters want a strong China, but their approach to the problem and their temperaments differ so widely that it is fascinating to bring out just a few points of comparison. Not only because of the psychological interest but because they represent the two progressive trends in the China of today.

Madame Sun, modest, warmhearted, understanding, believes in building the country from below upwards. She wants a sound, happy China.

Madame Chiang, ambitious, temperamental, subtle, believes in building it from the top downwards. She wants an efficient, model China.

Madame Sun is a patient revolutionary, ready to accept martyrdom, if need be.

Madame Chiang is a passionate reformer, ready to brush away any obstacle standing between her and her goal.

Madame Sun is an enlightened democrat; she has, for the past twenty years, consistently upheld Dr. Sun Yat-sen's *Three Principles of the People* — she wants a politically independent China, a constitutional government of the people by the people for the people, and a decent standard of living for everyone.

Madame Chiang does not identify herself with any party; she is a sparkling political cocktail — radical by nature, Christian by education, capitalist by circumstances, pseudo-democrat by conviction, and temperamentally a dictator. Democracy to her is not the inalienable right of the people but a candy which the Government may in time dole out as a reward for good behavior. When Wendell Willkie said, on his return from Chungking, "You cannot present democracy to China on a silver platter next Tuesday," I thought I heard Madame's voice.

I asked Donald once to show me one instance where the New Life Movement had bettered the standard of living of the people. Visibly embarrassed, he said that that would come later. But obviously the trouble was that Madame placed spiritual values above material values.

Those spiritual virtues kept popping up in most unexpected forms and places. For example, it was largely due to Madame's influence that the Generalissimo created the "Officers' Moral Endeavor Association." The title alone was enough to convey the idea that it was a "kindergarten for recalcitrant war lords," but in reality the beautiful building housed a sort of Emily Post institute for the élite — an officers' club where smoking and liquor were prohibited. Lectures on every variety of virtue were the daily routine, and on Sundays, Madame Chiang Kai-shek conducted the singing of hymns and patriotic songs!

At other times, Madame, as Chairman of the Aeronautics Commission, would line up the volunteer pilots, bombardiers, instructors and mechanics on the airfield and give them a long Sunday-school talk. A lad of the International Squadron — daredevils who fought like mad and faced death every day — commented: "I'd be ashamed to talk like this to a football team of twelve-year-olds. She treats us like we were nitwits." Otherwise the boys liked her, though she made them squirm whenever she had a brainstorm and laid down some golden rules of air tactics for their benefit. There was not a subject in the world on which

Madame would not speak with authority, but only when it was off the record. Whatever was on the record was prepared by Donald or by one of the ghost writers chosen and supervised by him. Intent upon building her up as the First Lady of the World, endowed with all the qualities of the human race and an all-embracing knowledge, he would take no chances. Inside her four walls, May-ling had the right to be selfish, petty, and capricious as a prima donna. We got a taste of this in Headquarters — everybody trembled when Madame flew into a temper.

Madame could fascinate and enthrall some interviewers, she could dominate a crowd of courtiers, and she could keep the vast majority of missionaries enthused with her knowledge of things Christian. But she had no inner contact with mankind. It sounds strange, and I had to have many proofs before I myself was able to believe it. Madame did not understand the hearts and the minds of people. She could not gauge the reactions. She had admirers but no true friends. She was loyal only to Madame Chiang Kai-shek and to the goals she set herself. She did not talk with people, she talked at them. She demanded blind obedience and broke anyone who dared think differently.

Well, Madame did not have the loving heart of a mother, but she had the fighting heart of a lioness, courage, tenacity, and ruse. And that frail little thing carried on two tasks which no man in China would have dared shoulder: one was to intensify the collaboration with America, the other was to purge the government administration of inefficient, corrupt officials. Her influence on Generalissimo, and Donald's collaboration, were her chief weapons; and she used them with amazing skill.

The odds against this personal influence of hers were tremendous. Facing her like a solid wall was China's tradition-bound officialdom, and army officers, resenting a woman's influence on their chief and her interference in state affairs.

The curious phenomenon in present-day China is that — notwithstanding divergent policies and acute dissensions among themselves — all parties and political groups support Chiang Kai-shek's leadership. At the same time, each is trying to win him over to its particular point of view by means of loyalty, persuasion and pressure. In other words, unlike the practice prevalent in other countries, there is no candidate to oppose him.

Thus the small but powerful coterie of appeasers leave no stone unturned to induce him to make peace with Japan and line up with the Axis Powers. The conservative elements of the Kuomintang, jealously safeguarding their privilege as the only legal party, oppose the recognition of any other existing party and demand that he take a clear-cut stand as chief of a totalitarian state. The Communist Party and the so-called "little parties," ranging from conservative to socialist, which have recently formed a Federation, work towards a constitutional, representative government, recognition of all parties, and a Chinese Bill of Rights. They look to Chiang as the symbol of China's United anti-Japanese Front and hope that he may, someday, develop it into a democratic government. Last, not least, there are China's reactionary militarists who worship their leader and hope for his eventual military dictatorship. They claim that the ties between them and the Generalissimo are more ancient and more binding than his ties with Soong May-ling. He grew up among them. He was their fellow-cadet at Paoting, their co-officer in the revolutionary army, their instructor at Whampoa Military Academy, their leader during their bloody campaigns. They shared his hardships with unswerving loyalty. They claim him as their very own. And their own he was — a stolid, old-time Chinese war lord — they say, until Soong May-ling and her foreign friends injected novel, non-Chinese ideas about statesmanship and international relations into his mind. Partly, they blame her also for defending the United Front, to which many have never reconciled themselves, although they admit that she is anti-Communist and sees in the unity only the most effective weapon against Japanese aggression.

What made it worse was that Madame neither cared about their criticism nor minced her words. The climax of indignation was reached when she published her essay on China's "Seven Deadly Sins." *

Cliques seem to hold sway in many places [writes Madame Chiang]. They are like dry rot in the administration. They stifle enterprise and initiative. They operate to oust honesty and efficiency by preventing a patriotic "outsider," or a stranger to the clique, from gaining a position, no matter how capable he may be.

She speaks of "human, unproductive deadwood which encumbers the pay roll of almost every department of public service," and of

. . . the Grand Army of the Paid Unemployable. The rank and file of this army are too incompetent to work — and their superiors were too spineless or too conscienceless to dismiss them — but they are not too proud to collect their unearned pay.

In the course of time, Madame had learned from her opponents the subtle procedure practised in China for many centuries. With Generalissimo's consent, high officials who were found wanting were tactfully invited, "in recognition of their outstanding services rendered to the country," to undertake a "study tour" abroad, at government expense. A gorgeous farewell feast preceded the departure. Smaller fry were transferred to other posts "more worthy of their remarkable talents." And the road was all clear for the new experiment.

The only trouble was that she did not apply the same measure to her own family — and to her friends.

Madame was too dynamic to be a good organizer; in fact, the remarkable progress achieved by national movements and welfare institutions over which she presided was due to the intelligent and self-sacrificing work of thousands of nameless young men and women. But she had brainwaves — brainwaves that followed each other in rapid succession and set Generalissimo's Headquarters a-rocking. There was hardly a field where she did

* Later included in Madame Chiang's book *China Shall Rise Again*, Harper and Brothers, New York and London.

not attempt to introduce reforms. She was the exasperating nightmare of China's officialdom, and Generalissimo often had a hectic time straightening out matters between his beautiful wife, who was quivering to turn China upside-down within twenty-four hours, and the seasoned politicians and bureaucrats who still thought in terms of centuries. Sometimes, when he had given Madame too much leeway, the Party or the Army would step in and remind him most respectfully of the obligations he had towards his ancestors, his brothers-in-arms, and the Kuomintang, and complain of Madame's un-Chinese irreverence to thousand-year-old tradition, to existing state institutions, and to venerable dignitaries. If they won out, Madame's new scheme would be dropped or modified with the usual fair measure of face-saving.

This is exactly what happened to the publicity venture which Madame had so expertly mapped out. With our three-day investigation, she had stolen a march on her adversaries. By the time they caught up with the game, Cheng Kung-po had reached Italy on his "study tour," and Generalissimo, furious over the conditions revealed in our report, had ordered the Fifth Board (Propaganda Ministry) abolished. The sad, aimless staff continued to hang around awaiting further developments. But when it came to firing the sixty men who were supposed to do foreign publicity without knowing a foreign language, the Party sent a delegation to Chiang who made it clear to him that they could not be dismissed because they were either Party members themselves or they had weighty relatives who were loyal members of the Kuomintang. And when the delegation had succeeded in persuading Generalissimo on this point, negotiations continued and Madame's program underwent other changes. The ultimate result was that the Supervisory Body with Madame as chairman was never created; the Kuomintang's Mr. Shao Li-tse was appointed Minister of Propaganda, and Generalissimo's Hollington K. Tong became Vice-Minister, in charge of foreign publicity.

The personnel was to be kept on and gradually reduced by redistribution among other ministries.

Madame had a nervous breakdown. Donald told us that she was "through with publicity." And I, in my capacity as "expert without executive power," found myself in the very midst of sixty colleagues who knew that I had suggested that their "rice bowls should be broken."

I must mention that, a few days before Generalissimo's decision, I had incurred Madame's displeasure. I had dropped in for tea at the Magees'; some friends were there. As usual, the conversation drifted to Madame Chiang Kai-shek and I said a few friendly, enthusiastic words about her. Next morning I received a letter from Donald at home saying that I had not heeded his warning and had mentioned Madame's name in the presence of a stranger. Madame had heard of it ten minutes later and was very indignant. He, Donald, was convinced that I had meant no harm and had the best of intentions, but he must call my attention to this unfortunate mistake! The only "stranger" at the Magees' was a foreign military attaché who was a good friend of Madame's. I never saw Madame again, but as the whole city was in a turmoil, with the Japanese drawing nearer and Nanking being evacuated, it occurred to me only much later that I had joined the ranks of the "dropped ones."

The hospital on my compound was emptied within two days. I saw touching scenes of convalescent soldiers carrying their disabled comrades on their backs to the rallying points. There were not enough vehicles to go round. The Government was doing a splendid job and all services worked on schedule, with remarkable discipline. The wounded, the children and the aged came first; then, orderly, one after another, the government services. Civilians evacuated by the thousands. All roads were crammed with refugees, all river boats and trains loaded to capacity. People were squatting and sleeping on the quais and around the station clinging to their children and to the belongings they could carry, waiting for transportation.

Then came the day when Donald told May and me to move into the city, because all buildings outside Nanking's walls, including the houses of President Lin Sen, Generalissimo, H. H. Kung, our hospitals and bungalows, would be dynamited so that the enemy could not take cover there.

The Cinderella dream had come to an end. I bade farewell to my servants, to my dear little black bungalow, to the beautiful park, where Guei-Guei and I had spent so many happy hours playing hide-and-seek. We went back to the American Church Mission. Two days later the Fifth Board was ordered to leave by special government train for Hankow. Each of us got a yellow silk ribbon tag with his number and name, and chop of the Ministry. This was at once our identification and free ticket. We also received special labels for our baggage which was collected punctually by government truck. Everything was done on schedule. The only one who did not conform to orders was that cat of mine. He hates traveling. When he saw me pack, he went into hiding. John Magee, the servants and I turned the house upside down before we found him under some rugs in the attic. I could have murdered Guei-Guei at that moment. The truck had to wait fifteen minutes just because of his idiosyncrasy! But this excitement made parting from John and all other *Sheng Kung Hwei* friends seem easier.

VI

Hankow

WE ARRIVED at Hankow at 5 A.M., in a pouring rain. I went in a ricksha from hotel to hotel and could find no accommodation. Hankow was the new capital and half of China had sought refuge there. At seven, drenched, starved and utterly discouraged, I telephoned Bishop Roots's house. He had invited me to stay there. I feared to inconvenience them, but there was no other way out. Frances, his daughter, answered the phone: "Come along right away — we will all be delighted."

My host and his two daughters were so charming and hospitable that after a few days I gave up the vain apartment-hunting, and stayed in the room which I shared with Frances. The big, walled-in mission compound, with its red brick church and school and teachers' bungalows, and the old bishopric with its weather-beaten wooden gallery and its warm, congenial atmosphere, became my Hankow home.

Slender, blue-eyed, thin-lipped Bishop Logan H. Roots was a quiet, kindly gentleman. He had the best qualities of an old China hand: exquisite manners, a philosophical approach to men and events, and a precious sense of humor. He never imposed his will and was never rushed or ruffled. He respected everybody's opinion and tried modestly to learn from every person. This curiosity about things human had kept him young at sixty-eight and had broadened his mind to an unusual degree. He had become Bishop of Hankow at thirty-six — and with open benevolent eyes had watched history go by: the Empire and its doom, the Revolution and the birth of the Republic, Sun Yat-sen's death, Chiang Kai-shek's advent, the Hankow Revolutionary Government, civil wars, and now the United Front. He was on a friendly though priestly conventional footing with the Chiangs, the Soongs, the Kungs and the whole hierarchy of officials. He was the father confessor and spiritual adviser of Colonel J. L. Huang and many of his Christian lieutenants in the War Area Service Corps (the amalgamated Officers' Moral Endeavor Association and New Life Movement Headquarters). At the same time, he was fair to the Communists; he had not hated them in 1927, quite on the contrary, he understood their motives and pointed out the social improvements they had brought about, to his fellow Christians. Somebody had called him the Pink Bishop then, and the nickname stuck. Now he rejoiced in the United Front as the great Brotherhood of all Chinese, his dearest dream come true. And he welcomed in his parlor with the same enthusiasm anyone — from the bluest Blue Shirt to the reddest Communist. Upstairs the guest rooms were always full. Stanley Jones, the evangelist, Anna Louise Strong, Bishop Huntington and Agnes Smedley, slept in the same bed — at different times, of course. When Dr. Maxwell, Hankow head of the International Red Cross, a man of sterling character and baffling abruptness, heard this, he barked his verdict into the air: "A bishopric? No, sir, a menagerie." This nickname stuck too.

The three cities designated under the name of Wuhan — Hankow, Hanyang situated at the mouth of the Han River flowing into the Yangtze, and Wuchang on the opposite, the left, bank of the Yangtze — geographically and industrially the heart of China, now also became its political heart. Hanyang was the smokestacked manufacturing center and arsenal, Hankow the treaty port and seat of foreign and Chinese concerns, Wuchang the university town suddenly become the emergency capital for the Government with Army and Party Headquarters, training centers, and so on.

Except for its pulsating war activities, Hankow, with its wide streets and rows of houses, was as unromantic and dull as any prosperous second-rate business town anywhere in the world.

The new Propaganda Ministry was divided. Its Minister, Shao Li-tse, and the majority of the staff, handling national propaganda, established their offices at Wuchang. Holly, the Vice-Minister, entrusted with international propaganda, called his section the Central Publicity Board and remained with his staff in Hankow, to be in close contact with all foreign diplomatic and consular officers and with the international pressmen.

Our offices were too small, and very crowded, but Holly had given the boys a talk or two — he had that personal, comradely touch and knew how to rally his collaborators to the cause, and every one of them was doing his best. They were no journalists, they had had no training, and news from the competent authorities was as unavailable as before. Holly and I had agreed and explained to the boys that they should write two-page eye-witness accounts on any subject connected with China's war effort. It sounded simple and common sense, but we met with passive resistance. There is no such animal as a Chinese reporter (at least there wasn't then at the C.P.B.). First of all, why should an educated man debase himself to the extent of looking at things which he can just as well find in his own imagination? Second, how can an artless statement of facts be a good article? To be good, an article must give historical background and be educational.

So all were editorial writers, animated by uncanny zeal. They never went out, they just sat, inspired, and wrote "eye-witness" stories by the yard. You can't clip the wings of Pegasus; with supreme disregard to orders, articles ran from ten to thirty pages. Mine was the task of revising and editing them. They were all in pidgin English, and I was lucky when they started with Sun Yat-sen, and not with Confucius or Huang Ti! My discussions with the individual authors were anything but refreshing. They had a grudge against me for the suggested dismissal, and they were enamored with their prose. One day the Board met to appoint the editor in chief. Young Frank Liu came to me with tears in his eyes. They had appointed him editor. He was not interested in words, he said, he was interested in cows. The people were starving. He was an animal husbandry man from the Ministry of Agriculture, and he wanted to go back there. They had made a fine start importing and breeding cattle and had it all mapped out for the future: by and by every peasant was to have livestock, every Chinese would eat meat.

It seemed so irrational to force a specialized man into a new profession which he despised! I asked Frank for a possible reason. "Because I understand English and because I am a Christian. They want Christians in representative positions."

We made a bargain: I would correct the English for him and would ask Bishop Roots to arrange for his retransfer. In the meantime Frank would stick to Holly and train the other boys to do plain reporting. Our duty was to keep the world steadily informed of China's tremendous struggle and to tell how the big and the small men and women shared in it. We were surrounded by acts of heroism; all we had to do was put the facts on paper. What the people abroad were interested in was essentials, and essentials only.

A day or two later something happened to remind me of the relativity of all things. This was about the fifth or sixth of December. The Chiangs and Donald were still in Nanking, with the Japanese closing in on the city. Communications were disrupted and we were all terribly worried. No one could tell whether they were still alive.

Epstein, representing United Press, burst into our office, headed straight for my desk.

"Ralf," he asked breathlessly, "what's the color of the polka dots on Madame's sweater? Remember the one in her photo with Generalissimo? You ought to know."

For a split second I thought Eppie was shell-shocked. He was our youngest and one of the most levelheaded correspondents. Then he showed me the urgent cable from his United States headquarters; it asked for the color of Gissimo's cape, Madame's sweater and polka dots. The cape was brown. I had never seen the historic sweater. I telephoned to everyone who might know. Holly did not know, neither did J. L. Huang. I tried Jeanette Kung. She was unobliging and sulky as ever, but this time, at least, her temper was justified. "I am not interested in my aunt's trousseau," she snapped. "Tell that journalist he can go back to Nanking and find out." She hung up. U.P. sent a second cable, dated a half hour later than the first, asking why he had not yet replied about the polka dots.

"Hell, Eppie, cable them it's yellow with brown dots. Who cares?" I suggested.

I don't know whether he took my advice, but one thing was sure — this little incident put Frank and the others into a meditative mood. What, in the eyes of Americans, was essential, and what was not?

Right from the start, Hollington Tong had established close friendly contact with all foreign correspondents. We had daily press meetings, with tea and a variety of Chinese cookies served. Try as he might, poor Holly had a hard time getting information. When he came in, embarrassed and mopping his forehead, we knew that he would invariably start his speech by saying: "My dear friends: Unfortunately I have no news for you, but we will have a friendly cup of tea together and some Chinese sweets — we call them *dien-hsin*, which means 'touch-heart.' I hope they will touch your heart and you will forgive me. . . ."

Whenever he had information, he shared it with the boys. If he had none, he invited interesting speakers from the Government, or visiting newspapermen. He arranged for group and special interviews with the Chiangs and other personalities, facilitated transportation, mail and telegraph service. He was courteous, cordial, and seldom failed the boys. Holly played ostrich only so far as the Eighth Route Army was concerned. He had written in his biography of Chiang Kai-shek that the Generalissimo had exterminated all "Red bandits." The mere mention of the existence of the "remnants" of these subversive elements was very painful to him. Nobody ever visited the Eighth Route with his permission or help.

There was no use pretending that my worthy Kuomintang colleagues had any friendly feelings for me. With one or two exceptions they sabotaged my work and my position. It was just futile telling them anything — they would not listen. Holly saw it and tried to arrange matters.

As a first step he engaged Buzz Farmer — a tall, blond, blue-eyed, naïve and friendly Australian boy, who had done some journalism elsewhere but to whom China was The Great Oriental Mystery. He shared the office with Holly and me and got the job of rewriting all articles. We all liked Buzz, but I could not help laughing when I saw him struggle with the produce of our "editors." His clear, matter-of-fact British mind could not readily follow the twists and the nonchalance of Chinese imagination.

One day he jumped up from one of those articles with a half-suppressed "My God" and proceeded to measure the height of the door with his ruler. "Say, Ralf, have you ever seen Feng Yu-hsiang, the Christian General?"

"Yep. What's worrying you now, Buzz?"

"This boy here writes Feng is seven feet six tall. . . . Surely, he can't be taller than this door?"

The next step was that Holly gave me a "highly confidential" job. I became foreign press censor; in other words, no press cable written in French, German, or Russian, and handed in at the Hankow telegraph office, was dispatched without my O.K.

This put me automatically out of contact with my colleagues and publicity proper. I did not like the idea of keeping tabs on my friends without telling them. But Holly insisted upon secrecy. I told Francis Yao, of course, and that relieved my guilty conscience a bit.

In reality, I was the one on whom tabs were being kept. I was on duty from 8 A.M. to 3 A.M., and the Post Office had to know my whereabouts every minute. From eight to five, during office hours, the telegraph messenger would find me at the C.P.B., wait while I read and initialed the cables, and take them back to the Post Office. From 5.30 P.M. till 3 A.M. he would bring the little envelopes to the American Church Mission. The regular gateman could not stay up so late, so I had a special boy at the gate. He was about forty, a giant with a shaved head, wearing an immaculate wash-blue gown. His steps were as noiseless as a cat's, and he was as mute as a Trappist. As a matter of fact, I never heard him say anything else than "*Shih, Ssu hsiao-dzieh*" ("Yes, Miss Ssu") and "*Dien-pao!*" ("Telegram!"). He was the only outsider who had the run of the compound at night. He would climb the usually squeaking stairs noiselessly, and pussyfoot into the room I shared with Frances Roots, at any unearthly hour. He would turn on the lamp on my night-table and then shout at the top of his lungs, "*Dien-pao!*" which never failed to make me sit up straight in my bed. Sleep-sodden, I would run through the message, blue-pencil it, and turn over on my side again, while he put out the light and vanished into the night. At first Frances found this interference with her sleep objectionable (who wouldn't?), but soon she got so used to it she did not even wake up.

Whenever I was out, he would bring the cables to me at friends' houses, at the cinema or theater. Towering over the crowds, he would spot me at my seat, and work his way imperturbably through the rows of chairs and spectators. He was not altogether inconspicuous, holding the envelope high above his head and shouting *"Dien-pao!"*

Even now he and my censorship period come back occasionally as a nightmare.

In the morning, copies of all cables I censored the day before had to be translated into English for Generalissimo's Headquarters (Donald). The English text was then translated by two or three members of our staff into Chinese, and then transcribed by others on those bewildering huge Chinese typewriters for distribution to other government departments. A sheer waste of time . . .

I envied the boys, especially the German correspondents, who, with no news available, could write cables by the yard, twice and three times a day, on nothing but impressions. They would describe dark, wet, empty streets, falling leaves, sadness, or any other sentimental scene that reminded one of their *"Lorelei"*: *"Ich weiss nicht was soll es bedeuten, dass ich so traurig bin."* On second thought, this weird prose may have had quite a different meaning to their superiors in Naziland, but how could I tell whether it was code or trash?

Things were different so far as Tass correspondent Vladimir Rogov was concerned. He was quite a personality. This stubby, blond, blue-eyed peasant boy had hiked barefoot to Moscow from his village, illiterate at twenty-two, and hungry for learning. They gave him a chance. He was brilliantly gifted and clear-headed. At thirty, he had the all-embracing knowledge that makes a first-class journalist, with that particular Russian stress on history, economics and sociology. He spoke English, knew some French and German. Tass sent him first to Manchuria, then, in 1936, to China, as Number One. He organized the Agency's branch there and studied Chinese "at odd moments." A year later he read the Chinese newspapers, conversed and wrote letters in Chinese, and in another six months he took part in debates with Chinese politicians and scholars, who stared in amazement at this blue-eyed phenomenon quoting freely from

the Chinese classics which he had read in the original. Alert
and interested in everything, Rogov knew more about inside
China than most of us; his articles in *Pravda* were little master-
pieces of concise information, keen observation and vivid accounts of what was really happening in China. He found time
for everything, yet the fellow was so easygoing he never seemed
to work. We could drop into his office, which was the big dining room in his apartment, at any hour of the day or of the
night, and find him ever ready for a chat, a *zakuska* and a drink,
always witty and ironical. He was serious only when dealing
with essentials; at such moments one got glimpses of his real
personality and the earnestness with which he approached life.
The rest of the time he was clowning. When, at a press conference, an official made a statement that was not true, he would
avoid looking at Rogov, who had a special sheepish grin for
such occasions.

Hankow was bombed almost daily. The *China Press* Building
was the only house where we were allowed to stand on the roof
to watch the raids. Reuter's occupied the ground floor. J. L.
Huang lived on the second, and Rogov on the third floor. Invariably, when the Japanese planes were overhead, Rogov would
make a sweeping music-hall gesture and sing: —

> *Madame, uzhe padaiut bomby,*
> *Pulemioty gremiat na uglakh . . .*

> (Madame, the bombs are already falling,
> The guns thunder at the street-corners . . .)

and we would run up to the roof to watch things happen. There
Rogov and J. L. Huang would look at each other like two por-
celain temple dogs and stand as far apart as space permitted,
J. L. fearing the cholera bacillus less than contamination with
Communism, against which there was no serum.

While we all moaned and complained over the lack or in-
accuracy of news from the front, Rogov did the only sensible

thing: he asked the Chinese Government's authority to send ten Tass correspondents to the different fronts. The request was met with a howl; negotiations followed, and finally he imported ten crack reporters, obtained the necessary passes, and dispatched them to their posts. They reported to him by wire as often as they came near a field station. Thus Rogov's cables to Tass, which I had to censor and to translate, contained the only accurate, detailed and reliable information from the various battle zones which gave a comprehensive picture of the war situation. They were highly appreciated by the Government, though this was, of course, never admitted — but the fact that officials would go to the trouble of telephoning or dropping in to get them was proof enough.

There were American and British war correspondents like Jack Belden and James Bertram, traveling with one or another army unit and doing good work, but no other country had arranged for as complete a coverage as the U.S.S.R.

Rogov is now back in Moscow.

After a few weeks, I could not stand it any longer. "Look here," I told my boss, "this is not the expert talking to the vice-minister, but Sues talking to Tong: I am fed up with this job, which is idiotic and unconstructive. I am overpaid, doing work which any damn fool could do. I don't want to be called a quitter, so you've got either to let me do something else or fire me." Holly was embarrassed and nothing happened for another week. Then I wrote a short memo suggesting improvements in our service; this he had to submit to Headquarters. Thereupon I received a letter written in Donald's prose, but signed by Holly, saying that the Publicity Board contemplated moving further west and was very sorry not to be able to take me along, as the only woman in the service, and ending with the usual complimentary phrases about my valuable services.

"Thank God, I am fired," I told the Roots family, but I did feel queer, never having been fired before; the fact that Donald had dictated the letter hurt me more than anything else. Why in hell couldn't these people be frank? What was the real reason for my dismissal?

I called on Holly to say good-by. We were very sorry for each other: I, because he had had to sign such a categorical letter, and he because I had to leave. At that moment we positively meant it.

When he heard of my intention to return to Europe, he grew suddenly animated: would I consider opening a Chinese News Center for the Central Publicity Board in Europe and run it in accordance with the outline I had submitted to Madame Chiang? Earl Leaf had been commissioned to open one in New York, with my memo as sole instructions. I could choose Geneva, Paris or London as headquarters and carry on, independent of any government agency abroad. He made me an interesting offer. I just listened.

"You understand this arrangement will be confidential and entirely a matter between you and the C.P.B.," Holly concluded his enticing offer. "Mr. Donald will know nothing about it — at least not for the present."

This was just one sentence too many. Doing anything behind Donald's back was out of the question.

Not wanting to hurt Holly's feelings, I thanked him for the offer and promised to think it over.

I arranged for air passage to Hong Kong and phoned Harry Timperley, who was to leave there by train, to ask if he would take some of my luggage along. Sure, he said, and would I have breakfast with him next morning? Tim, with his handsome young face, white hair, blue eyes, lithe elegance and refined tastes, looked like a marquis from the court of Louis XV, who had dropped in on this brutal century by mistake. But the Tim who welcomed me that day was not the dainty rococo Tim. He boiled with indignation. "Do you know why you've been fired?" he asked, and when I looked blank, he said hotly, "I can't give you the reason here, I might someday, somewhere else. But you ought to know one thing: when you go near Headquarters

you've got to reckon with caprice, caprice, nothing but caprice."
Now I was sure that it was not Donald's doing.

Tim took my suitcases to Hong Kong and I wrote a farewell
letter to Donald. Here is what he replied: —

Wuchang, December 29, (1937).

Dear Miss Sues,

I have your letter of the 27th. I fully realize how you feel about
having to leave. It is apparently unavoidable. Developments have
rendered curtailment necessary in many directions, especially financial. With all Customs and Salt revenues coming into the hands
of the Japanese; with the wealthy tax-paying regions also being cut
off from the jurisdiction of the Central Government; with the
necessity being acute to purchase materials with which to keep
up resistance, combined with losses in all directions, make it im-
perative for economies. The economies have to be made not only in
money but otherwise. Personnel cannot be transported easily, and
conditions out back are against easy living. Supplies will be in-
creasingly difficult the further the departments [move] westwards,
and they must keep up the trek. Personnel is being cut down wherever possible, and so are plans for reorganization. Therefore, the
hope of putting publicity upon an entirely new basis has been
destroyed by the pressure of war. In the circumstances the best must
be done with the means at hand. This would be the situation in
any country placed as is China, and it is not solely because "this is
China."

I am sorry that the situation slipped so rapidly out of the hands
of the Chinese military leaders. Had they received the support
that China was entitled to expect from the Democracies, and especially from Russia, things would have been different. That support
has been denied, especially by Russia. I mention Russia because that
country has the nearest interests to China. She is menaced more by
a Japanese victory. Yet she now demands that China pay her aviators the same as American, and also pay cash for planes. (This is
confidential and merely for your interest, and, perhaps, surprise.)

Britain and America talk mostly of their own interests being protected by Japan. They speak no more about violation of treaties and inhuman slaughter and rape and ruin. One would almost think that civilization had at last been tried and found wanting. What is happening seems to admit to the Dictators that their assumption that might is right has been proved. Here is no war, but savagery that could not be dreamed of under the terms of international law governing war. And the world has thrown up its hands.

How long China can hold out no one knows. You have to leave because there are no means to carry you out west and take responsibility for a woman. I expect very shortly to leave because the end has come. It is merely a matter of time, I think, since the Powers have indicated to Japan that they are not going to do any more than express gratification for Japan's apologies and readiness to pay for damage. As a result the terms of Japan will make the withers of China wilt, for she will demand an indemnity to settle with Britain and America, and the conditions she will require to get the indemnity out of China will cause her to want control of everything that is China. She will be triumphant if the Powers do not move, and no doubt the Powers will be quite happy if she pretends just now to leave the way open for them to sell their goods. The Powers overlook the fact that the Chinese people will (if many are left) have nothing to buy with, and it is on the cards that the regions from which Chinese have been killed will be colonized by Japanese who will not buy other than Japanese goods. All the rich country between Shanghai and Nanking will be cleared of Chinese and if Japanese are not put in to fill that region up then my guess is wrong, or something will interfere with Japan's plan. The same in the areas of the North wherever the Japanese can get the chance to slaughter the able-bodied men and growing youth. The rest will be slaves of Japan. That is what the world is watching develop. The world did little or nothing when the Japanese put into operation the plan to wipe the population out of the North with opium and narcotics. That system was the best the Japanese could follow before they had an excuse for invasion, but now they can put the blame for annihilation upon military necessity. If the world stands for that, think a minute what will happen to India. Japanese lessons to the discontent and Japanese war supplies will soon effect the wiping out of the handful of British military and people there and soon the whole country will be run by Japanese advisers and there will be settlements of Japanese people there. And so on.

I am sorry that everything went smash before it began, but this is China and this is worse than any war ever staged with modern armament. So it is no use having any feelings based on mere human disappointments and feelings of injury. Forget it. I have been injured and bumped ever since I have been in China. Some day there will be a last bump, of course, but when it comes believe me I'll not cry or quit, or squeal. The Chinese did not ask me to come to China; lots of them don't want me now. Why should they? Every move I make is against their interests. So why should they want me? If they do not kick me out with a resounding thud, I'll kick them out if I get a chance. If they do contrive to eject me I'll take it in good part — and anyway, I won't mind, for I am just a wee bit tired of the strain and the monotonous hearing of everyone's troubles, and of seeing the difficulties that have to be removed in order to have reorganization in China. So it was in our own countries. We have nothing to spurn China about. Only we went through it decades ago. China is not to blame. She did not want any foreign devils here. She wanted to be left alone, and she should have been left alone. She would have been much better off, and maybe so would the world, but a lot of us foreign busybodies got in and tried to put over a lot of our notions that our own peoples have not properly digested themselves, and what a mess?

I hope that you have a good trip; that you are philosophic enough to laugh. I think I told you that whenever I tried hard to do something and failed through miscalculation, by ignoring the "concatination of circumstances," or just by damphoolishness, I first laughed at myself, then at my folly, then at my stupidity, then at my ignorance, then at anything that could be laughed at. Thus I preserved my sense of humor, my physical strength, and my mental balance. The latter may be questioned quite legitimately, however. I often question it. Nevertheless it is never worth while taking either oneself or one's troubles or one's difficulties, or one's failures, too seriously. Damn it, anyone can succeed if things are easy; but it takes a real person to endure the stings and arrows without squealing and without quitting but with just as much laughter as can decently be indulged in. So smile, even if you can't feel like laughing. With best wishes,

Very sincerely,

W. H. DONALD

P.S. Excuse the haste. My only chance to get a line over to you. *Bon voyage —*

D.

And I should double-cross a fellow who wrote such a letter? Never.

I did not leave Hankow after all, at that time. Anna Louise Strong arrived, on her way to the Eighth Route Army. She stopped with the Roots and upset all my plans without ever noticing it. I knew her by name as the editor of the *Moscow Daily News*, one of the papers I subscribed to in Geneva. Her brother Tracy was the head of the World Federation of the Y.M.C.A. And her father was the only stranger I had ever buttonholed in the League of Nations lobby. He was a slim, stooping, kindly-faced little old gentleman, and I had singled him out among the swarm of private idealists who had invaded Geneva during the Disarmament Conference, because of the badge on his lapel: a big white button with a big "2%" on it. "Pardon the intruder, sir," I had said, "but this is highly intriguing . . . " "That is why I am wearing it," he had replied, friendly. "People get curious, which gives me a chance to tell them that, if only two per cent of the world's population honestly worked for peace, there would be no more wars." I had spent a wonderful half hour listening to him.

I had not pictured Anna Louise so — solid, massive, authoritative. She combined the rigid intransigence of the *Mayflower* pioneer with the lucidity of a revolutionary historian. Those cold, light-blue eyes in her hard, determined face awed me, and I was not the only one — the entire household seemed to stand at attention. And yet, at moments they were soft and limpid and made one visualize what she had looked like as a girl of twenty. She had known the Bishop in 1927, during the days of the Hankow Commune and the split of China's first Communist-Kuomintang United Front. She had come back now, ten years later, to investigate and report on the new United Front.

Anna Louise had no patience with individuals. When she shook her white mane lion-fashion and barked, or when she paced angrily up and down in her room overhead and made the candelabra tingle in the parlor, we all trembled, even the Bishop. But when she spoke on any subject that interested her — Soviet Russia, China, workers' movements in general — we all listened, fascinated by that harsh, matter-of-fact voice, to her reasoning which went right to the core of the most complex problems with merciless logic, amazing clarity, and remarkable vision. Her delivery was like machine-gun fire: impersonal, unemotional, penetrating. Facts and figures that spoke for themselves — never an attempt to persuade or proselytize. If you understood, so much the better; if you didn't, it did not make a bit of difference. In either case you felt that, so far as she was concerned, you could go to hell with her compliments.

To me it was the opening of new horizons. Now I could not leave China without seeing the Communist regions; without a firsthand experience there, my picture would be incomplete. Anna Louise wanted a secretary and an interpreter to accompany her. I volunteered as secretary and suggested Francis Yao as interpreter. After considerable palaver Francis got the permission but not I. The Foreign Office was stalling and Holly pretended sweetly he could do nothing. Miss Strong flew in a temper and told me if I didn't know how to take care of my affairs,

United Front: Bishop Logan H. Roots, Anna Louise Strong,
P'eng Teh-hwai, Frances Roots, Agnes Smedley

TOP ROW: Dr. Logan H. Roots, Comdr. Lo Jui-ch'ing, Ralf Sues,
Charley Higgins, Mme. Chou En-lai

MIDDLE: Bishop Logan H. Roots, Agnes Smedley, Frances Roots

FRONT: Po Ku, Chou En-lai, Wang Ming, Mme. Wang Ming

I could stay put. As a last resort, I phoned Donald; he raised hell and ordered Holly to obtain all visas for me immediately. I got my papers, but not till twenty-four hours after Anna Louise and Francis had left. This is China. There was no possibility of catching up with them. Traveling in war-torn China, and particularly to the Northwest, was a minutely scheduled expedition, with escorts, fixed itinerary and timetables.

So I stayed "put," crying and foaming over the bedding roll I had had made specially for this trip. Later I saw that a benign fate had preserved me from traveling with them. Miss Strong returned after a few weeks with a great deal of information, a bad cold, and in execrable humor. She hurled an avalanche of invectives upon my poor head on account of Francis — the most unruly, obstinate non-co-operative person she had ever encountered. At interviews with Chu Teh and others, she said, he did not interpret but asked the questions himself and took down their replies, telling her that he would let her know afterwards. And on the way back, in Chengchow, she lost him; he never came to the train. I was nonplussed by her account of Francis' strange behavior.

He came back a few days later, a gloomy, different Francis. It was difficult to get anything out of him at all. Then it seeped through that "that woman" was the only person that ever got his goat. "This a Communist? Forget it. She is a damn foreign imperialist," he said quietly, restraining his bitterness. I could not help laughing. "She treated me like a yellow dog of a Chink," he continued, "yelling, stamping her foot. I have never been so humiliated in my life." I put my arm round him and tried to comfort him by explaining that Anna Louise drew no color line, that she treated us all like yellow dogs; that, aside from her temper, she was one of the outstanding personalities of our time. "Maybe," he said, "but don't expect me to thank you for this experience."

"And how about the Eighth Route? Chu Teh? P'eng Teh-hwai?"

"I turned in my reports. Hsiao would not publish them. The subject is taboo with Central News Agency."

"Can't you tell your impressions to *me?*"

"What for? She's got all the information."

"You need not have dropped her in Chengchow, Francis," I rebuked him gently.

"It was not my fault. I was detained downtown. Good-by." He left abruptly.

The next thing I heard was that he had asked to be sent as Central News reporter into the firing line and that he was in beleaguered Hsuchowfu.*

A few days after Anna Louise had left for the Eighth Route Army and I still sat in my room with Guei-Guei brooding over the failures of my life, Frances Roots came up excitedly with the sensational news that Agnes Smedley — that legendary Agnes, who had marched a whole year with the Eighth Route Army — was in the parlor downstairs. She had come straight from the front and asked for Anna Louise Strong. "Father is out. You've got to help me persuade her to stay with us." We raced each other downstairs.

Straight from the front? She looked it, in her dusty khaki uniform, threadbare putties, and torn, mud-covered cotton shoes — a plain, blue-eyed, stub-nosed soldier, sun-tanned, wiry, but thin from privation. Nobody would have taken her for a mature woman. She took off her large fur cap; her short-cropped sparse sun-bleached hair accentuated her boyishness even more. "We were covered with lice," she explained, showing two rows of white teeth in a charming smile. "So long as I didn't have them, the comrades said I couldn't really claim belonging to their army."

---

* I learned later that the Chengchow Blue Shirts had detained and threatened Francis and his family if he refused to collaborate with them. He dodged the issue by becoming Central News' daredevil battlefield reporter. According to Hollington Tong he later joined the New Delhi Broadcasting Station.

Then she gave us a vivid description of her trip. She spoke of the ghastly poverty of that population. The partisans fighting the Japanese night after night in a temperature of forty below zero had neither shoes nor gloves. Their hands would swell and turn black. Then there was only amputation to save their lives. In one night, Agnes said, doctors had had to amputate forty pairs of those black, frozen hands. And there was no food — nothing but millet and salt turnip twice a day, sometimes not even every day. No medicines, no surgical instruments — the Eighth Route and the partisans lacked everything. Yet they fought and they sang and they shared everything they had with the civilians.

Frances and I were stirred so deeply that we remembered only hours later that Agnes might want a bath and something to eat. Then we took her upstairs to "her" room, and while Frances prepared a hot tub and selected from her own wardrobe a blue skirt, a white blouse and feminine underwear, I kept Agnes company. She took off her shoes and assured me laughingly that those black socks of hers were really white and that, originally, they had even had feet to them! One wouldn't have believed it!

She conquered the Bishop's heart as easily as she had conquered ours. She had come to Hankow to get funds, medical supplies, shoes, socks and gloves for the Eighth Route and the Partisans, and she lost no time getting them.

Agnes could not have chosen a better place than the Bishop's house; it gave her that prestige which she had never had in Kuomintang-ruled China. Her hatred for that party kept oozing out of her, try as she might to stick to the United Front line in her speeches. She never swore in these days (it was very hard on her, she did not want to shock those friendly Christians) but whenever she pronounced the word "Kuomintang" it sounded like swearing. Yet she was accepted even in Kuomintang circles without anyone's ever taking a pot-shot at her. She organized a real collection campaign, giving two and three talks a day.

Lieutenant Colonel Joseph Stilwell and other American officers would spend entire evenings bent over Shansi and Shensi maps spread on the huge dining-room table, with Agnes tracing and explaining to them the strategy and tactics of battle after battle fought by the guerillas against the Japanese. She knew all the figures and details they wanted to know, the plans, the terrain, the exact results. "Vinegar Joe," who is today the big commander in chief in the Far East, was known for never growing stale; there was not a military detail that escaped his attention, and he considered everything worth studying. We never found him sour; he could be very jolly, though pretty sarcastic occasionally, but most of the time we saw him with his thin pointed nose following a mountain range or sniffing a particularly strategic valley on that Shansi map.

Bishop Roots's house became the center of the United Front. All the missionaries had read Edgar Snow's *Red Star Over China*. Sillily enough, I did not read it until after my return from the Eighth Route, as I wanted to get an unbiased firsthand experience. It would have helped me a lot up there. Agnes called the Bishop affectionately "Comrade Bishop." Chou En-lai, the Political Director of the Communist Party, who had played a preponderant role in the Sian discussions, was stationed in Hankow as liaison officer between the Eighth Route and the National Government. This slender, refined, cultured man, with a brilliant mind and a kindly understanding soul, gave us the outlines of China's Communist program for the next fifty years. I can still see his pale, ardent face above the black Chungshan uniform under the soft light of the standing lamp in the parlor, telling us in his mellow, earnest voice that the first and foremost task was to rid the country of the invader. In this war for national survival party feuds and class differences did not count — whoever was against the Japanese militarists was a friend. This emergency collaboration was a boon for China, as it brought all elements into close contact. Mutual understanding was the very foundation of postwar China. Education, not revolution, he said, would emancipate the nation. The Party's demands, therefore, tallied with Sun Yat-sen's Three Principles in their broadest interpretation. This embraced a constitutional government of the people by the people for the people, universal franchise, recognition and equality of all parties, and the democratic freedoms: freedom of education, freedom of speech, press, assembly, freedom from want and from fear. After exercising their rights for some fifty years, Chou En-lai concluded, the people would be in a position to determine freely and knowingly whether they wanted to adhere to this the democratic form of government or to adopt some other form — socialism, fascism, or communism.

Such was the political credo of the Chinese Communist Party. Later I learned from many talks with workers, peasants, soldiers, students and school children in the Northwest that it was not only expounded by the leaders but had penetrated deeply into the consciousness of the people. Democracy was the first step in the national evolution.

On her evenings off, Agnes Smedley, with Frances Roots at the piano, would teach Bishop Roots and old, white-bearded Bishop Huntington from Anking to sing "The Death of a Cowboy" and "The Man on the Flying Trapeze." Sometimes she also sang the anticlerical "You'll get pie, in the sky, when you die"; the Bishops smiled, but would not join in.

She organized a small group of us into the Northwestern Partisan Relief Committee, kept book meticulously of all monies collected and sums expended for supplies.

We rounded up anything we could get from the International Red Cross and the Chinese Red Cross in the way of medical supplies for the Eighth Route. Among other things they needed Thomas splints, for broken arms and legs. These were usually imported and none were available in Hankow. So Agnes borrowed one of each kind from some hospital and found a local factory which manufactured 150 in a short time and made a fine job of it. They were stacked up on our terrace and Agnes examined every piece carefully before they were shipped.

I had to attend to the gloves, socks and shoes. The Y.W.C.A. became the headquarters; here the gloves were cut and distributed among members and other organizations for sewing. There was a regular competition as to who could turn them out better and faster. The spirit prevailing in the Y.W.C.A. and the other associations was remarkable: wives of high officials and poor orphan girls worked side by side. They were all animated by the same zeal for comforting the heroes, the brothers, the defenders of the nation at the front. Then someone hit upon the idea of letting the boys at the front know that they were not alone, that the people behind loved them and appreciated their heroic sacrifice. Like everything in China, this idea was immediately put into practice. There was not a pair of gloves or socks that did not have a message rolled in it. "I am a student," some would read. "Thanks to your valiant struggle I may continue to widen my knowledge in safety. A group of us have pledged ourselves to sew a thousand pairs of gloves for our soldiers. Please accept this pair as a small token of our deep gratitude." "My parents were massacred by the Japanese. More power to you, valiant avenger." "While you are fighting the ruthless invader, we are preparing a better China for you to come back to."

Never before had anyone in China thought of soldiers in these terms. It was a novel feeling, part of that extraordinary phenomenon of awakening patriotism. It is difficult for anyone in Europe and America to picture the status of the Chinese soldier prior to this war. There were many armies — every warlord and provincial governor maintained one — and none of them, not even Chiang Kai-shek's Central Army, well clad and disciplined and relatively well behaved, was considered the pride of the nation. They were accepted as an unescapable evil. The soldiers were hirelings driven to the ranks by sporadic compulsion, by acute poverty, or by a spirit of adventure. Their own families were ashamed of this dishonor, and no decent Chinese girl ever went sex-mad at the sight of a uniform. A fellow with a gun was a bandit, and his uniform a warning to the population that he could rob, rape, and kill with impunity. Neither was his relationship with the officers educated in any of the swanky military academies any better. To them he was the cannon fodder whose loss did not matter, the imbecile coolie who had to be walloped into blind submission. I have seen officers in the streets of Shanghai and Nanking and Hankow beating and kicking a soldier bloody and unconscious.

Thus the doughboy was treated as the anonymous outcast. Villagers bolted their doors at his approach, and shopkeepers kept a trembling vigilance over their goods when he entered. Who could tell whether he would pay or stage a hold-up? The soldier felt it. He knew that it did not make a bit of difference whether he was whole or wounded; that so far as his officers or the civilians were concerned, he could croak by the roadside like a mangy dog.

Then, to the utter amazement of the great majority of the nation, Generalissimo Chiang Kai-shek in one of his speeches called the soldier the defender of the country, the protector of China's homes, the hero giving his life on the field of honor. The words of the Commander in Chief were taken up by all. The administration and the brass-hats accepted and expounded them as a theory. The progressive elements put them into practice. Thousands of students and politically conscious boys and girls from every walk of life organized educational centers throughout the country.

Chen Li-fu, who paradoxically had been promoted from Minister of Education to Minister of Mass Education, was considerably upset over this spontaneous movement. Unable to stop it openly, he resorted to the old tested methods of clandestine suppression. Incidents which inevitably arose out of this policy were many. For instance, a student from Peiping, well known as a National Salvationist, obtained permission to speak at a Wuhan University patriotic meeting. The big crowd was orderly and everything went on schedule. In the meantime police surrounded the compound and when the meeting was ended and the people were leaving the grounds many of them were beaten up and one young man was shot. When the private organizations filed a joint protest, they were told that "it had been an unfortunate misunderstanding."

It must be remembered that 1937–1938 were the first years of the United Front, which was going strong, carried by popular sentiment. The reactionary factions were stunned by its impact; they pulled in their horns and went under cover. Mass education was banned only in the restricted areas which they controlled; there people were jailed or disappeared. The rest of the country was free to learn and rally to the popular anti-Japanese front.

Chiang Kai-shek had called for total economic and spiritual mobilization because he and his generals realized that military power alone could not win the war. As the Japanese advanced one fact became clear above all, namely, that popular resistance was strong and effective only where the people knew what they were fighting for. In regions untouched by political education, the army was left high and dry in the midst of an indifferent, often hostile population. This compelling reason induced the High Command to insist upon greater freedom for the political educators. A number of the more advanced generals invited propaganda groups to their armies and incorporated them in their staffs as a sort of public relations unit.

Major Hu Lan-hsi, a short, stocky woman in her thirties with the set face of a military and an aggressive nose, had just such a position when she descended upon us at the Hankow bishopric with eighteen of her subordinates. All these girls looked like boy soldiers in their gold-button khaki uniforms.

Bishop Roots had invited Hu Lan-hsi to dinner. On occasions

like this we were often ten or twelve at table. She told us how her group came into being.

"When the battle of Shanghai started in September," she said, "the whole rural population evacuated in panic. They abandoned their huts and left the crops standing in the fields. Our troops had the enemy in front and a real desert behind them. Not a soul for miles around. No supply of vegetables, rice, or even a drink of hot water. No one to take care of the wounded who limped or crawled to the rear with open wounds, armless, legless. The roads were strewn with soldiers delirious with pain, thirst, hunger. Our defenders, dying there like mad dogs.

"I was then in Shanghai, teaching factory girls in a vocational night school. We decided to get the villagers back. Three of us set out to one of the small towns where they had taken refuge. We asked the mayor to announce an open air meeting for next Sunday, and we pasted our own handwritten posters on street corners, and handed out some to be distributed in surrounding villages. The people did not care a hang. It rained cats and dogs at our first 'mass meeting.' Our audience consisted of sixteen people, including the mayor. We were all drenched. That gave us the idea of speaking about the hardships of our troops at the front. The public listened and did not run away. We sang a battle song; this drew a few more people. We told them what Japanese invasion meant, and what the soldiers defended, and what obligations we, the civilians, had to the country, to the army, and to our own families. Then we sang again and asked them to bring as many of their friends as they could to our next meeting, next Sunday. Some two hundred came to the second meeting, and over a thousand the following Sunday.

"The great majority of the population drifted home and went about its normal tasks. We were delegated to report on this to army headquarters and to promise regular supplies, transportation of ammunition and care of the wounded, if the soldiers would behave. We obtained the promise and permission to organize joint soldiers' and peasants' mass meetings. We lived in an abandoned house right behind the front. The growing friendship between us and the peasants and between soldiers and civilians was one of the most thrilling experiences in my life. Of course there were frictions, many frictions. The complaints were brought before us and we had to arbitrate.

"It was high time to harvest, but the fields were so near the front, with shells and bombs dropping there occasionally, that no one dared go near. The Shanghai front was growing shaky and retreat was imminent. The crops had to be saved at any cost; nobody wanted the Japanese to reap them and the hinterland to go hungry. We discussed the problem with the villagers and decided to make a one-day trial. We girls went with the farmers. It was a success; the shells were bursting behind us, between the village and the field, so no one was hurt, and we worked at top speed. Next morning at 5 A.M. the villagers themselves came to knock at our door: 'Hurry up, sleepy ones, it's late, we've got to bring that crop in.'

"Not one stalk was left standing when we finally had to evacuate."

Then she told us how her unit grew in number and wisdom and became part of a central army. They had officers' rank and pay but were practically autonomous so far as educational and liaison work with the civilians was concerned.

"To give you an example," she continued, "one day at a joint meeting, a village delegation complained to me that a soldier had 'bought' a pig, but instead of paying for it, he had threatened to beat up the owners. 'Do you know which soldier?' I asked. They knew, but before they had time to point him out, a soldier just in front of me whipped out his gun. The people were scared and some started to run. 'Ai-yah, comrade,' I said, 'look what you are doing — you have frightened the whole crowd — what's the idea of pulling a gun at a meeting?' He grew red in the face, looked down at it, and explained lamely, 'I thought I heard something rustling in yonder bush,

maybe Japanese . . .' I smiled, the audience laughed, the
soldier grinned and put the gun back where it belonged, and
the meeting continued. I made quite a speech about the highly
unpatriotic deed of that unknown soldier who had stolen a
brother's pig, and expressed the hope that he might think it
over and pay it after all . . . This was our usual procedure:
instead of reporting the offender to his officers, who would beat
him up or have him shot, we put him on his honor and gave him
a chance to make good. In ninety per cent of the cases, we were
right. After dark, this particular soldier came to me with two
dollars — all he had — to pay for the pig; he and some comrades
had feasted on it after many meatless weeks, he said; they had
never meant to steal it, but they had no cash. Would I save his
face and arrange the matter with the owner? I told him I had
never doubted that the whole thing was only a misunderstanding.
He left and I ran over to the peasant, very happy at heart.
There I was told that the price of a pig was ten dollars. What
now? We made up the difference from our unit's fund. The
soldier never learnt of this; such a precedent might have under-
mined the morale."

These stories may seem fantastic to people in America and
in Europe, but there is no doubt in my mind that these nameless pioneers for unity have made China's nation-wide resistance
possible. Incurable diehards in China and in Far Eastern colonies
ridiculed the movement then. Today we know better; experts
assert that Indo-China need not have surrendered if the French
armies and the population had joined forces, and that Singapore
might still be in the hands of the British if the people in the
hinterland had not been so totally ignored.

Chinese reactionaries went even farther than foreign diehards
in ridiculing and despising democratic mass education. Typical
of their spirit was General Theodore Tu, of the Officers' Moral
Association. Teddy was a stocky, fat man in his late thirties,
jovial and amusing in company. Educated in America, he had

brought back with him an amazing knowledge of popular songs and that jaunty arrogance which so many foreigners admire. He had a very fine baritone voice and solid backing from higher-ups; for these two reasons he had been given the title of General and sent to Hollywood as artistic and technical adviser while they produced Pearl Buck's "Good Earth." It is his voice one hears singing the Chinese song in the film.

Teddy, a couple of his fellow officers, Agnes Smedley, and a few missionaries were gathered for tea at the Bishopric when I came back from one of my visits to the Y.W.C.A. and told them a story just heard from a twenty-year-old girl educator.

This girl had hitch-hiked from Shanghai to Hankow at the head of a group of ten students, stopping at many places to hold meetings and organize popular resistance. When the young-sters arrived at the gates of Ihsing they were asked to stay out. The wounded and convalescent soldiers had gotten out of hand and were terrorizing the place; they refused to leave the hospital and return to the front. They had pillaged the foodshops, and they had even thrown hand grenades into the municipal build-ing. The kids insisted upon trying to settle the problem and were finally admitted. They made a hurried investigation, ques-tioning the civilians, who had barricaded in their houses and lived in mortal fear of the mutineers. Then they called on the hospital's self-appointed "soldiers' committee," and asked po-litely if they might entertain the wounded with songs and theatricals. The Chinese who would refuse such an offer has yet to be born. They obtained the permission at once.

"We held a preparatory meeting," the girl had explained to me. "You know, most of the time we do not write our plays, we just invent the dialogue while we are on the stage. Every place has its local problem, and the people are first and fore-most interested in their own local problem. It is up to us to prove to them that their local problem is part of the nation's problem, and to show them how and where they fit in in our struggle for

liberation which will ultimately solve everybody's problems at
once." So much wisdom behind this pink-cheeked baby face
with its merrily twinkling big brown eyes amazed me, but the
girl said that system was just plain common sense, other groups
used it too, and it worked.

"In Ihsing," she had continued, "our play was all there in the
exciting situation. All we had to do was to put it on the stage,
with the war as background. At the preliminary meeting we
fixed the general outline and the scenes . . ."

"How?" I had asked curiously.

"Well: —

"SCENE 1: Japanese invade China. Big talk. Cruelty. Fascist ideology.

"SCENE 2: Chinese defend their country: Heroism. Patriotism.
Democratic ideology.

"SCENE 3: Villagers praising the defenders, increasing production.
Their place in the war effort. Hopes for the future.

"SCENE 4: Wounded soldiers at a hospital. The patriots and the
instigator. The bad spirit takes the upper hand. Mutiny.

"SCENE 5: A town tyrannized by the evildoers. Physical and moral
suffering. A mother makes a dramatic appeal to the pillaging mutineers, at the risk of her life. 'Think of China first.' Evildoers
bend their heads in shame.

"SCENE 6: Hospital. Meeting shows change of heart. Patriotic
speech by former instigator. Back to the front to defend our
families, our country, and to build a free, democratic China.

"That's how we played it," the girl said. "We wound up with
the Volunteers' March. It was a real success; we had touched
their hearts and the bad leaders were ashamed. They asked us
to stay after the performance and told us many things to justify
their behavior, and we knew from experience that their words
were true. They said that nobody cared for a wounded soldier
on the battlefield, that many of their comrades had bled to

death. That medical care at the hospital was bad enough, but the thought of lying again wounded in a ditch was worse. For this reason many soldiers refused to go back to their regiments. And the food was very bad, starvation rations. So the wounded had to take food from the shops, and as they had no money, they could not pay for it. They were ready to do their duty as good patriots, but would like to be treated as sons of China, and not as her stepsons. We promised them to intervene with the military authorities, and we did. The convalescents agreed to go back to the front. We gave a big market-place performance for the population and left very happy and satisfied."

When I told the story, all those present were visibly moved, except Teddy Tu. He was livid with rage and fairly spitting venom; it was hard to recognize the jovial jester under those contorted features.

"Ihsing?" he reminisced with a sneer. "I saw their last performance on the market place. We had come just in time. This girl and her accomplices and all such so-called patriotic groups should be hanged. All they do is demoralize the people. They incite the populace to disobedience and undermine the military discipline. The morbidity of those girls, displaying their charms on the stage 'for patriotic reasons'! Of course the men get wild with enthusiasm — for the legs, not for the country."

Frances Roots, Agnes and I protested vehemently, but he brushed our arguments aside with a sweeping gesture, and went on: —

"Don't let this rascal tell you that she and her boy and girl friends brought about a change of heart in Ihsing. What a joke! Ha-ha-ha!" he laughed boisterously, cynically. "I'll tell you who brought about the change of heart — our troops. The actors walked out one gate, and my soldiers marched in through the other. We had orders to punish the guilty and straighten matters out. We surrounded the hospital and turned the whole damn bunch out into the market place — "

"The wounded? The bedridden?" I asked.

"Every one of them. I had no time to bother and investigate. And they would have lied anyway. And then *we* gave the town a performance. We had them flogged publicly, before the eyes of the whole population. And believe me, after fifty bamboos each, the lame and the blind and the crippled were ready to gallop back to the front. That is how *we* brought about a change of heart."

Some time later the military authorities in Changsha lined up fifty wounded soldiers in front of the shops where they had stolen some green vegetables, and shot them. These were some of the hundreds of wounded who had to live and beg in the streets, as there was no room in the hospitals, no canteen, and no pay for them.

In areas administrated by reactionaries, conditions are not any better today. On the contrary, they have deteriorated to an appalling extent.

The Northwestern Partisan Committee got news from the Eighth Route Army that 10,000 pairs of sturdy warm winter shoes were urgently needed for the Northwestern partisans. Our Committee had the money, we found two manufacturers ready to execute the order. Agnes, wary and experienced, said that "any kind of shoe" would not do. The fighting peasants, on their feet day and night, needed the best, the sturdiest footwear that money could buy. And she sent me to Eighth Route Hankow headquarters to get a sample pair.

As instructed, I asked for Comrade Po Ku, former chairman of the Northwest Soviet Government, who together with Chou En-lai and others had played a big part in the Sian negotiations and now headed the Hankow office. When he entered, tall, broad-shouldered, in black Chungshan uniform, with that young, energetic, conscious face of a revolutionary leader, his thick black hair standing up like a new brush, his keen eyes scrutinizing me from behind the black-rimmed spectacles, I was so impressed I sat up straight and reeled off my message as fast as I could. He listened, his eyes narrowed, and he said he had not understood a word. I realized I had made a mistake talking so fast, for Po Ku spoke better English than most of his comrades.

"Shall I repeat it in French or in German?" I asked slowly.

"No," he retorted impatiently. Then an idea struck him. "*A ty pozhaluy po russky ne govorish?*"

Sure, I spoke Russian. We brightened up and got along fine. He called in a bodyguard and asked for a sample pair of winter shoes. The lad came back and handed me a black felt shoe, not unlike those high house slippers elderly people wear here indoors in wintertime. The thick soles were made of many layers of cotton cloth, tightly pressed and stitched. I put my hand inside to examine the fluffy lining and felt that the shoe was warm, as though someone had just taken it off. When I wanted to take it with me as a model, Po Ku, who had talked with the lad, said he was very sorry but he could not let me have it as this was the only whole pair of shoes in headquarters. It belonged to a bodyguard, who had sent it in to oblige and was waiting outside barefoot. I asked him who had manufactured these shoes; we could perhaps contact the same factory. Po Ku replied that they were handmade by peasant women in Shensi on a co-operative basis; the Eighth Route had helped them organize and distributed the orders and the necessary material among the different villages. These women were patriots and familiar with guerilla requirements. They considered themselves the mothers and sisters of China's defenders, and the best was just good enough for the fighters. That's why their shoes were comfortable and lasted.

A couple of days later, we got a cable from the Eighth Route asking us not to place the order in Hankow, but rather to send the money to Shensi. They were disappointed in a former shipment which had not come up to sample and standard; the shoes fell apart after a few days of marching.

* * *

No sooner had the war started than the Japanese stretched out their peace feelers. They have continued to do so consistently up to the present day, counting upon the pro-Japanese sentiments of China's reactionaries and isolationists, to whom the United Front was a thorn in the side, and hoping to win Chiang Kai-shek over eventually to the anti-Komintern idea.

In those early days Nazi Germany was the natural mediator. Hitler was sitting on the fence: politically he sided with Japan, the fellow-fascist and partner in the anti-Komintern pact; economically he followed the Kaiser's traditional policy of maintaining profitable friendly relations with China. And while the pro-Chinese democracies shipped scrap iron, oil, and other valuable war material to Japan and extended very little help to China, pro-Japanese Germany increased the volume of her barter trade with China, taking tea, tin, tung-oil and tungsten in exchange for desperately needed war matériel. Up to the outbreak of the war in Europe, Germany was China's largest supplier. The United States came second, Russia third, Great Britain fourth. China could, therefore, ill afford losing this precious friendship, and the Government had to use all its diplomatic resourcefulness to parry the German-Japanese peace offensives. Most of these latter were kept secret, but the one undertaken at the beginning of 1938, following major Japanese victories, blossomed out on the surface.

Right after the fall of Nanking, the "bamboo wireless" started vibrating with rumors of peace negotiations.

The vernacular "mosquito" press followed suit, discreetly hinting that Germany had a hand in the game.

Then, one after another, the big Chinese and foreign dailies carried lengthy editorials featuring the Reich's endeavor to mediate peace between the two Far Eastern belligerents. Official dispatches of the *Deutsches Nachrichten-Bureau* emphasized that Germany alone was friendly to China and Japan, that she enjoyed the confidence of both and was therefore eminently well suited to safeguard their respective interests, and to bring about an "equitable, lasting peace."

And finally came the staccato of cable reports from all over the world: *GERMAN AMBASSADOR TO CHINA CONFERRING WITH JAPANESE AUTHORITIES; REICH SPONSORS FAR EASTERN PEACE; JAPANESE DRAFTING PEACE TERMS; GERMAN AMBASSADOR RETURNING TO HANKOW WITH JAPANESE PROPOSALS.*

Hankow was a buzzing beehive. From the Executive Yuan down to the last ricksha coolie people discussed nothing else but the question of whether or not the Government would make peace. Generalissimo Chiang Kai-shek had repeated as forcefully as ever, in his New Year's message to the nation, that China would resist to the bitter end. But the people were nervous. His all-out anti-Japanese attitude was only a few months old. Would he hold out now, in the face of adversity? The people wanted to believe in him. Yet no one ignored the presence of powerful men in the Government who were opposed to the war. To say nothing of the German advisers who were rushing in and out of Headquarters as if they had the run of the show. Generalissimo listened to all opinions. Whose advice would he take this time?

Headquarters had issued no denial. The country was kept in the dark as to the Government's attitude towards Hitler's peace maneuvers.

One day, early in January, all feverish talk and speculations ceased abruptly. The ominous moment had come. Ambassador Trautmann's appointment with the Generalissimo was scheduled for 11 A.M.

Leaving the house in the morning, I was shocked by the gloomy expression on people's faces. Nothing can be more soul-stirring than a mute manifestation of the Chinese masses. Whoever said that Chinese faces are impassive? As I walked down to the Bund, I read it in every pair of eyes, in every stooping shoulder, in every weary step — life or death for the nation depended on this morning's decision in Headquarters, and the people knew it.

Half an hour after the interview I got the inside story from one who was present. Here it is: —

The German Ambassador arrived at Wuchang Headquarters punctually. He was conscious of the extremely important historical mission his Führer had entrusted to him, and confident that the painstaking efforts of the past weeks would be crowned with success within the next hour. Germany would bring peace to Asia. And the fact that *he* was instrumental in pulling the historical wires made the jerky little man look bigger and gave him an air of dignity and self-assurance.

He was politely informed that very important state affairs unfortunately prevented Generalissimo from receiving him, but that Madame Chiang Kai-shek was expecting His Excellency instead.

If this change of program ruffled His Excellency, nothing in his acquiescing bow betrayed his disappointment. Madame had always been very friendly . . . She was her husband's right-hand man in international affairs . . . Of course, her rather pronounced pro-democratic feelings would render his task more difficult . . . But she was clever and would see the advantages offered by the Japanese in the proposals he carried.

Madame hurried across the room with light footsteps and greeted him like a welcome guest, with both hands outstretched. She seemed more graceful and beautiful than ever with this lovely, excited smile on her lips.

"Oh, Doctor Trautmann," she cried, jubilant, "welcome back in Hankow! You are bringing us good luck — I just had a telephone call saying that our pilots have brought down two Japanese planes this morning."

The ambassador nearly lost his countenance and looked forlorn and embarrassed.

Madame motioned him into an easy chair, took a seat herself, folded her beautiful hands and waited for him to speak. He composed himself and started slowly.

First, a well-prepared preamble featuring the historical background . . . She listened attentively, without interrupting him. Encouraged by her silence, he read the Japanese Government's proposals — the customary ultimatum offering to extend Nippon's sovereignty over China's economic life, and to protect China against communism and chaos by maintaining strong military garrisons throughout the country.

Still no protest from Madame? Trautmann launched his final speech, a masterpiece of eloquence and diplomacy, where everything had its proper place: the whole gamut of convincing arguments prepared by the Wilhelmstrasse, and the extraordinary advantages that would arise to China out of an early conclusion of peace with her great neighbor, under the benevolent auspices of Greater Germany.

Madame listened. And when he had finished, she leaned over to him with a most gracious smile and asked solicitously: —

"And how is your family, dear Doctor Trautmann?"

It came like an icy shower. Mechanically, he tried to reply in the same tone. Mechanically, he rose and bowed. This was worse than a diplomatic defeat. It dawned upon him that China's exquisite First Lady had been entrusted with the delicate mission of intimating to him that the Government was not prepared to discuss terms.

When he crossed the anteroom, the young garde-de-corps officers noticed with relief that he had left his buoyant self-assurance behind Madame's door.

The immaculate sentries outside, in the courtyard, noticed it too. They presented arms and shouted *"Chin lee"* correctly as ever, but with an imperceptible tremor of joy.

And an hour later the people of Hankow knew it. One could read it in every pair of eyes, in the swinging gait and the triumphant smile of every passer-by — Headquarters stood pat. There would be no peace. China would win the war.

One day, coming home, I was astonished to find two big, bulky bodyguards in mufti at the entrance gate of our compound. Two others, just as big, and tough-looking, stood before the church, and by the time I reached the Bishop's house, where another pair of huskies eyed me with suspicion, I had made up my mind that something phony was going on. Either they were looking for somebody — maybe Agnes or Anna Louise — or they had come to arrest the Bishop who carried on so openly with the Reds! I slowed down in my stride, clutched the key in my pocket, and dared not enter. What if they followed me into the house to murder him? I passed them with studied indifference. A look over my shoulder reassured me that they had not budged. This was my chance: I dashed across the path, up the steps in a beeline, unlatched the door, entered, slammed it behind me and stopped dead. The biggest of the bulls stood in the hall, towering over me. I swallowed a couple of times before I could ask him in my most polite Chinese, "Who is the gentleman waiting for?"

"For Dr. H. H. Kung, who is having tea with Bishop Roots in there," replied the giant with a reverent bow in the direction of the parlor door. Something said "*oof*" inside me with immense relief. But I only nodded condescendingly, offered the fellow a cigarette and sauntered upstairs to my room.

There I let loose and told Guei-Guei what I thought of the Minister of Finance and his bodyguards. The cat was horrified at my vocabulary and hid under the bed.

Bishop Roots walked on clouds the rest of the day.

Our Northwestern Partisan Committee was more successful than Agnes had ever expected. The International Red Cross Committee and the Chinese Red Cross contributed money and medical supplies. Dr. Borciê and Dr. Eric Landauer, both League of Nations men, helped us draft the lists of medicines and surgical material most urgently needed.

Borciê, a Yugoslav, was the technical expert of the National Health Administration and, as such, the moving spirit behind the astounding progress China had made in the field of public health.

Eric had just been appointed director of the First Anti-Epidemics Team — three other units had recently arrived from Europe. He went to cholera- and typhus-infected regions as to a picnic. He was indefatigable, trekking from district to district with his team, vaccinating and inoculating the population in a mad rush to outrace the epidemics, which were spreading like wildfire among the stable population and the floating millions of wayward refugees coming from the invaded areas and fleeing in all directions. As soon as he could pocket his hypodermic, Eric would make a minute study of the district and prepare a concise report on its social and economic conditions, listing the needs and making concrete suggestions for improvement and development. The reports went to government organs, to the League of Nations, to the China Defence League, and to anyone able to help. Significantly, the only people who took a constructive interest in them were Madame Sun Yat-sen and her group, and the Eighth Route Army people.

One beautiful day Agnes came thundering down the stairs, late for breakfast, into the parlor where we were reading the latest papers.

"Comrade Bishop," she beamed, "P'eng Teh-hwai is coming for lunch. Is this okay with you? Do you know him personally?"

The Bishop liked Agnes and his new honorary title. He looked over the rim of his spectacles and smiled his kindly, amused smile.

"Agnes, this house is your house; all of your friends are always welcome. I have never met P'eng, but I know him by reputation. He is the fiercest of them all. . . . Didn't they call him 'the Tiger' during the civil war?"

"He is China's greatest guerilla strategist, and today he is the Vice Commander in Chief of the Eighth Route," said Agnes, eagerly. "Chiang Kai-shek has summoned him to Hankow to discuss the plans for a joint defense of Wuhan."

"I shall be delighted to have him here. By the way, we have had some experience with him, a few years ago . . ." Bishop Roots paused deliberately, timing his effect, and his little blue eyes twinkled with contained mirth. "He once kidnaped two of our missionaries and carted them through half of China."

There was suspense in the air. Agnes' face was a battlefield of emotions. She frowned: here was a formal accusation, so often repeated by diehards, that her beloved Red Army behaved like bandits. And yet, she must not flare up: this Bishop was such a decent fellow. She was puzzled, too: had he not just said he would be delighted to meet P'eng? Would she ever be able to follow the mental processes of these queer Christians? Well, Bishop or Pope, she wouldn't let anyone get away with this kind of a statement. Throwing back her head with that characteristic jerk of hers, ready to fight, she challenged: —

"P'eng never tortured or killed any of your priests, did he?"

"I never intimated that our missionaries were maltreated by your friends," was the Bishop's conciliatory reply, but the ripple of good humor could not be suppressed. "I believe it was just a matter of letting them have a free ride cross-country. You know, sort of a compulsory educational expedition. P'eng released them eventually and never asked for ransom. So don't be aggressive, Agnes — run along and tell P'eng that the gates of the bishopric are wide open to receive a welcome guest."

"No need. I have already told him so last night."

The cloud had passed. Agnes beamed again. She squeezed the Bishop's arm: "Oh, Comrade Bishop, you're a grand fellow."

*　　*　　*

P'eng Teh-hwai came, accompanied only by a pale, intellectual-looking interpreter. We looked curiously at this man who had the rank of a general and moved about Hankow without a bodyguard, as though he were among friends. The prize set for his head had been NC $100,000; Generalissimo had rescinded the order only recently, but any one of the reactionaries would have been only too glad to pay an even higher price out of his own pocket for the Tiger's skin.

P'eng did not look at all like a tiger. Not even like one of those legendary Eighth Route Army men Agnes had depicted to us. Where were the blue padded uniform, the torn cotton sandals? It was almost disappointing to see this perfectly well-mannered, well-dressed officer in khaki uniform. He had even shaved his head! Just like any general staff officer, except for the absence of insignia and the lack of pompous self-assurance. He was much more himself when I met him later in Chu Teh's headquarters; in Hankow he obviously made the concession of fitting into the official surroundings. He had a nice, cordial handshake and little wrinkles in the corners of his eyes which betrayed a keen sense of humor. And yet he seemed preoccupied or worried, and his restraint contrasted strangely with the Bishop's hearty welcome.

Anna Louise Strong grinned like a Cheshire cat and immediately buttonholed him.

While the Bishop, Anna Louise and P'eng Teh-hwai were exchanging preliminary phrases, Agnes poked me in the ribs, her eyes blazing with indignation.

"Look what they have done to him," she whispered fiercely, "just look how they've dressed him up."

"Do you mean that khaki uniform?" I whispered back.

"No, he's got to wear that in the capital. What I mean is the officer's belt, that shoulder-strap! What a disgrace! The poor fellow must feel wretched. . . . And the thing keeps slipping down his shoulder — he isn't used to such fancy stuff. Nobody ever heard of such a thing — an Eighth Route Commander with a belt! I bet you it's that pale-faced interpreter of his who persuaded him to put it on. There you've got it again — an intellectual's conception of smartness. Oh, I'd twist the neck of every one of those intellectuals. The sissies . . . never fired a shot in their lives . . . don't even know how to load a rifle . . . won't march with the rank and file for fear their feet might blister. . . . Their only ambition is to dress up like a Kuomintang officer."

The word "Kuomintang" sounded like swearing again. Fortunately, the boy announced that lunch was served, and she stopped in the midst of her tirade.

For the first time, we sat down without the traditional blessing of the food by the Bishop. Comrade Bishop had omitted it tactfully, to put P'eng Teh-hwai at ease. But P'eng seemed seriously worried. He sat motionless, stared into his soup and did not touch it. What on earth could be the matter with him? Did he disdain foreign food? Or was he simply intimidated by the unfamiliar surroundings? This might be an explanation for his strange behavior. After all, Eighth Route men did not as a rule sit at Bishops' tables. There was a long moment of awkward silence.

Suddenly P'eng raised his head resolutely, took a deep breath, and turned to the Bishop: —

"Bishop, do you know our past?" The words rang out clearly, earnestly.

"Of course I do," our host hastened to reassure him. "I have lived in China for the past forty years and know a lot about the civil war." The merry twinkle was again in his eyes. "I even know a little of your own activities — do you remember having captured two of my missionaries?"

P'eng remembered, slightly embarrassed. "But they came to no harm — we treated them well, didn't we?"

"Oh, you treated them like real comrades. You took them across a good many provinces, and gave them a lot of political education, and showed them all your democratic institutions —

schools, co-operatives, free medical treatment, and what not. . . . Why, when they finally came out, we were faced with quite a problem — they had almost turned Communist themselves!"

We all laughed, P'eng loudest of all. The Bishop's good-humored account of the incident had broken the ice; still P'eng felt that something more had to be said, and he said it, slowly, reflectively: "Mistakes have been committed in the past . . ."

Whereupon Bishop Roots replied significantly: "Mistakes were committed on both sides. But, thank Heaven, now all this belongs to history. Today we have a United Front, and all men in China are brothers. I am happy to have met you, Comrade P'eng."

The two men smiled into each other's eyes. Then P'eng reached for the spoon and attacked his cold soup with appetite. Now he could enjoy his meal. He had made sure that hospitality was extended to him with a perfect knowledge of his background. The idea of eating at a man's table under false pretenses would have been unbearable to him.

From that moment on, the Bishop and all of us accepted him as a friend.

"The people are the water, and we guerilla fighters are the fish," said P'eng Teh-hwai. "Without them we cannot live or fight. So long as they do not understand what this war is about, so long as they do not look upon it as their very own struggle for political freedom, for economic independence, for national emancipation, they will not move their little fingers to help us. But as soon as they understand, they become our staunchest and most reliable allies."

P'eng stuck to the United Front line with remarkable self-discipline; he mentioned no names and refrained from criticizing the Government. But he did not need to tell us that the Kuomintang was as dead-set against popular education as had been the Russian Government at the time of the tsars. There was no telling just how far a literate coolie would go. He might, someday, read Dr. Sun Yat-sen's *Three Principles* and demand a constitution, a democratic government, and the right to vote! And where would the Kuomintang be then? Already some very disrespectful people had circulated a nickname for it among the populace: they referred to the Party not as the *Kuo*mintang (*Kuo*= "State," *min*="people," *tang*="*party*"), or in other words as the State or National People's Party, but as the *Kua*mintang (*Kua*= to scrape), that is to say, "The Party which Scrapes the People."

The Kuomintang was thus standing at a crossroads. Mass education spelled ruin to the Party. Refusal spelled defeat at the hands of the Japanese. A difficult choice . . . The various government groups were hotly debating the burning question of how to eat their cake and have it. They were all in favor of a formula by which organized mass drilling — mental and physical — might take the place of mass education.

And while they debated, Generalissimo and his National Defense Council had just set out upon the first noteworthy experiment along United Front lines: rightist General Ch'en Ch'eng and communist General Chou En-lai were appointed director and vice director of the Political Department of the Military Affairs Commission. Here, at least, was a beginning of collaboration.

Our animated discussion round the Bishop's table was drawing to an end. Over the demitasse, we told P'eng of our goodwill mission planned to the Northwest. He was delighted and promised us a hearty welcome. Then we asked his advice what small gifts we should take to the boys in the Army. All contributions we had received were expressly earmarked for the civilian population — no one wishing to anger the Government, which discouraged gifts to the Eighth Route. But Anna Louise Strong had fortunately earmarked hers for the fighters, otherwise we should have had nothing for our hosts themselves.

It didn't take P'eng long to reply: —

"Pencils and notebooks would please them more than anything. We lack paper, and the boys are crazy about their studies."

"What else?"

"Flashlights and batteries — nights are pitch-dark up there, when we go to battle. And another thing, tooth brushes and tooth paste — these are scarce since Japanese dumping stopped."

I took notes. "Anything else you can think of? Any sweets? Cigarettes?"

He shook his head disapprovingly at this frivolous suggestion. "No, but if you would bring them some ping-pong balls, there would be no end of joy."

Chou En-lai and P'eng Teh-hwai had impressed upon us that we must change the NC $20,000 we were taking along to the Eighth Route for the partisans into ten-cent, twenty-cent and one-dollar bills, as there was no possibility in their region of changing a five-dollar bill. Agnes entrusted this errand to me. Money was scarce and small denominations difficult to get. It took me several days to do it. I had a fixed itinerary, called on every big bank every day, patiently awaited my turn with the rest of the crowd — there were always crowds — persuaded the clerks to change as many of my large bills as possible, and to reserve some more change for me for the following day. I insisted upon new or clean bills. Most of the small bills in circulation were repugnant: filthy little rags which did not even resemble paper; one had to guess the value by the size! It was a lucky day when I could obtain a few hundred dollars' worth.

The clerks were all polite and serviceable with the exception of a young fellow in the Central Bank of China, who treated me as a nuisance. Either he was anti-foreign or he disliked me in particular; whichever it was, he did it so ostentatiously that the crowd, always ready to make fun, responded by grinning. It became a daily sport for him. I could not afford to give him a piece of my mind, because the C.B.C. was the biggest issuing bank, so I decided to look upon this as an exercise in holding my temper. One day, however, when he (there were no tellers) tossed two NC $100 bundles of bills across the counter, which looked too dirty even for a garbage can, I objected. He grinned, and so did his colleagues and the clientèle.

"Will you please give me some clean money?" I pleaded.

"You no need clean money. No can buy things for ten cents. This clean enough for pay ricksha coolies," he said snootily, evidently playing up to his public.

I raised my voice: "This money is not for ricksha coolies but for the Northwestern partisans." And I repeated it in Chinese.

The effect was immediate. The clerk blushed, ashamed, stammering excuses, and pulled in the bundles. A sympathetic excitement ran through the crowd. Everybody seemed to talk at once. The employees were curious too and stopped working. A fine gentleman interviewed me in English and translated my replies to the people. Ayah, a friendship expedition to the Eighth Route Army! Ayah, it deserved help, the fightingest army of China. They wanted to know all the details, and I was so glad and surprised at this manifestation of popular sympathy here in Kuomintang Hankow and, of all places, in H. H. Kung's own lion's den, that I replied with as much enthusiasm. Then my ex-tormentor let me have two bundles of brand-new bills and promised more for the following day. He kept his promise and I got preferred treatment ever after.

We sat on the top of the world, preparing for our trip. Frances Roots and wiry, active, old little Deaconess Judy Clark were the ladies in our party. Lanky, affable John Foster with a touching inferiority complex, and intelligent vivacious Charley Higgins, whose healthy outlook on life could never be marred by any complex, completed the missionary quartet.

Chou En-lai advised us to take only as much baggage as we could ourselves carry in case of emergency: a bedding roll with our toilet articles and change of clothes rolled into it. If we wanted any foreign foodstuffs along on the trip, we could take them in cardboard boxes which could be thrown away. He emphasized the necessity for warm clothing. Frances and Judy selected an assortment of canned goods. Charley and I thought only of coffee and requisitioned Cook's biggest percolator. Po Ku came in to cast a last glance at our outfit and found everything perfect except the bulging thing under the oilcloth of my roll — our percolator. There was no room for it elsewhere. He ruled it out.

"This is impractical," he said, inspecting it critically. "*Bei wo* must be packed flat, so as not to hurt the tiny donkeys which may have to carry them."

I fetched a low casserole, but Po Ku shook his head. "Still too bulky. . . . Must you people make coffee en route? You will get hot tea everywhere."

We raised a howl of dismay. Po Ku laughed. "Well, if it is a matter of life and death, you can take a frying pan along. That will be flat enough." And that's what we did.

The NC $20,000 in ten- and twenty-cent notes was another headache. Judy made five wide cotton belts with big pockets all around which we were to put on under our sweaters. So much publicity had been given our expedition already, that we feared to lose the money "by accident." We felt very important and worried only over the elephantine dimensions of our waistlines. Po Ku grinned amused and asked us to hand the money over to Comrade Ch'iou, a gay, intelligent youngster who accompanied us as interpreter. Ch'iou counted the bundles, asked for old newspapers, wrapped the whole NC $20,000 up like a laundry parcel and shoved it under his arm. He certainly did not feel important. From then on until we reached Commander Chu Teh's headquarters, he and our Eighth Route Bodyguard, whose name was also Ch'iou, carried it alternately.

We left for the Northwest equipped as though we were heading for the North Pole. As a special favor, Frances had lent me one of her father's woolen union suits, just as she had a few weeks before to Anna Louise Strong. But Frances herself, Agnes Smedley's pet, was the luckiest of all: she wore Agnes' patched-up uniform and looked so smart in it that we were all bursting with envy.

Guei-Guei had to stay in Hankow with the Bishop.

VII

Shansi

THE TRAIN was crowded with soldiers and refugees.

Traveling was very slow. The Japanese bombed railway lines frequently, and though the Chinese repaired the tracks with amazing speed, timetables had gone out of fashion. Troop trains, heavily camouflaged, had priority. We stopped for hours in open fields, and long enough at every station to have a meal and a good look around.

Inside station buildings and all around them the ground was covered with sitting, squatting, lying refugees — thousands of homeless families, waiting for transportation: tense, tired, weary people with sunken cheeks, clutching small bundles in their hands — all they had saved in their hurried flight — and hanging on to their little ones. They did not complain or wail or even sigh. They just sat there, proud, patient, silent in their sorrow, waiting for transportation. This great silence was more heart-breaking than the most strident scream of agony I had ever heard. I never dared look into the sad eyes of these crowds. I tiptoed past them with an unbearable feeling of guilt. I belonged to those who did not help.

I was so depressed that I hardly looked at the old historic towns. I have to get over this haunting feeling, I told myself, or else this whole trip will be a flop. And while the others went souvenir hunting, I stuck to my corner in the railway carriage, resolved to analyze matters down to the last shred. Gordon Lum's words came back to me: ". . . If you can go through

China and take in all the beauty and grandeur, all the horror and misery she has to offer, and still continue to love her . . ." Still continue to love her — did I? I did, each day more fervently than the day before. "Rather sweeping and sentimental statement," mocked the joker in me, "a trifle more precision would do no harm." All right.

I liked the country: the tropical, radiant abundance of Kwangtung; the grayish-brown, grave-mound-studded planes of Central China; the pale, tender green rows of young rice plants set in frames of liquid silver; and the night-blue majesty of Shantung's gigantic mountain ranges. I liked the bamboo groves with their deceptive air of austere chastity — those secret sanctuaries rustling down voluptuously upon the first timidly aggressive abandon of adolescence; adding spice to the lust of a wise, subtle seducer; fondling between their smooth stems the obscene loveliness of nimble-fingered nymphs gamboling with virile playmates; fanning with trembling leaves the lascivious grace of slender Sybarites. . . . Bamboo groves, symbols of languorous, tantalizing caresses, echoing the delicate crescendo of Oriental erotic . . .

"What a libidinous flight of fantasy from the corner of a dusty railroad carriage," remarked my inner joker drily; "open a can of tomato juice and cool off."

The tomato juice had a sobering effect and I resumed my inquest. That much for the country. How about the Government? *Hm.* What precisely is a government? A régime and a group of individuals. I thought that a few of them could, with good advantage to the country, be made a head shorter. But I enjoyed all of them because they were so candidly uninhibited in their greatness and in their foibles, in self-sacrifice and in selfishness, in generosity and in corruption, in gentle refinement and in bestiality.

Then whom did I love? The anonymous, harassed, selfless pioneers scattered throughout the country, courageously preparing the people for democracy. And the coolie bending under his burden, and the peasant toiling for the absentee landlord, and the beaten, underfed soldier, and the wounded bleeding to death on the roadside. All of them — the down-trodden, under-privileged Chinese masses. . . .

"Holy Moses, where did you pick up this subversive vo-cabulary? Holly would faint at the mere sound!" sneered my joker. "We haven't yet crossed the Yellow River, and you are all set to lap up Marxist doctrine!"

No, I wouldn't. I would keep my eyes and my mind open in the Border Region, exactly as I had done in governmental China.

"Donald too would have a good laugh, after all the baloney you gave him about your being immune to hero worship! Isn't this a flagrant case of hero worship?"

I did not object. Perhaps it could be called this. I went down to the platform and up to the refugees. I could face them now and smile, and exchange a few words with some. An old woman was mending a pair of black pants. A young mother with an infant at her breast smiled up at me and responded to my foreign-sounding greeting with the peasant's customary: *"Wo-men ch'ih k'oo."* ("We eat bitterness.") I had heard it often before, but never so consciously. And then, this smile . . .

I realized that there was no pity in me for these people. One can pity only somebody inferior. They stood head and shoulder above me. I felt compassion and friendship and deep admiration. And I felt very humble and very useless and ready to speak up for them, if I only knew how.

Worship was perhaps too emotional a word, but I had found my hero for life — the little man, the little woman in black garb — the country's backbone and only hope for the future: the Nameless Builders of New China.

I paced up and down the platform, among the usual hundreds of curious gapers, and suddenly almost bumped into someone taller than the rest, a white man without a hat — Dr. Eric Landauer, of the League of Nations First Anti-Epidemics Unit.

"No?" I shouted surprised. "Yes," he shouted back, and we hugged each other to the amusement of the crowd. Funny how love for China draws quasi-strangers together. A brief case under his arm was his baggage; he was going south, and his train would be in any moment. There was so much I wanted to know. "Eric, those refugees?" "They stand up magnificently." "How many are they?" "An estimated thirty million." "Where are they going to?" "Many to distant relatives — you know how far-flung their family relations are. But the great majority just trek ahead, as far as wheels or barges or their legs will carry them." "No help from anywhere?" "Precious little. The Government has some funds for the purpose, most of which stick to the hands of squeezers and do not reach the refugee. Private associations do as much as they can, which is insignificant, as they have more good will than money. Missionaries distribute some food, preferably to Christians. But all efforts are a drop in the bucket. It's a tremendous problem. Charities won't solve it." "What will?" I asked anxiously. Eric gave me a look which told me that I had touched upon the thing that occupied his mind. "Co-operatives," he replied. "I am working out a project for Shensi. We will start small. The army needs shoes, bandages, soap, blankets, cotton cloth, and a million other things. And so do the civilians. There are thousands of skilled workers among the refugees — just waiting for a chance to work. They can be grouped in smaller and larger units — mobile units to move with the army, if necessary. If we get the necessary funds — we don't need much, just to buy the simplest tools for handicraft — like looms and spindles, no elaborate machinery — we can start to industrialize China on a co-operative basis."

"In the Border Region?"

"Yes. The government there is reliable and Shensi has already worked out a very successful refugee organization. Refugee relief committees exist in every border *hsien*, with subcommittees in special Receiving Stations. They co-operate with a number of self-help organizations, mainly with the National

Salvation Association, Labor Unions, Women's Unions, Youth Organizations, who either raise funds or take care of a certain number of refugees. Each local relief committee is obliged to dispose of a refugee within ten days of his arrival: able-bodied men may join the Army or one of the partisan detachments; boys and girls may join one of the new Yenan schools, where tuition is free; people with vocational training are put to work whenever possible; positions have been found already for a large number of teachers, skilled workmen, farmers. Families without members capable to work are sent to the farmers in the country, ten host families taking care of one refugee family. The Border Government provides medical care, shelter and transportation. People who do not wish to stay — usually the wealthy — are helped in transit. Quite a number of refugee families can be persuaded to return to their homes behind the Japanese lines. Every assistance is given to them; they are put in touch with, and taken care of by, the partisan units of their home district and can often be developed to be of great help in the war."

A train thundered into the station. "So long!" Eric joined the hundreds of refugees in their wild assault on the train, noisily scrambling for seats or standing room, climbing through doors and windows in mad frenzy. When it pulled out a few minutes later, it had passengers sitting on the locomotive, on car roofs and buffers.

The old walled-in town of Tungwan on the bend of the Yellow River was one of the most fascinating trading centers I had ever seen, with camel and donkey and human caravans carrying cotton, tea, silk, food from and to the four corners of China, as though there were no war, as though the railway had never been invented, as though civilization had stopped five hundred years ago. A kaleidoscope of all Asiatic races (minus Japs, of course) in their characteristic costumes — slow-gestured Tibetans with bead-embroidered gowns, short, squat Mongols wearing long sheepskin coats, the fur turned outside, tall, broad-shouldered, ponderous, blue-clad men from the Northeast; vivacious, gesticulating Cantonese in black . . . Soldiers and officers of many armies, buoyant or wounded, some well-equipped and warmly dressed, others shivering in their flimsy cotton uniforms . . .

The Eighth Route had a communication station there, where we enjoyed a hearty meal, a hot sponge bath and a good night's rest on wooden army cots. From then on we were the guests of the Eighth Route.

Early next morning we crossed the Yellow River aboard a huge mud-brown, weather-beaten wooden structure which had neither bow nor stern and looked like a Chinese version of Noah's Ark. It was propelled by light-footed, bronze-colored athletes deftly juggling with long bamboo barge-poles.

The Yellow River is called "China's Sorrow" because of its obstinate spirit of independence. Every now and then, at unpredictable times, it rises in savage vehemence, bursts all fettering dams, and breaks loose in search of a new bed, flooding entire provinces, bringing death and despair to countless humans. Man has never subdued it. It is not navigable. It may be crossed at certain points, but even there it often takes its toll.

Contemplating this immense, impenetrable stream of heaving, gurgling mud, torn by whirlpools, furrowed by uncanny cross-currents, I had the weird impression of looking into a human face. A proud, strong face lined with a lifetime of sorrow, ravaged by unbridled, elemental passions . . . The face of one who knows the nonsense of good and evil, the futility of life and strife and progress, and yet rolls on, disillusioned beyond despair, obeying destiny, ready to crush the world in another spontaneous, wanton embrace . . .

We reached Fenglingtu on the opposite bank at breakfast time. Shansi province was officially old General Yen Hsi-shan's domain, with Generalissimo's own General Wei Li-huang at the head of military operations. In reality the Eighth Route had the run of it.

A few months before, Yen's troops had been routed and fled in wild panic, throwing away ten thousand rifles. The Eighth Route had stopped the Japanese onslaught, picked up the rifles it needed so badly, and held them at Chiang Kai-shek's disposal. Chiang ordered them returned to Yen, and the Eighth Route had obeyed. He had dispatched Wei Li-huang to supervise the retraining of the Shansi troops in a specially established military patriotic reform school, and entrusted the Eighth Route with the defense of Shansi.

P'eng Teh-hwai came all the way from his headquarters to receive us, which was sweet of him and put us all into a wonderful humor. He was so different here, in his own blue padded-cotton uniform, natural, easygoing and in high spirits.

In the late afternoon we took the narrow-gauge train for Linfeng. P'eng stayed behind to attend to some military business. A freight car was reserved for us and for our honor guard — eight fighters and a young commander. The first question those fellows asked was, "What is the last news from Spain?" And they told us what a wonderful meeting they had had recently to express their sympathy with the Loyalists. We settled down comfortably on our *bei-wos* and left the sliding door open for air and light. And after a snack the songs started. They sang a marching song of fight and freedom and sacrifice, and the young, joyous, self-confident voices sounded wonderful with the rhythmical accompaniment of the wheels. I had never heard any other Chinese army sing. Mass singing was as taboo as mass education.

"Now it's your turn; *wai-guo t'ung-dzhemen ch'ang.*" ("Foreign comrades, sing.") So we sang Frances' favorite "My Bonnie lies over the ocean," and when Judy translated it, the boys said "Ai-yah" and giggled, because it was not a patriotic or revolutionary text. So Charley saved the situation with "Carry me back to old Virginny," which thrilled them as much as his beautiful baritone voice. They rewarded us with the most beautiful song of all, *"Ch'i lai"* — "Arise, you who do not want to be slaves." It was then still forbidden in Central China. I shall never forget this first time when I heard it, and I know my companions felt the same. The night fell, we lit a candle and continued to sing alternately. Suddenly a gremlin whispered into my ear: "Put them to a test. See how far their United Front discipline goes."

"Do you sing the *San Min Chu I?*" I asked the song leader. *San Min Chu I* — the Kuomintang's national anthem. For a fleeting second there was dead silence. Then he turned to the lads and repeated in an even voice: *"San Min Chu I."* They stood at attention, took off their caps, those faded blue caps which never left their heads. We rose. The solemn tones of the anthem sounded as orthodox here as in any Kuomintang memorial hall — a ritual which had lost its meaning. I was never more ashamed of myself than at that moment. But the boys had stood up to the test.

When the sliding door was opened next morning, we were traveling in a deep narrow valley between two softly sloping mountain ranges of sheer pale mat gold. The sky was blue, the rest of the landscape golden — the tiny villages with their mud houses, the wells, the donkeys, the people. And within half an hour we ourselves looked steeped in gold, covered with the finest, softest, pulverized sand one can imagine. Our eyebrows and eyelashes looked like gilded little temple roofs. Since time immemorial the wind had continued to carry loess sand from the Gobi Desert, building mountains so soft that it is easy to dig caves into them. We saw our first cave villages. And the roads were so soft that they were sinking deeper and deeper.

"The Japanese have a hard time advancing with their heavy equipment on these low roads," the boys explained. "They are at our mercy when we swoop down from the mountains for the kill."

The sand penetrated everywhere. Our eyes burned, every bite creaked between our teeth, and it irritated our windpipes and made us cough. But we were happy.

The only things that remained clean and shiny were the submachine guns and rifles. The boys kept oiling and wiping them every few minutes, never forgetting to put the gaudy little woolen tassel into the barrel to keep out the dust. Two of the submachine guns were Shansi-manufactured. All the others had been taken from the enemy.

We arrived at the little village of Mamoo by a rickety Ford bus from Linfeng. Our quarters were three rooms in a large house built by a rich landowner who had escaped with his family. The rest of the house was occupied by poor peasants. The Eighth Route had invited all absentee landlords to come back, but none dared. So their land was tilled and harvested by the families who formerly had no land.

A long table and rough wooden benches occupied practically the entire hall-dining-room. A huge iron incense burner, which must have come from a temple, served as stove. The room to the right was reserved for John, Charley and interpreter Ch'iou, the one to the left belonged to us girls. A rustic cement *k'ang* occupied three quarters of the room. To our great surprise and joy, it was warm; I looked inside and saw an iron pot full of burning charcoal. Dazzling white paper had been pasted over the large, carved wood window, in lieu of glass. There was even a dressing table which must have been manufactured specially for us, as its rough planks smelt so fresh under the clean white paper napkin.

We had not been there five minutes when a couple of *hsiao hung kwei*, "little red devils," brought us piping hot water to wash, and announced that Comrade Chu Teh had just arrived.

"We've got to tidy up first," said Judy and Fran with female coquettishness, but I didn't give a hang and ran to see Chu Teh. He was in our "parlor" already, shook hands with the boys and with me. We sat down and started talking of our trip. Chu Teh wanted to know all the details and news from Hankow, and whether we were comfortable, and what we would like to see first tomorrow morning. The little muscular man with his ready, jovial smile and hearty cordiality was so unlike all the pictures I had seen of him. He wore the same faded blue uniform as his men, and was sun-tanned and agile like the youngest of them, notwithstanding his fifty-nine years.

"Comrade K'ang is really the one who is organizing the whole program for your stay," he said. "She will be here first thing tomorrow morning."

"Who is that lady?" we asked.

"K'ang Keh-chin, my wife," grinned Chu Teh. "And Ting Ling, the playwright, is here too with her theatrical group."

The little red devils brought hot wet towels for each of us to wipe our faces and hands, and then placed washbowls with soup, vegetables, pork and noodles on the table.

Suddenly the left door was opened a bit and Judy's frantic yell — "Ralf, for heaven's sake, can't you hear me calling?" — brought me to my feet and to our room.

"Fran has fainted. Get some cold water and John's first-aid kit."

Fran lay stiff on the *k'ang*. Chu Teh and the others were very much concerned. I rushed back to Judy with the stuff, and while I was handing it to her, she too keeled over and passed out. I yanked the little slim body up on the *k'ang* and threw cold water over both girls' faces, but they did not move, that is to say Frances didn't, but Judy kicked and boxed in all directions like an acrobat — gentle, soft-spoken Judy — who would have thought she had so much temperament in her? I tried to pour some brandy down their throats, but Judy nearly knocked me off my feet. So I called Charley. He climbed on the *k'ang* and tore big holes in the white paper window.

"Come on, rub Fran's chest with some alcohol. I'll attend to Judy."

We went through routine first aid.

"Don't you smell anything, Ralf?" asked Charley, wrestling with Judy.

"Smells like something is burning," I said and went to tell Chu Teh.

"Ai-yah!" he said, and ordered the *hsiao kwei* to take the charcoal pot immediately out of our room. "With some people carbon monoxide does not agree," he explained.

As soon as the charcoal was out of the room, both girls opened their eyes. But they were sick and headachy and could not even say hello to Chu Teh.

Next morning at seven, Chu Teh came to ask how they were and how we had slept, and had breakfast with all of us. Then came K'ang Keh-chin, a stocky, jolly, resolute girl a little over twenty. She was Chu Teh's second wife. The first Madame Chu Teh had been executed by government troops on a public square in Changsha in 1927.

Ting Ling, who accompanied her, was older and had a whole revolutionary career behind her. She was China's foremost playwright and had now organized a small group of progressive artists: actors, poets, painters, musicians, who played for the soldiers and people at the front, conducted mass singing, organized art exhibits, and so on.

K'ang Keh-chin had some classes for the fighters, teaching them character reading and writing. The village women had selected her as adviser in their mothers' club, where war relief, household and child-care matters were debated. She had some girl helpers and was the busiest woman round Headquarters. How she managed all this and kept her healthy girlish smile was a riddle.

Next to her in cheerfulness were our *hsiao hung kwei;* four or five of them were always around, cooking and washing for us, serving hot tea the day long and hot towels every fifteen minutes. We *had* to use these, they said, because "cleanliness

Front Service Corps: Comrade Tsen, K'ang Keh-chin (Mme. Chu Teh) and playwright Ting Ling, all wearing captured Japanese uniform coats

Ting Ling's front-line theater

was the most important thing to keep army and nation fit."
Those kids either were orphans or had left their families and
joined the Eighth Route. They were the Army's adopted sons,
received the same pay and education as the fighters, and were
real fiends when it came to fighting the Japanese. The only
order they ever disobeyed was to stay away from battlefields.
Chu Teh said they always managed to sneak out. War prisoners
admitted the Japanese were afraid of these youngsters, who had
not the slightest conception of danger and enjoyed the blood-
iest fight as though it were a football game. As a result of
criticism in some quarters, the commanders had decided to send
the boys to schools behind the lines, but they never succeeded.
The boys formed *cadres* of their own, the "Young Vanguards,"
and sent a delegation to Chu Teh, protesting against the decision
and demanding that their "democratic right of defending their
country" be respected. Who could turn down such an appeal?
When telling us about it, Chu Teh was so proud of his boys!
Now, wherever they went, they organized the village children
into self-defense groups and made them nation-conscious. All
of which did not prevent them from taking dancing lessons at
Ting Ling's, singing and acting in her plays, playing ping-pong
and croquet and basketball. Chu Teh, though a bit clumsy at it,
was a basketball fan and joined them whenever his older part-
ners were busy elsewhere.

The commander in chief was referred to as Chu Teh or as
Chung-sse-ling ("Generalissimo"). I could not help comparing
the two Generalissimos of China, both legendary figures. The
one of Nanking and Wuchang, in his superb remoteness and
seclusion, unapproachable to common mortals . . . I had
worked next door to him and had never felt the urge of asking
for an interview, because all people who interviewed him came
out with the same stereotyped report about his slim figure, his
compelling eyes, and his reluctance to speak. To know Chiang,
one had to follow the trend of his policies; no interview ever
disclosed his human side. . . . The one here in Mamoo was

always around. He would drop in for a chat, or take us round to see "our link with the outside world," a two-by-four portable dynamo which serviced the radio telegraph station in a tiny shed behind the school building. Then he would go to attend a wedding, or look in on a sick old peasant or on some wounded fighters who were cared for by peasant families. The villagers knew at all times where he could be found. When two neighbors had a dispute, or when a husband and a wife or parents and children were at odds, they would bring the problem before Chu Teh, who would go into all details and give his advice. There never was a case of people not accepting it. Chu Teh was invisible only when meeting in conference with his military staff in the "strategy hall" of his headquarters. This room contained the most valuable detailed maps and operation charts and was always locked and strictly guarded. Otherwise, if we were told that he was "somewhere around in the village," we just had to look for a grown-up surrounded by a flock of urchins, the youngest clinging to his padded jodhpurs — that was always Chu Teh, the Father of all Guerillas. And it had been like this for years, and everywhere the former Red Army passed during the civil war. No wonder the Government's offer to pay NC $150,000 for Chu Teh, dead or alive, had not tempted the people. They had laughed at the leaflets dropped by airplanes, and had shown them to Chu Teh, wagging their heads — "Ai-yah, aren't they crazy?"

The very first afternoon, Chu Teh and K'ang Keh-chin called for us to go to the welcome meeting. An Army comrade came with a yo-yo pole. He tied the bundles of money we had brought to one end of the pole and put the other presents in the basket dangling at the other end. Our procession walked through the village to the meeting hall. The Eighth Route Propaganda Section had plastered welcome posters all over the place. "Welcome good friends of China"; "*Soyez les bienvenus, bons amis de la Chine*"; "We are fighting for world peace and democracy" — and so on, in English, French and Chinese.

The square courtyard was packed with standing fighters, and so were three of the thick walls that surrounded our meeting place. A primitive stage with a gay hand-painted curtain leaned against the fourth wall. In front below stood two long tables and benches for the leaders and for us guests, with teapots and cups and peanuts.

The audience cheered. Chu Teh smiled and bade them sit down, and down they went on the ground, hugging their knees, chatting, laughing, full of expectation.

Chu Teh went up on the stage and made a short welcome speech, introducing each of us in turn. We had to stand up. "Long live America," "Long live Poland," "Long live the Brotherhood of Nations," cheered the blue boys. Then he gave an account of the last few days' fighting at the various fronts, flavoring it with some anecdotes which made the audience roar with laughter.

Then came our turn. One after another we told them just what this visit meant to us, and what their heroic fighting meant to the democratic-minded people throughout the world. An interpreter translated sentence by sentence. Judy brought the house down when she made her whole speech in Chinese.

And we had to sing, of course. "*Wai-guo t'ung-dzhemen ch'ang.*" After which the stage was set for Ting Ling's Little Red Devil Ballet and for two or three patriotic sketches which were so realistic and so excellently well played that the best Western producers might have envied the little theater with its settings painted on brown wrapping paper.

Throughout the meeting, the cheer leader would seize any intermission or opportune moment to shout slogans. The audience took them up in a chorus. We knew a few of them and shouted with the others. Some were too long for me, so I abbreviated them conveniently. At one moment, when I was just standing up because the bench was somewhat hard, they shouted, "*Da dao Zhih-pen di guo dzhu i.*" ("Down with Japanese imperialism!") I raised my hand with the others and shouted "*Da dao Zhih-pen.*" ("Down with Japan.") Someone pulled at my sleeve; I looked into the round face of a peasant boy in uniform. "Foreign comrade," he said, "you must not say, 'Down with Japan.' We have no grudge against the people of Japan. What we are fighting is Japanese militarism. Do you understand my language?"

"Yes, I do. Go on and tell me — don't you hate the little devils who invade your country? The soldiers, I mean?"

"We do not hate them. They are forced to fight in a foreign land, far from their families. They suffer as we do. They are peasants and workers, as we are. And when they are killed, their mothers and wives and children weep as our womenfolk weep."

One cannot talk in China without arousing curiosity. By this time I was surrounded by a dozen youngsters nodding approval to their comrade's explanations.

"How can you kill them without hating them?" I asked.

"We fight invasion just as we fight a flood or a fire or an epidemic. Our national existence is at stake. But that does not mean that we hate water or fire in general, or despise the cholera-stricken people. That is why you must not say 'Down with Japan.'"

"My Chinese is so poor," I finally admitted shamefacedly, "that I can't say that long a sentence."

"What you have learned, you can say," sloganed the lads in unison.

"Repeat after me, '*Da dao Zhih-pen di guo dzhu i*,'" said the first. I obeyed.

"And now after me: '*Da dao Zhih-pen di guo dzhu i*,'" said another. And I repeated.

And when I had repeated it after the third and the fourth and the twelfth, it stuck for life.

"Now you have no more excuse," they laughed when I thanked them.

*   *   *

We spent several mornings from nine to twelve interviewing Chu Teh at his headquarters. We had so many questions to ask that once did not suffice. And we loved those talks in the tall stone hall, with its gray bare walls decorated with a single huge map of China. Chu Teh sat at one end of the long teakwood table, with one or two interpreters, and right and left sat we, with our notebooks and pencils, and questions, carefully prepared the night before, many of which must have struck him as awfully silly. We sat and listened like school children to his frank, simple replies which opened a new world to us — the Chinese People's China. It was all common sense, sound economics, human understanding. No tutelage, no compulsion. No witchcraft either.

The Eighth Route Army was born of the people, he explained. Only volunteers were accepted, and before admission they underwent a thorough physical and moral examination: Are they healthy? Are they anti-Japanese? Are they loyal to the cause of new free China? They were organized as the People's Army, and they acted like the People's Army.

Commanders and fighters ate the same food, shared all hardships, discussed their own problems, China's problems, world problems jointly. They sang and played games together. Such comradeship brought about mutual confidence and an esprit de corps.

"The fulfillment of any military plan depends primarily on the courage, self-confidence, fighting power and esprit de corps of commanders and fighters," Chu Teh said. "Mere inspiring slogans and posters do not help matters to any great extent. The most important thing is gradual education to awaken national consciousness, to acquaint the men with the designs and conditions of the enemy, and to convince them that victory and national independence cannot be had for nothing. To understand the meaning is to raise the fighting morale."

We asked Chu Teh to describe the process of forming the spirit of a fighter.

"A new volunteer is welcomed by the old-timers in a friendly spirit; no contempt or ill-treatment is allowed," he replied. "He is told about victories at the front and living conditions in the Army; the veterans are kind to him, guide him, help him acquire some military and political knowledge and solve his personal problems. This gives him peace of mind and confidence in the future.

"Another way to help the fighters in strengthening their confidence in the final victory is to acquaint them with the comparative strength of China and Japan. It cannot be a comparison of guns, airplanes, and tanks, because we have none, but a comparison of man power and resources. Here we are decidedly at an advantage over the enemy, and our men ought to know that this will determine the final victory.

"Harmonious relations in the Army must be based upon rationalized command and self-imposed discipline. No scolding or beating is allowed. Commanders and fighters share the work and overcome difficulties together. Rationalized command consists in explanation, persuasion, influence, and example. Self-imposed discipline is conditioned upon a knowledge of the reason for good behavior and a law-abiding spirit.

"We lay great stress on education. Commanders and fighters attend classes and discussion groups every day, except when we are in battle or making preparations. Short, inspiring speeches are made before engagements, in order to increase the fighting morale of all men."

Speaking of the great importance of the unity and co-operation between the Army and the people, Chu Teh said: —

"Our men must do a few simple things: they must pay for what they buy, be polite in speech, in attitude, return what they borrow, pay for any breakage. Before troops leave for another place, they must submit themselves to a disciplinary investigation, lest they should have done wrong to the people. We have only to observe good conduct to win the confidence of the people and to enlist their support.

"But we are doing more. Wherever there is a shortage of men because the male inhabitants are at the front, our men volunteer and help in the fields. We help the people to sell their foodstuffs and oppose unfair requisition or any other act detrimental to their interests. We help the local authorities to mobilize men for transportation; every transport corps has a political worker telling the men the meaning of their help. We pay for their services and for the hire of their pack animals. We cannot tolerate the work of the press-gang. Our hospitals and medical units give treatment to military and civilians alike.

"We organize mass meetings, with mass singing, patriotic plays, and discussions. The aims of our political work among the masses are: To awaken in them their dormant and yet powerful national consciousness. To organize, arm, and train them to resist the invaders. To develop guerilla warfare and organize the people's self-defense corps. To mobilize them to help suppress the activities of traitors. To enlist their help in obtaining information about the enemy and in guarding our own military secrets. We must always remember that the people are a living bulwark against the invaders."

"And how do the people react?" we wanted to know.

Chu Teh smiled a proud, happy smile: "They react exactly as all human beings react to friendliness. They are with us, hearts and action. They don't run away, they don't hide their possessions. Wherever we come, they share with us what little food they have. They volunteer to transport our supplies and our wounded and take care of them in their own huts. They organize their partisan and defense corps units under our guidance and are in constant touch with us. Thanks to the alertness and co-operation of the people, we know of every movement of the enemy, we know the positions of the Japanese, the number of troops, guns, tanks, planes, the supply trains en route to them. This enables us to choose the time of attack, the most favorable terrain for us, the weakest spot of their camp or advancing column. We attack them always by surprise, mostly by night. With their heavy equipment and clumsy tanks they cannot turn or run; they must keep to the low roads. We hide in the mountains, swoop down on them — army and partisans in co-ordinated action. The Japanese hate hand-to-hand fighting, especially at night. We kill as many as we can, destroy as much of their equipment as possible — we could not take it up the mountain or use it anyway. But we capture all food supplies, ammunition, light weapons, horses and mules. That's where Ting Ling, K'ang Keh-chin and all the others got their Japanese uniform coats. It is just like going to market. The enemy is our sole source of supply. I am sure you have heard our boys sing: —

> We have no food, we have no clothes;
> The enemy will send them to us.
> We have no rifles, we have no artillery;
> The enemy will make them for us.
> Here we were born and here we were raised,
> Every inch of the soil is ours;
> Whoever tries to take it from us,
> Him will we fight to the end." *

P'eng Teh-hwai was terribly busy preparing for the imminent Japanese offensive. He had no time for interviews. Once, however, we got hold of him for half an hour. The Tiger was considered the strategical genius of the Eighth Route — a few months later Generalissimo placed him in charge of all Shansi operations. Also, he was the tough disciplinarian among the other commanders.

We asked him about his views on wartime army education and on political training.

"Some people say that military men need not have political knowledge," he started. "Such an idea is either a policy to make fools of military men or an insult to them. We are fighting at

---

* From Evans Fordyce Carlson: *Twin Stars of China*, p. 77. (By permission of the publisher, Dodd, Mead and Company.)

all risks, but we must know what we are fighting and dying for. If we know that our sacrifice has its great value for our people and for mankind, then we are willing to spill the last drop of blood.

"Our aim is to defeat Japanese imperialism," he continued. "Our commanders and fighters must understand the theory and practice of strategy and tactics. As we are at present engaging in guerilla and mobile warfare, they must know and apply the principles and methods of guerilla and mobile warfare. At the same time we must familiarize ourselves with the theory and practice of strategy and tactics employed by the enemy. The training in war tactics and techniques should lay emphasis on real conditions and cover intensively and thoroughly a small bit of ground at each lesson period. Formalist and mechanical theories and methods of war should be discarded as useless. Theory should be co-ordinated with practice throughout all courses of study.

"Before our men go into battle, we explain to them its meaning and the importance of their duty. In a joint meeting, we review the strong and weak points of the enemy, his position, numbers, and so on, and our own strong and weak points. We lay down the general strategy of the engagement and discuss possible tactics. The execution of the plan is left entirely to the initiative of the individual. A man is on his own in guerilla warfare. He must act and react on the spur of the moment. After the battle we get together for another review: what were our good points and what our shortcomings? What technique should we develop, and what mistake must we avoid next time? The discussions are illuminating; they give us an insight into the thinking and the aptitudes of the fighters. This is where we pick the most courageous, intelligent, and clear-thinking young men and send them to K'ang Ta Military Academy, to be trained as commanders."

Then P'eng summarized the basic principles for mobilizing and organizing the masses: —

"All parties and groups, all classes and organizations, must pledge their loyalty to the national United Front and place the interests of the nation before partisan interests," he said. "We must support the National Government and national armies, and spare no efforts to make for better relations among Government, people, and army, and solve all obstacles in the way. We must carry out a campaign against Trotskyists, traitors and spies who are at work to destroy our national united front. But leniency should be shown those elements who have been deceived and pressed into such treacherous service. We must also oppose those who, under the pretext of guarding against traitors, merely work to suppress patriotic activities.

"Any attempt on the part of the Government to unify all forces organizing and mobilizing the people must not depart from the aims of national resistance and national salvation. Agreement upon common objectives must precede co-operation or, if necessary, compromise. But collaboration must be based on spontaneous enthusiasm, and not on compulsion or command, which leads to friction, and not real unity.

"All such forces and efforts must be democratic and public-spirited in nature. Suppression or monopoly, intrigue or secrecy, can never lead to any success.

"Plans and slogans must be flexible, so that they may be adapted to changing conditions.

"The success of such work depends in a large measure upon the correct attitude of those who play the leading part. The more progressive elements should keep in close and friendly touch with the less progressive elements and help them to catch up.* The more progressive elements ought to have ample room for the exercise of their abilities, but must guard against arrogance, adventure, or leaps in the dark. They should have patience, politeness, and considerateness toward the less progressive

---

* In this respect Mr. Wendell Willkie's idea, on his recent visit to Chungking, of getting H. H. Kung to invite Chou En-lai to his party was a real inspiration.

elements, but not contempt, insults, or raillery." And P'eng Teh-hwai concluded: —

"We must have decision, confidence, resourcefulness, fair play, perseverance, and endurance, so that we may succeed in training and turning out thousands and tens of thousands of staff members for all the agencies connected with mass organization and mobilization. We must guard against cowardice, unsteadiness, hesitancy, retreat, escape, corruption, narrow-mindedness, self-conceit, and the play of sentiment.

"Any questions?" he asked.

Just for the sake of seeing him smile again, I asked: "What is the basic difference between the training of the Central Army and the training of the Eighth Route?"

Here it was, that charming, roguish grin that sent all girls a-raving!

"The difference?" he repeated. "Well, I can train a fighter in four weeks. The Central Army takes six weeks to teach a soldier how to salute."

Our whole group laughed. P'eng made an attempt to tone down his statement: "Of course our boys salute rather nonchalantly, and their manners are not as snappy and elegant as the others'!" But when he saw that this apology only added to our merriment, he became candidly precise: —

"The difference is that our system of training is based on the idea that the average Chinese is intelligent, reliable, resourceful, and an individualist. We show him how to load his rifle, swing his sword, and throw a hand-grenade. We give him something to fight with, and something to fight for. The rest he does himself. And they are splendid boys."

The first time I saw J. L. Huang on my return to Hankow, I verified P'eng's statement.

"How long does it take to teach a recruit to salute, J. L.?" I asked.

"Six weeks," was his prompt reply.

"As long as that?"

"Well, you know, they are uneducated country boys, so stupid . . ."

The United Front being dominant in his mind, Chu Teh's historical survey of the development of the Red Army was unique. He did not mention the civil war! He spoke of the aims, the routine, and the spirit within the Eighth Route Army and its relationship with the people. He gave us a brief, vivid description of the Long March, which had taken them over 6000 miles, from Kiangsi through many provinces, Tibetan mountain ranges, across vast Western grasslands, to Shensi. He told of the many hardships they encountered, of the difficulty of feeding thousands of men for many weeks on nothing but grass, with occasionally a slice of tough yak meat "cooked" under the saddle; of the murderous frost on 15,000-feet high plateaus, where they were cautioned not to speak, lest their lungs burst in the rarefied air; and of the many brave comrades they had lost en route. But he passed over in silence the fact that the fifth "bandit suppression" campaign had been the cause of the Long March; that Chiang Kai-shek's best, heavily armed troops with artillery and bombing planes had thrown an iron ring round the Kiangsi Soviet territory; that the Red Army, whom everybody considered doomed, staged a spectacular breakthrough, and that neither the pursuing forces nor the mobilized provincial armies had succeeded in stopping it.

He told us what their Kiangsi Soviet administration had accomplished in six years. Opium poppies were "pulled up" and replaced by rice, soy-beans and vegetables. This automatically rid the province of opium smokers and drug addicts and provided sufficient food for every mouth. Taxes were lowered to the minimum required for administration and defense. Usury was stamped out; a farmer could borrow money at from 5 to 10 per cent interest, whereas he formerly had to pay from 60 to over 100 per cent or forfeit his land. Mass education made rapid progress. The people were given political franchise and

P'eng Teh-hwai, Chu Teh and James Bertram at Eighth Route
Shansi headquarters

Little red devils at a game of croquet

elected most of the officials. Schools were opened, co-operatives organized, hospitals established. The people responded warmly and collaborated unflinchingly.

In this connection again Chu Teh omitted to say something which amused Far Easterners talked about even in the lobbies of the League of Nations. When government troops took over the Kiangsi stronghold in October, 1934, Chinese press despatches contained horrible accounts of the devastation perpetrated by the "Red bandits." Barely a month later Generalissimo had "rehabilitated" the area. Kiangsi was now *the* model province of China with schools, co-operatives and health service. Better still, Dr. Victor Hoo presented his Government's report to the Geneva Opium Advisory Committee, pointing to Kiangsi as the first province where poppy cultivation and opium smoking had been totally eradicated, in compliance with Generalissimo's Six-Year Opium Suppression Plan presented to the Committee during its May session!

Again, Chu Teh skimmed over the Sian incident and explained to us the importance of the United Front.

I was in a battling mood that morning and asked: "How about Chang Hsueh-liang? He is still detained."

"The Young Marshal has rendered the greatest service to Chinese unity. He may be of great value to the nation in the future," he replied.

"Which of the Chinese leaders were for the United Front?"

"Madame Sun Yat-sen, Madame Chiang Kai-shek, the adviser — what's his foreign name?" he turned to the interpreter.

"W. H. Donald."

"That's right." Chu Teh continued to enumerate: "T. V. Soong, Generals P'ai Chung-hsi and Li Tsung-jen, Feng Yu-hsiang . . ." He gave us about fifty names.

"How about General Chiang Kai-shek?" I wanted to know.

There was a pause. Chu Teh was searching for the truthful answer. "Generalissimo saw the necessity of the United Front," he said finally.

And then he spoke in the highest terms of Chiang's leadership in this war, of his military talents, of the difficulties he had to cope with owing to the fact that "some of the generals and government officials were still opposed to the United Front because they lacked the necessary education." "Generalissimo Chiang Kai-shek is the symbol of China's unity, and the whole people stands behind him like one man," he concluded.

Judy, Frances, John and Charley sensed my impatience and Frances cautioned me by giving me a kick under the table. I kicked back; it was none of their business, after all; I had come to learn something about the Red's psychology. I understood the importance of the United Front and the remarkable discipline of the Eighth Route, but Chu Teh going out of his way to pay such high tribute to a man who had been their deadly enemy . . . All this was simply beyond the scope of my mental faculties.

"May I ask a question in which my friends here have no share?" I asked.

Chu Teh nodded.

"I am a Western barbarian," I said apologetically, "and I have great difficulty in understanding your extraordinary loyalty after all the sacrifices you and your comrades have suffered and still suffer . . ." I hesitated and stopped.

Chu Teh looked down at the table with so painful an expression on his face that I wished I had never touched the subject. But this lasted only a fraction of a second, then he looked me full in the face and said with calm forcefulness: —

"When the life of the nation is in peril, we put all private grievances in our pockets. And whatever we do is not a sacrifice but our duty as soldiers and citizens of China. We are the People's Army, and Generalissimo Chiang Kai-shek is our Commander in Chief."

These few words were the deepest impression I carried away from Eighth Route headquarters. They still ring in my heart.

They are the only explanation why the United Front is still alive in China — despite the fact that reactionary troops ambushed and killed 4000 men of the New Fourth Army in January 1941 — despite the fact that, since 1939, the Eighth Route has been blockaded by a triple "sanitary cordon" of the best Central troops, who attack it periodically and prevent any supplies from reaching it, even medical supplies sent from America and specially earmarked — despite the fact that many in high places spend their time savagely suppressing all those who dare mention the words "United Front" and speak of democracy. The Eighth Route continues to fight the Japanese, to blame the "difficulties" on "lack of education of some reactionary elements," and to maintain that Chiang Kai-shek is "the symbol of China's unity."

One day Chu Teh welcomed us with great excitement. He grabbed my arm and pulled me to the large map on the wall, spluttering words in German. It was the only foreign language of which he had some notion, having spent a year in Germany. And I was the only one in the group to understand it.

"*Kampf, Kampf . . . ganze Nacht . . . neun Städte . . . Japaner weg, tot . . .*" were the only words I could understand out of the whole speech he delivered, bouncing up and down exactly as he did when playing baseball.

The interpreter came to the rescue, and this is what had happened. The three-pronged Japanese offensive, of which we had already heard before leaving Hankow, had gained momentum and was actually coming down through eastern Shansi like an avalanche, with the Wuhan Cities as objective. All towns on the Peiping–Hankow and the Chengting–Taiyuan railroads, down to Shihchiachuang, were already in enemy hands. Chiang Kai-shek issued an order to the Eighth Route Army, to retard the onslaught, so that Hankow might have time to prepare for the attack.

The Eighth decided that nine walled-in towns had to be recaptured. Lin Piao was commander in that sector, but he was ill, so Vice-Commander Nieh called a meeting of all commanders, fighters, and partisan leaders of the region, and they all deliberated together how to carry out the plan without a cannon or a plane available. Fire would be the best thing, they agreed. But how set fire inside the thick walls? They had never heard of flame-throwers. Then someone in the crowd suggested "Everything works two ways: If a machine can be used to put out fire, the same machine can be used to start a fire." That settled it. All fire-engines in the region were "borrowed" for the purpose, and makeshift "tenders" with anything that looked like a tank or a barrel and did not leak were attached to each engine. The Reds had no gasoline, of course, but the Japs had a big depot somewhere near. Their sentries were overpowered, the tanks filled. With characteristic Eighth Route circumspection, the men even found a means of silencing the clattering battle-wagons. They cushioned everything with straw. They tied straw even round the wheels and round their own feet! The Japanese never heard a sound.

The nine towns had been surrounded last night, soon after the gates were closed.

"And this morning at three," Chu Teh continued, "all of them were attacked simultaneously. The water-hoses spat gasoline over the walls. A shower of hand grenades followed. The towns were ablaze in no time, and garrisons and inhabitants rushed to the gates in panic. Here they were met by our boys. Every Japanese who refused to surrender was shot. By 10 A.M. eight towns were in our hands. Street fighting is still in progress in Paotingfu."

Now it was our turn to go wild with joy. Chu Teh, however, commented soberly: —

"Of course we cannot hold any town without equipment, but before the Japanese can send reinforcements, all rails, telegraph and telephone lines will have disappeared. All bridges and roads will be blown up. Trained volunteers are busy dismantling everything, and every bit of metal is carried West; the Government needs it for the new railways it builds," he said with a satisfied grin.

Victory Bulletins are always red on white. Even in Hankow, red lettering attracted big crowds. Ordinary news is black on white. One gets so used to such detail that I stopped short one day in Mamoo at the sight of a wall gazette written partly in red and partly in black. A peasant was reading it aloud to an eager group. My interpreter explained: —

"This is the speech President Roosevelt made yesterday, so it is news. He spoke of democracy and of China. So it is a victory for China."

Since the monoxide incident on the first evening, our *k'ang* remained cold and the window torn open for air. The thermometer remained below freezing point, and we slept with our sweaters and caps on. But the nights were wonderfully quiet after the almost nightly air raids in Hankow. Also there was an atmosphere of security here, of confidence and self-reliance which the capital often lacked. "It's because one cannot find defeatists so near the front," P'eng Teh-hwai had explained. The sentry marched up and down the courtyard as inaudible in his cloth slippers and as sure as a guardian angel. He would call us in case of any danger. Now and then he shouted "*Chin lee*" to salute someone passing.

But on that Sunday morning someone shouted "*Chin lee*" right in our room. I sat up straight on my cement berth. A little red devil at the foot of my *bei-wo* repeated the salute. Fran and Judy groaned.

"*Chin lee, hsiao tung dzhe* — what do you want?" I asked.

"Generalissimo bids you good morning and invites you to attend High Mass with him at ten."

"*Shen-mo?* What?" I asked bewildered, blinking. "Say that again."

"Generalissimo wants you all to come to church at ten o'clock," the lad repeated with an obliging smile.

That was too incongruous. "*Shen-mo chung-sse-ling?*" I asked. ("What generalissimo?")

Now the boy laughed. "*Shen-mo chung-sse-ling?* Comrade Chu Teh, of course. The Bishop invited all of us to come. Will you come?"

"Hey girls, wake up," I turned to my *k'ang* mates. Fran continued to snore. Judy sat up. She looked like a little mouse in her gray woolen bonnet — a pensive little mouse.

"A Catholic Church?" she muttered half to herself. "I have never been to a Catholic Church in my life . . ."

"*Hao-la,*" I told the boy. "Tell the Generalissimo we accept his invitation with pleasure. *Chin-lee.*"

"*Chin-lee.*" But he lingered. Obviously we needed some enlightenment, and the Army had taught him not to laugh at ignorance but to educate the underprivileged minds. "In this war all friends unite. Christians too are our friends. This is the United Front. Long live democratic China. *Ming-pe pu ming-pe?*"

"*Ming-pe,*" replied Judy and I in unison; "long live democratic China."

The youngster left with a satisfied smile.

I reached the little rustic white church later than the others. The barnlike inside was festively decorated with green and pink paper garlands. Chu Teh with our group sat right in front of the altar. The rows of plain wooden benches were tightly packed with blue-padded soldiers and black-padded peasants.

I stopped a moment at the entrance and took in both the ear-piercing discord of the chant and the perfect harmony of the atmosphere. Where else in the world would people so deliberately discard party politics and religious feuds for the sake of one common aim?

Somebody pushed me gently forward, somebody else made a little room for me on a bench. Now I could see the solemn face of the officiating Bishop better. Suddenly I made the startling discovery that the assisting clergyman had blue eyes. One can't overlook a pair of light eyes in the interior of China any more than one could miss noticing a pink horse trotting down Broadway.

"Who is this blue-eyed Chinese?" I whispered to my right-hand neighbor.

"Lei Ming-yuan," he whispered back. "He comes from Belgium, but his heart truly is Chinese.

High Mass terminated, tea and dry biscuits were served at the parish house. The Bishop made a short, hearty speech welcoming "brothers of the Eighth Route" and us. Chu Teh spoke next. He was as simple and direct as ever.

"Our dogmas and our methods may vary," was one of the things he said, "but the fundamental truth is the same — the love of mankind. We both believe that all men are brothers, we both fight to save humanity from evil, we have dedicated our lives to this cause, and we are ready to die for it."

Judy gave a vivid description of how Protestants, Catholics and Communists collaborated in the same spirit. Lei Ming-yuan followed. Father Vincent Lebbe was his real name. He had become a Chinese citizen and had organized a Red Cross unit with 260 stretcher bearers at the front.

"If anyone had told me two years ago that I would fraternize with the Reds, I would have said he was crazy. How we hated each other! And today you are my best friends. Why? Just because we have come to know each other. We realize that there are no fundamental differences between us. Hatred is an unnatural feeling. The natural thing for humans is to associate and to collaborate. If nobody interfered by playing up to religious, to racial, to political differences, and if the artificial barriers between peoples, like frontiers and tariff walls, were abolished, we could have heaven on earth and a perfectly decent, happy worldwide community.

"I don't know whether you believe in the Devil, but I do. He is a very clever and versatile sort of fellow. He no longer shows his horns and hoofs. He changes with the times. Today he gives the Fascist salute, he backs capitalism, he pays the international press and calls the tune, he generates hatred and foments wars, and does everything conceivable to spite our Lord and keep mankind in bondage."

When Japanese planes were overhead, and there was danger of machine-gunning, your Eighth Route bodyguard would throw you on the ground and lie on top of you, actually protecting you with his body. Apart from being awkward, this struck me as unreasonable, and I argued it out one day with my bodyguard.

"Why should you expose yourself for the sake of a foreign devil like me? China needs every man," I said.

"I am a sworn bodyguard," was his reply, "and you are a friend of China. I protect you just as I protected the Chinese commander who was in my care before."

"It is inconsistent with your policy of making the Japanese waste ammunition. Don't you see that if we lay on the ground apart, he would have to fire two bullets, but if you lie on top of me, he can do the job with one?"

There was a pensive frown on the round peasant boy's face, then he figured it out: —

"But when the bullet strikes, it will kill me first, so I will have done my duty," he said soberly.

The proximity of the front became clear to us when one day Mamoo was overrun by a transport of wounded. Partisans had picked them up on the battlefield; trained volunteer first-aiders had practised their primitive art and at least bandaged the wounds to protect them from dirt and dust. The lighter wounded limped and hobbled in, others came on stretchers, handcarts, wheelbarrows. The Eighth Route Army had a list of villagers who had offered beds, and care in their homes for sick or wounded fighters. They were all present in the market place to receive the men assigned to them and take them home. I watched the extraordinary spectacle of these men and women welcoming the strangers as though they belonged to the family, asking questions, comforting them in that peculiarly touching unsentimental way peasants have. And I compared this with what we had so often seen in Hankow: ragged, hungry, blood-stained wounded begging at street corners, lying on the pavement at night, because hospitals were crowded, and no one ever stopped to look at them.

"We can get enough coolies to fight," bragged official China with a shrug.

"We must save every Chinese brother we can," was the slogan of the Eighth Route, and the people agreed that this was the right thing to do.

When I spoke about it to some Hankow officials later, they foamed: "It shows you to what length those Reds will go to spread their subversive propaganda."

There was another big meeting with theatricals and speeches to celebrate the capture of the nine towns and at the same time to bid farewell to us. Jim Bertram had walked in that day, coming from Ho Lung's army, with which he had spent several months, gathering material for his book *North China Front*. He told the meeting of the fighting there.

Chu Teh had agreed to let Charley Higgins and me go to Yenan, and we pestered Jim to tell us about Mao Tse-tung. "He is not as easygoing as Chu Teh, and very much more reserved," was one thing he said. "He thaws up after about the third interview, and then he is wonderful." Jim left for Hankow.

The last night in Mamoo we had a picnic. We invited the Propaganda boys, Chu Teh, P'eng Teh-hwai, and the *amazones*. Judy and Frances opened the remaining cans of vegetables and fruit. Our little red devils brought in some Shansi specialties.

P'eng heaped peanuts and candy on the table. But the height of the meal was three pheasants cooked by Chu Teh himself. I am a gourmet and I have always managed to find the best food any place I go, but I have never tasted any pheasant so delicious, or any gravy so exquisitely flavored. Chu Teh laughed at my enthusiasm and was delighted that we liked it.

"It is not so difficult to season food when one knows botany," he explained good-humoredly. "I have studied it . . . in the grasslands. There I have picked, tasted, and cooked thirty-six different varieties of herbs to feed the comrades."

And then he told us that the pheasants were not his idea; the little red devils had pestered the life out of him: "You can't go to the feast empty-handed. You've got to bring something special. Just as an exception, for this one occasion, give us some bullets to shoot a pheasant," they had begged. Ammunition was so scarce that every shot was reserved for the Japanese.

"Finally I gave them six cartridges. They selected the two kids who have the highest marksmanship. The boys came back triumphantly with these three pheasants and handed back the three remaining cartridges. 'One bullet is enough to kill a bird,' they said, but inside they were very proud of themselves, and I am proud of them too."

We sang and talked until late at night. Next morning they all came to see us off on the rickety Ford bus. When I spotted P'eng in the background with his arms round the shoulders of two peasants, talking animatedly, I snapped the group. Someone saw me do it, shouted it to P'eng. He and his toothless old friend with the infant in his arms turned round and laughed at the joke, and I took a second shot.

With Commander Chu Teh, father of China's guerillas

Farewell, Shansi: P'eng Teh-hwai (*background*), K'ang
Keh-chin and Chu Teh (*front*)

VIII

Yenan

CHARLEY AND I parted company with the others, who returned to Hankow. Stupidly enough, we had asked for a more experienced man as interpreter, because we burned to go to Yenan on horseback. Thus we lost our charming comrade Ch'iou and were accompanied by a lackadaisical intellectual whose name I forget. His main characteristic was that he opposed all of our suggestions with a lymphatic: "Maybe better not." He liked comfort and, best of all, he liked to sit somewhere undisturbed. Riding was off, under these circumstances, and we took the train to Sian, where Lin Pai-ch'ü, former red Finance Commissar and now head of the Borderland Government, received us cordially at the Eighth Route communication station. He was a white-haired kindly man with the manners of a university professor, and as full of valuable information. We were to spend the night in the building. Lin asked us not to go out without a bodyguard and made us promise that we would be back before 5 P.M. Sian was controlled by Blue-Shirts; some people had already been kidnaped; and Lin was responsible for our safety.

I suddenly remembered that there was a League of Nations Anti-Epidemics Unit at the Sian Guest House, men whom we wanted to see.

We found Dr. Mooser and Dr. Etter on their beds. We had never cast eyes upon them before, but the old country, common interests and a stiff highball brought us near within a few minutes. The two were disgusted with the non-co-operative attitude of the Sian authorities, who laid every possible obstacle in their way. There was nothing to do but cool their heels. As both were active, they concentrated upon one task, at least, which the Blue-Shirts let them do, having never heard of any equally crazy hobby. They established a louse farm, collecting the largest and healthiest specimens. Typhus patients were the pasture, and these were abundant. The infected lice were "milked" for the serum. As it took approximately ninety of these parasites to prepare one dose, and as they needed millions of doses for this area, which has periodical typhus epidemics, the Sian authorities saw no objection. They figured that it was a nonpolitical activity which kept the foreigners from investigating such military secrets as civilian and army health conditions. The rest of the time they dined and wined and feasted the honored guests.

"Drop in on your way back from Yenan," Dr. Mooser said when we took leave; "you'll need a bath, judging from Dr. Jettmar's accounts. If we should be out, you will find disinfectants and eau-de-cologne in the bathroom. Drinks and cigarettes are over here; sardines, Swiss cheese, and canned stuff in the other case. Make yourselves at home. Here is the only thing I would not advise you to touch." He pulled open the desk drawer containing an array of test-tubes. "That's where we keep some germ cultures."

We were delighted to make use of their invitation on our return. They were not in. We never touched that drawer. But the next thing we heard was that Dr. Etter had nearly died of typhus. "No wonder," commented Charley, "running a vermin ranch and keeping the dairy products right in their bedroom!"

Charley Higgins was a splendid traveling companion, always in good humor, ready for every adventure, expansive in his boyish hate of injustice and love for everyone who did not get a square deal.

Lin Pai-ch'ü had a military truck loaded with supplies for Yenan, and some twenty boys and girls, three officers and the two of us could perch on top of the pile of wooden boxes, tins and bundles. It took some skill to squeeze our legs in between. We had to hold on to whatever strap or handle we could, as the road was full of holes, and every bump might mean a broken neck.

When we first saw the three officers in their beautiful winter uniforms and valuable fur caps, Charley and I exchanged a quick, supercilious glance: Kuomintang. We turned away, but the fattest of them approached with quick steps and a genial smile: "Hello, Miss Sues, what a pleasure to see you again." I recognized General Walter Yang, one of the nicest members of the War Area Service Corps, whom I had met at one of those congenial Yangtze crab feasts given by J. L. Huang shortly before the fall of Nanking.

Yang and his two companions were the first good-will mission Generalissimo sent to the Borderland. They carried money to distribute among the Eighth Route wounded as rewards for bravery. The Service Corps had about twelve units traveling from hospital to hospital throughout China, distributing Generalissimo's personal gifts.

First came the plain round Sian, studded with the huge round grave-mounds of the Chow Dynasty, and one of the officers told us so many historical facts and legends that my head buzzed. Then came the mountains — nine ranges of them, and every one different. Some were so steep that we fairly lay on our backs during the climb, and on our noses on the way down. Others with vast flat tops — cultivated land 6000 feet above sea-level, overlooking black-green abysmal canyons. Sometimes the road was so narrow that we passed with one wheel in the air, with the precipice below. Charley grew eloquent in his rapture — this reminded him of some canyons in his homeland. Canyons? I had never heard the word before. I did not want to dampen his enthusiasm, but I was horror-struck at this kind of scenery, and kept my eyes tightly closed. No canyons for me; I see them whenever my temperature rises above 103!

It was bitter cold, about forty below zero. I donned all the woolies I had with me: Bishop Roots's union suit, two pairs of heavy knitted skiing pants, with my riding breeches over them, three sweaters and a fur-lined leather jacket. Incidentally this latter protected my Leica from dust, at least to a certain extent. All the others looked just as padded as I did.

"A field of forget-me-nots," suddenly called out Charley, and we stared in utter amazement upon the huge bright blue patch covering a softly undulating hill slope. An incredible sight in this gray, arid landscape where nothing seemed to grow! Our truck drew nearer and Charley had just time to yell "Birds," when our forget-me-not field took to the air and flew over us like a snow-white cloud. They were doves, we learned, and their undersides were white.

We stopped at inns and temples for food or rest. There was practically nothing to be had but grayish water-noodle soup, stale steamed bread, and an occasional egg. No meat, no vegetables. Oh, yes, some dark-brown pickled turnip, which at least had a taste. Dire poverty, tumbledown huts, swarms of half-naked beggars in every village. Walter Yang and his companions were sweet; they not only distributed food and coppers to the kids at the stops, but actually talked and played games with them, and enjoyed it.

One day, at a crossroads, we saw some hundred men marching in our direction, carrying long bamboo-and-iron spears with floating red ribbons. Our driver stopped, and soon they surrounded us for a talk. Tall men from Shantung they were, volunteers marching to Yenan to join "our army," they said. The spears signified that they had completed military training with their home defense or partisan corps, that they were ready to fight with these spears or exchange them for uniform and rifle. They were cheerful and confident that they would lick the enemy. The Kuomintang men shook their heads in amazement. These peasants had walked for weeks to join an army of have-nots, while the Government had to use force and men-catchers to get recruits for its best-fed, best-paid, best-clad divisions!

From then on we met many such groups, from Yunnan, from Szechuen, from Kwangtung and Anhwei — from all over China, marching, singing. Some were students, some illiterate; girls and boys — marching with their light bundles 100, 500, 1500 miles, just to get to those Reds, who would teach them how to win the war and build a better China.

Three days and nights from Sian, we reached the Borderland frontier. Shortly afterwards we passed the gate of old, walled-in little Yenan, a town like many others we had seen, and yet so strikingly different: the first thing we noticed was that there was not a single beggar to be seen.

We were welcomed cordially off the truck by two men of the Receiving Station, and taken to a small co-operative restaurant for a simple meal. There was no official reception; Charley and I were on a study tour, and treated just as friendly visitors. But we had not finished eating when we heard a marching song and were asked to step outside and meet a student delegation from K'ang Ta Anti-Japanese Military Academy and from Shen Pei, the Northwestern Training School. Some fifty girls and boys in their teens marched up, carrying self-painted banners and placards with WELCOME slogans. They lined up at the sidewalk; and one boy from each school, speaking good English, stepped forward and shook hands with us.

"We came quite informally," they said, "to tell you how glad we are to have you here, and that you will be welcome at our campuses whenever you come. You must come often: just drop in and feel at home and see how we live."

Then came the usual storm of questions until someone remarked that our food was getting cold. But the cook had kept it hot.

Our bodyguard was a veteran of twenty-six, wounded four times. He sniveled dismally, telling me that he would never be able to go into battle again because the last bullet had struck his left kneecap. He did not limp and could outrun Charley and me any time, but his speed was insufficient for guerilla warfare. He was a sturdy boy, or else he could not have succeeded in handling me in this mountainous region. Most of the people and institutions we had to see were not inside the town walls but in caves in the mountains — hospitals; schools; the nursery; the offices of the various commissars; and other offices. Each was located in a different mountain, at a different height, with steep climbs and slippery loess footpaths. After the first fifteen minutes of watching my un-co-ordinated attempts with concentrated attention, the lad established a routine: going uphill, he pushed me from behind, as unceremoniously and as carefully as an amah; on the way down, I had to place my hands on his shoulders and follow. He ran so fast I never could do it without closing my eyes.

Either we could eat at the Eighth Route mess or the bodyguard brought the meals home to us. As guests we often got noodles instead of millet, some fresh vegetables imported with heaven knows what difficulties, and even some pork. The army, the schools, even the hospital and nursery were on a strict millet-and-salt-turnip or millet-and-pickled-cabbage diet, with an occasional egg. Rice could not be got for gold. No oil or fats of any kind; no sugar; no fruit; no milk, of course. Bean curd, so common all over China, was here a delicacy. And peanuts were the only luxury; they at least were abundant.

Another privilege: as guests we got fresh *hsiao-bing* (unsweetened crisp biscuits delicious with jam and peanut butter) every morning to go with our coffee, lunch at noon, and dinner round seven. The Army ate twice a day: at 10 A.M. and 4 P.M.

People dropped in from the various departments, to have a talk and help us with our schedule. One of the very first was Dr. Ma Hai-teh, a foreigner, notwithstanding this Chinese name. He was a man in his thirties, not tall but muscular, and bent slightly forward when he walked, as though headed against a storm. He had an energetic, handsome tanned face and deep-set, kindly forget-me-not-blue eyes under fierce black shaggy brows. He spoke English like an American, French like a Frenchman, Chinese like a native, and some Near Eastern languages. To our puzzled question he replied with a smile that we could take him for an American Turk or a Syrian Yankee, but that — like Lohengrin — he would prefer that we did not ask whence he came or what his real name was. "I was a young good-for-nothing until I came to the Eighth Route," he told me once. I could not believe it, seeing the fellow at work.

"You have the run of the place," he advised us, "you can do and see and photograph everything you like, except three things: take no photo of any landscape because it might, inadvertently, fall into enemy hands; and take no photo of me and Li Teh. We put you on your honor." Ma Hai-teh was responsible for the health of all students and in charge of epidemic prevention in the region.

Nobody was idle in the Borderland. This explained also the absence of beggars. When the Communists took over the region with the National Government's approval, conditions were not any better in this poorest of all Chinese areas than anywhere else.

"How did you clean up the beggars?" we asked the competent commissar.

"We called them together, or picked them up in the street, if necessary, and we sifted them. Whoever could work was given work. The sick were taken to the hospital. The very aged or seriously crippled are housed by better-off families, clad by the community and fed by the Army. The smaller children were put into the nursery, the bigger ones attend school and learn a profession; many are in the Young Vanguards. Whoever works, fights or studies gets a monthly allowance of one dollar. Instructors get two or three dollars, Mao Tse-tung gets six dollars plus cigarette money, because he is a heavy smoker and because he has the best head of us all."

"Where does the money come from?"

"The National Government contributes NC $500,000 per month for the upkeep of the Eighth Route Army, that is to say the pay for three divisions, according to Central troop standards, where a soldier gets from twelve to sixteen dollars. The Government also provides the uniforms for three divisions. However, we have nine divisions in the field, and we cannot allow the fighting partisans to starve and freeze. That is why we have to be so very thrifty. The men understand the situation perfectly and have agreed to the dollar-a-month pocket money. A short time ago, when some 1000 miners from Shansi flooded the mines so that the Japanese might not get them, and came to join the Eighth Route, we had no uniforms for them, but our boys called a meeting and voted unanimously that half of their pay that month should go to the miners. This is, very roughly, how the fighting is financed.

"As for the Borderland's administrative budget, we have revised all taxes. Farmers owning fifteen mow of land or less are exempt. All others are taxed progressively, with the richer landowners having to shoulder the heavier burden. But there are hardly any big estates in this region — the soil is too poor and our coal and other mineral resources have never been exploited for lack of capital, initiative, and transportation facilities.

"Money is a very rare commodity here, as you may have noticed," the commissar continued, "so taxes are mostly paid in kind. The Government sells the products to the Eighth Route and thus gets cash for its expenses. Education and public health are the major items. Just now we are installing the first modern public bathhouse in Yenan. The incinerator on the hill opposite the hospital has recently been completed, and this, together with a large disinfecting station, which is in the process of being built, will go far in preventing the spread of epidemics."

* * *

Very shortly afterwards we met Peter Chang, the enthusiastic young sanitary engineer "borrowed" from the National Government to "discuss possible improvements." Well, Peter did not believe in only discussing, he just went to it and built whatever he could with the limited means and scarce material, and he did a remarkable job.

"You know," the American-educated young man told us, "I came here just out of curiosity, but now I am pulling all possible wires to be allowed to stay here. My friends in Hankow laugh at me, say that I caught the 'Red bug' or got addicted to millet. Never mind, I know what I am after. I have never dreamed of such opportunities. Here is a government — you won't believe it — that doesn't know what 'red tape' means. I am making a survey and wherever I turn I find something that's got to be done: wells must be drilled, deep latrines must be dug; we had to have a delousing and a disinfecting station; then the bathhouse; now we are building a laboratory in a cave for the Central Hospital. Now, when I see the need of some such thing, I draft it and make up my minimum budget, and talk it over with Ma Hai-teh and one or the other of the top men. They see my point, and that's not astonishing; they are educated people. But then I have to present the project to a meeting — communal or municipal. Most of the men and women there have never heard of such contraptions, and most are illiterate, though many more can read here than round the model Kiangnin Hsien, near Nanking, where I did the sanitary installations for the National Government. They listen to my exposé — I talk in as simple a language as possible, of course; then they ask questions, practical, earth-bound questions. Then they vote the budget and I can go ahead. People are ready for progress, anywhere in China, as soon as they see its advantages; but here there is something more. They are very conscious of their democratic rights to vote and to take part in government. They feel their responsibility. They are eager to do all the things they could not do before."

"Where do you get the skilled labor?" asked Charley.

"That's another phenomenon," Peter replied: "here you can do the job with unskilled workmen. We have some carpenters and blacksmiths, of course. Well, all my men are ready to learn — it's fun, they say, and they catch on very fast when I show them a new method and explain the reasons and the use. They are interested, and the fact that it is not slave labor for a boss, but their own improvement of their own living conditions, has a tremendous effect."

Later we saw some of the new installations and were greatly impressed. Only the brand-new incinerator gave us a shock. It looked so arrogantly civilized in its rectilinear whiteness; an insolent intruder among the soft slopes of a golden-gray legend.

The Yenan Central Hospital was a row of caves dug in a semi-circle into a golden beehive-shaped mountain — like an ornament. There were seventy caves at that time, others were being dug with feverish zeal as fast as wooden supports could be obtained which would prevent the "wards" from caving in during the rainy season. The interiors of the caves were light, due to the beige walls and the large entrance; the wards were deep enough to hold a *k'ang* with eight to twelve patients. These patients had to climb, or be carried up on stretchers, 450 feet on a narrow, steep, slippery footpath. Two or three doctors, a few nurses and helpers, coped with disease under the most heartbreaking conditions I had ever encountered. Aside from the scantest supply of medicine, which the hospital sometimes received "by chance," there was literally nothing. Amputations were performed with ordinary woodsaws, operations with tailors' scissors or kitchen knives, and the rest of the instrument chest was filled with make-shift utensils which the doctors had manufactured out of any available pieces of scrap.

The operating room was a small cave with a white enamel operating table and a little one for the instruments.

"We can only operate between ten and noon, when the sun shines into the cave," the doctors told us. "And it is very in-

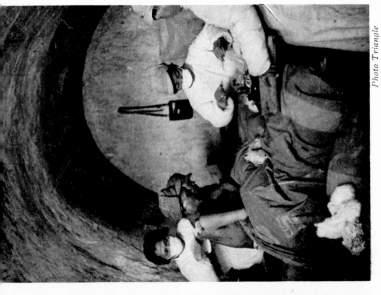

Yenan Central Hospital

Hospital ward in a cave

convenient without glass windows. We have to keep the door open for better light; and then sand comes blowing in. If we have to operate at any other hour, we call in some boys with flashlights." Poverty simply screamed at you out of every corner. The patients lay side by side on the bare *k'angs*, in their own clothes or rags. Here and there a rare dark cotton blanket was tucked around a more serious case. No bedding, no linen, no hospital clothing. A very few washbasins, hardly any candles for the night. No anesthetics, no sedatives. Bandages were so few that they had to be washed and sterilized before use on the next patient. Insufficient supply even of cotton and alcohol! And the diet? The same for the hospital staff and for the patients with anything from tuberculosis to a broken leg: millet and pickled vegetables! There simply was nothing else.

We had a long talk with Dr. Nelson Fu, then at the head, and went with him through some of the wards. And those feverish, emaciated, ailing men and women smiled welcome. Black, parched lips told us what an honor it was for them to receive us foreign friends.

Thin little Dr. Fu looked almost as ill as a patient himself. He was a quiet, hard-working man with sad eyes and a deep conviction that someday his hospital would get help. This conviction came from his faith; he had been a missionary in Kiangsi when the Red Army came, and when they asked him to become their doctor, he joined, and had stuck to them for ten years, through the Long March and battles and dire hardship. The comrades said affectionately that he was just a wee bit "off" because he said his prayers every morning and night, but he was one of the most beloved men in Yenan.

The Chinese Red Cross and the International Red Cross advanced all possible pretexts for not sending supplies to the Northwest. The two most common of these were (1) that the Yenan hospital cared only for civilians, and (2) that the Yenan hospital did not only care for civilians, but also for the military.

Charley and I were so impressed that we asked Dr. Fu for

a list of the supplies he would need to equip a 100-bed hospital. We had no authority to promise anything, but we resolved to get the stuff, even if it should mean beating up some tough Hankow officials.

As it turned out, we were the ones who got the beating — or rather a tongue-lashing from Dr. Maxwell, head of the International Red Cross in Hankow. Charley and I sat rather meekly in the bare office, facing this white-haired, steel-eyed, rigid and authoritative gentleman. With hearts pounding, we explained to him the whole horrible situation. He did not open his mouth, nor did he bat an eye. But he opened his mouth all right as soon as he looked at Dr. Fu's list. Heavens, what a voice! It exploded against the white walls and bounced right back, boxing our ears with merciless blows. The whole room was vibrating and echoing.

"I have never seen anything so absurd, so idiotic," Dr. Maxwell roared. "Two drums of vaseline? What does he want that much for? To lubricate the whole neighborhood and all his motor lorries? Ten gallons of iodine? That man's never practised medicine. . . . How do *you* know he is a doctor? . . . Fifty gallons of alcohol? . . . That is outrageous. . . . Whom do you think you and your doctor are going to fool? Such quantities for a 100-bed hospital? Nonsense. Subterfuge, that's what it is. The fellow thinks he is smart and can get supplies for all military hospitals of the region on this occasion. . . . Two autoclaves? *Two* autoclaves for one hospital? Well, that's done it . . ." he foamed, and flung the list across the desk.

We tried to explain that there were thousands of outpatients cared for by the hospital, but he practically threw us out of his office. And yet his parting words were: "Get him to draw up a reasonable list, and I may reconsider the matter."

Browbeaten and miserable, we called Eric Landauer. He sat down with us and dictated the standard maximum list for a 100-bed hospital, with a little extra "for the OPC" and some special items to take care of the regional diseases and epidemics.

Charley, our heroic Charley, who stood up under any bombing, backed out this time. "You can handle this lion much better," was his lame excuse.

I must confess that I walked at least ten times round the Red Cross block before I dared enter the lion's den.

Dr. Maxwell nodded, reading the new list.

"This is more reasonable," he commented evenly. Then he started scribbling something at the end of our list. "I am adding some items: sheets, hospital clothing, towels, stretchers. I shall see what other supplies we can spare. We will have to send them an extra barrel of cod-liver oil and a few more cases of condensed milk . . ."

I swallowed with emotion and started thanking him, but he looked at me with those cold gray eyes and said drily: "Be here tomorrow at five sharp, with a lorry. They must need the stuff up there." What a lion, what a man, what a heart!

Dr. Nelson Fu sent us a very touching letter of thanks and attached his passport photo as a souvenir. Part of it read as follows: —

In your letter you stated that Dr. Maxwell was critical of the lists presented and he has a right to be. I am afraid that we did not explain sufficiently the reasons for such large lists. In the first place we carry out complete outpatient department service completely free of charge and we have from four to five thousand patients a month who receive medicine free of charge. This is connected with the hospital. Furthermore there are run a number of health stations and hospitals throughout the region which receive their supplies from the Central Hospital, therefore the mix-up, I think.

The letter was typewritten, probably by Ma Hai-teh, the proud owner of the only typewriter in Yenan.

Among the poor, dark-padded, sandal-shod population and the faded, blue-padded, slipper-shod Army men of Yenan, the League of Nations' Dr. Jettmar stood out like a phoenix. He was taller than anyone around, with waves of well-groomed blond hair, gray bespectacled eyes, meticulously manicured hands. His silk shirts and light gray suits were expensive and immaculate, crease and all. His light brown shoes seemed to outshine the sun, and neckties and socks were artistically matched — exactly as though he had just stepped out of one of the fashionable Vienna salons. But the little red devils of Yenan knew nothing of Vienna salons, and to them Jettmar was an inexhaustible source of amazement and amusement. He was for Yenan what the Panda is for New York.

Why Dr. Rajchman had sent Dr. Jettmar to Yenan was anybody's guess. He was a plague expert and had done some fine research work several years before at Juichin in northern Shensi. Yenan had not seen a case of plague for the past five thousand years. So there was not much for him to do, particularly as the Eighth Route tolerated but never trusted this explosive professor, who showed his disgust with the people, their ways and manners, at every step. I strongly suspected that his dandyism was only another form of protest against the "mob," for all the rest of his makeup was that of a rabid scientist, totally absorbed in research and slightly befuddled when it came to practical matters. He was genuinely glad to see us outsiders, when Ma Hai-teh brought us to his two-room bungalow. The table was full of odds and ends. He made room in the middle and dumped a handful of candy, a piece of Edam cheese, and a few crackers on it. Intrigued by a long iron instrument that looked like a cross between a poker and fire-tongs, and lay next to the food, I asked its use. "Oh, these are pincers to hold the rat by its neck when I pick off the lice and fleas." Entomology was his second great hobby — he had a whole arsenal of little glass tubes with a variety of preserved insects and bugs.

Next day he took us up a mountain to see a beautiful pagoda and a temple. Biology oozed out of him for hours. Charley listened fascinated. I just panted. Every now and then Dr. Jettmar stopped in the middle of a sentence and rushed left or right to a piece of rock or a stone. He lifted it and peered underneath, or scratched the earth and dug something out. He raised the trophy triumphantly in the air, explaining excitedly: —

"This little spider just crawled out of his egg today . . ." He produced a little tube with alcohol from his left coat pocket, threw the struggling spider in it, and put the tube into his right coat pocket.

"How do you know it isn't two days old?" I asked aggressively.

"Because I saw the eggs yesterday and took some as specimens. Look, I mark the stones with white crosses, and follow up the processes that go on underneath very systematically."

We saw at least fifty of those little white crosses marking breeding stations before we reached the temple, and heard stories about the life and behavior of strange worms and beetles and butterflies. What a weird passion, to spy out peaceful families and snatch their eggs and progeny, I thought. Just then a wild rabbit zigzagged past us and Charley and I hailed this more familiar sight.

"There are quite a good many of them," said our professor, with his thoughts still deeply in the interrupted bug story.

"Do you ever go hunting for them?" I asked eagerly.

He looked at me with mild reproach. "They don't live on the surface," he replied with his charming Viennese accent, "I would have to dig five meters deep to catch one . . . And then," he added reflectively, "who could guarantee that I would find him at home?"

Charley took quite a fancy to Jettmar and often joined him in his climbing expeditions. I was satisfied with the anecdotes his little red devils told us. One or two of them would come at night to visit our guard and chat in the candlelight, chewing peanuts. The only thing they would always accept was peanuts, so we bought from the peddlers whatever our pockets and caps would hold.

"He is very curious," one would say. "He locks up everything, especially the two wooden cases with foreign foodstuffs and drinks. He thinks we are thieves. His food looks funny and smells awful — we would not touch it, anyway."

"And his bubbles rise [he gets angry] every time we look at him," another would chip in. "Give me your glasses, I'll show you how he acts." He almost snatched my spectacles from my nose, put them on askew, just like Jettmar, looked fiercely over the rim.

"He sits down and takes the first mouthful of noodles, then suddenly he gets all red and yelps like a tiger: 'Ahoa, you want to make fun of the foreign devil? Ahoa, you want to see the foreign devil use chopsticks? Well, the foreign devil won't eat.' And he throws down the chopsticks, kicks the chair, like this, and runs into his bedroom and locks himself in."

The lad mimicked the scene so masterfully that our whole company roared. Then, as an encore, he imitated me — the way I climbed a hill. (Mercy!) This was followed by our guard's demonstration of the way Charley and I brushed our teeth — a ritual which it was customary to perform on the porch.

The Northwestern Training School was not far from our house: a half hour's walk, with the frozen Wei River to cross. We went there quite a number of times and developed a real affection for the place.

The principal was a short, quiet little professor from Peiping, worshiped by the students. His office was a little cave, comfortably furnished with a polished desk and real chairs. What a luxury, I thought; then we heard that some students had gone to the infinite trouble of getting this furniture there, and that the co-eds had made and embroidered the cushions on the settee. Curiously, the light in this cave was like alpenglow, and I discovered the reason: instead of the usual white paper, the boys had pasted pink cellophane over the window in the door.

"A gift from Hankow; doesn't it look beautiful, like real

glass?" whispered student Fang, one of the two boys who had volunteered to be our guides on the campus.

The principal told us little. "Go and find out for yourselves; talk to the students, the teachers; see them live. Interviews are a poor substitute for the real thing."

The capacity of the school then was some 10,000, all housed in caves. The ages of the students ranged from sixteen to thirty-eight, and the preliminary education from the barely literate to college professors. The courses lasted from ten weeks to four months, over sixty per cent of the time being devoted to political training, the rest to military exercises. Students came from all over China. The strenuous curriculum prepared them to under-take mass organization of men and women into partisan and volunteer workers' units and to promote co-operation between civilians and the Army. They were encouraged to go back to their home districts after graduation, but could continue to study at K'ang Ta Academy, if they chose and were fitted for it.

The caves had the advantage of being cool in summer and warm in winter, bomb and fireproof, and easily kept clean. They had the disadvantage of caving in during the rainy season, as it was very difficult to obtain the necessary amount of wooden beams to support the ceiling. Five thousand new students were waiting to be received by the two schools, and volunteer corps of students dug ever new caves. We no more wondered at the rapid growth of little Yenan. In two years its population had grown from 3000 to 30,000. But how the Eighth Route solved the problem of feeding these multitudes, even on millet, re-mained a mystery to us.

The caves were dormitories, each holding a *k'ang* for nine, with blankets neatly rolled up against the wall. A shelf was dug in the wall; it served as table, wardrobe, and library. Next to it hung a rifle — one practice rifle per dormitory. There was no other furniture. Each dormitory had its captain. Black-and-white rough portraits of Mao Tse-tung, Chu Teh, Stalin or Lenin were pinned to the walls with thumbtacks. Right underneath hung "Resolution Sheets" for the week — the outcome of self-critical discussions.

The "dining room" and the "classrooms" had the sky as roof, as no cave could be built deep enough for those purposes. There was one larger cave, a sort of social hall, with class blackboards, poems, stories, drawings pinned to the wall, a "suggestion" box, and a bulletin board on which meetings and social activities were publicized. Each student had an unpainted stool manufactured in the school's carpenter shop, which he carried about to the different "lecture halls" and which he left outside the dormitory, together with his shoes, so as not to overcrowd the space.

Fang and his colleagues told us their daily work. Five hours regular study, competitive climbing of the surrounding hills, races, military training twice a week, singing, intersection basket- and volleyball games. Just then they were having a hectic time flattening their newly-made tennis court without a roller.

The boys also told us of their hardships: —

"The school is too poor. We have tried to raise money from private sources, but failed. We get five cents per day per person from the Army. The District Government gives the school a subsidy of five dollars to five dollars and thirty cents per month. Out of this, we get one dollar pocket money, which goes to buy shoes, toothbrushes, soap. Uniforms come from the Eighth Route; graduates leave them here for the next class."

There was no running water. Every drop had to be carried uphill by coolies; they got the same food and pocket money.

"There is not enough money to employ more water coolies," the boys said, "and there aren't enough basins for us each to have our own, so four or five must wash in the same water. Many of us get trachoma that way. Otherwise our health does not suffer so much. We have colds, of course, and frost-bites, because we wash and eat and attend lectures outdoors, with a temperature from twenty-five to forty-five below zero. Every day after lunch we can go to our clinic and get some treatment, but the frost-bites somehow do not want to heal and keep on bleeding."

Ma Hai-teh took the situation more seriously. He told us the kids were all underfed.

"Don't let the sun-tan deceive you," he told us sadly, "it's their youth and their energy that keeps them up, but their physical resistance is impaired. The slightest cold degenerates into tuberculosis. We vaccinate them against smallpox and cholera and typhoid, but I dread to think of the consequences if we should get any epidemic in this region."

We saw them eat their tasteless lunch with appetite, then they sang for us, then we had to sign hundreds of autograph albums — just as crazy as American kids, but those albums looked so strange in a place where even the simplest scrap paper was at a premium! It was so scarce that every leaflet the Japanese planes scattered in the whole Northwest (and they were abundant) was picked up and sewn into pads. We saw the students take their notes on the blank sides, with the Japanese propaganda pictures on the reverse!

Asked about the food, the students replied: "We get used to it. Of course, if we could get some vegetable oil to cook the millet, instead of the water, it would taste much better."

"We often eat bitterness, and sometimes the burden seems too heavy on our shoulders," young Fang said once, "but we just have to go through it to win the war. Anyway, life is paradise here compared with what our comrades at the front go through."

Perhaps the most touching thing was the loyalty to the school and the genuine feeling of gratitude those boys and girls felt for the great privilege of being able to study at Shen Pei.

"What really matters is not what we learn here. Nobody attaches any importance to exams. It is what we grow to be. It is our life direction that counts. We have a Life Director and a Life Directing Committee, composed of teachers and students. They lay down the general lines but leave us perfectly free to decide things for ourselves. Every night after roll call we sit on our *k'ang*, with a candle burning (when we are rich enough to afford one), and we discuss maxims and questions: political, economic, educational. When we are unanimous, our opinion is recorded in the school diary. When our views differ, we ask the Education Office who is right.

"At least once a week we have self-criticism, that means that we have to admit publicly our faults and mistakes, and when we forget any, or when we are too lenient with ourselves, our comrades help us remember! In the beginning it is rather hard on one, because it means losing face, but it is a great help in correcting our faults."

I struck up a particular friendship with young Fang, a frank, intelligent, broadminded lad of eighteen or nineteen, who thought of nothing but improving himself and serving his country, no matter what sacrifice might be demanded. "China has got to become a democracy," he repeated with determination, "and nothing can get us there except education. We must educate the people to want it." I met him later, and some of his colleagues in Hankow working in the hardest spots, as coolies, as workers in factories, as teachers, as minor government officials. They had to conceal the fact that they had been to the Northwest, lest they be ostracized and perhaps put in prison, under any pretext.

On Saturday afternoons Shen Pei had no classes; usually some outstanding personality — a commander from the front, or political leader, or professor passing through Yenan — would give them a lecture.

"Last time we had Mao Tse-tung," said young Fang with that deep affection with which all people there spoke of Mao. "He speaks beautifully — like a poet, like a philosopher and like a statesman, and yet in such simple language that everybody can understand. He does not use flowery meaningless expressions that one forgets immediately; he uses striking analogies, pictures that stick in our minds for life. This time, for instance, he ended up by telling us that we, the future guerillas, should be like fleas — mobile, stinging, persistent and uncatchable. 'You know that the strongest, the most heavily armed man can be conquered by a flea,' he said. 'If it keeps on stinging him, night after night, and he can't catch it, lack of sleep weakens him, he loses his appetite, his temper rises. Very soon he cannot think clearly. His nerves give way. He becomes a demoralized individual. The little flea has conquered him. It is the same way with Japan's powerful army and with us. Nothing worries them more than our night attacks. So let us be as quick and as tenacious as fleas; and remember — the night is the best time to sting.' "

The Students' Council was the chief self-government body; candidates were chosen from among the students of the whole school, and eleven members were elected at a mass meeting, by means of secret and universal voting.

A Selection Committee, also elected by the students, had the task of studying the character and the particular aptitude of each student, and of advising graduating students in what place they would be most effective. The Committee's motto was "the right man in the right place." It acted in consultation with the Life Direction Department.

One morning the campus was in effervescence, with a huge mass meeting going on. Comrade Fang lent me his stool to stand on, and interpreted the very lively and interesting proceedings.

The staff had found out that one of the students, a lad of eighteen, from Peiping, had weakened under Japanese pressure there and signed a "collaboration pledge." He then managed to escape and come to Yenan. At the time of matriculation he had not mentioned the incident. His case was now on trial.

The chairman of the Life Direction Committee presented the facts to the meeting with remarkable clarity and impartiality. One boy, whose name he would not state, he said, had committed an act of high treason, due to weakness of character or lack of political education. But he had done it before joining Shen Pei, and had admitted his fault frankly when the question was put up to him. Since the time he wore the school's uniform, he had not committed any unpatriotic act, and his record was good. A grave matter like this concerned the school, as a whole. The student body was therefore called upon to discuss it and decide by majority vote: (1) Whether the student was to be expelled from the school as a traitor — in that case he would be advised to prove his patriotism and loyalty by actions either on the battlefield or at any productive work he might choose, and if he made good, he could be re-enlisted in the school; (2) whether he was to be allowed to continue his studies — in which case he would be made to understand that this was a probation period.

The chairman wound up this exposé by saying that he personally was in favor of giving the lad another chance because he was young, had a good record otherwise, and could grow into a valuable member of the community under the influence of the school.

There was quite an uproar in the audience. The boys and girls wanted to know who the traitor was, and where he was. The chairman refused to give the name and said the culprit was under lock and key awaiting the sentence.

The next speaker was the lad's company commander. He said the accused was stubborn, preferred being alone, kept away from discussions, and had refused point-blank to admit his action in public. "Who are they to pass judgment over me?" he had asked. The commander pleaded for immediate expulsion.

A young student took the floor. He spoke with indignation. "Once a traitor, always a traitor," he maintained, and asked for expulsion. The audience applauded and shouted approval. An older student recommended leniency, but was shouted down.

The chairman took the vote: The whole assembly, with the exception of four, was for expulsion.

Shen Pei College anti-traitor meeting

Photo Triangle

Northwestern partisans transporting wounded fighters

Then pandemonium broke loose. "We want to see the traitor." "Show him to us." "Give him to us," demanded the youngsters. They rose and yelled and shook their fists menacingly. It was a real riot and for a moment I was alarmed. How about this self-government? I could almost see the "traitor" quartered before my eyes. Young Fang at my side seemed tense.

The chairman on the platform raised his hand to speak. The audience quieted down.

"I will show him to you," he said in a grave voice. "As soon as he is safely out of the Border Region, you may see his photo."

There were shouts of protest and laughter.

"And now I have another very important suggestion to make," he continued cheerfully. "Let us have lunch. The meeting is closed."

Now everybody laughed. They picked up their stools, and commanders and students walked off to the feeding station.

K'ang Ta, the Anti-Japanese Political and Military Academy, differed largely from Shen Pei College in its main purpose. Here political workers and military staff were trained for the army. They also trained partisan leaders.

General Walter Yang and his Omea (Officers' Moral Endeavor Association) boys were just taking leave of Commander Lo Jui-ch'ing, vice-chairman of the school. They had promised to let us know when the rewards would be distributed among the wounded, and I now asked them what had happened to the whole affair.

"We are negotiating," said Yang; "the Eighth Route Army leaders have different views on the matter. But we hope to find a satisfactory formula within a day or two."

When they left and we settled down to the interview with Commander Lo and half a dozen staff members, I asked, out of sheer devilment, what K'ang Ta thought of the New Life

Movement. This question caught them so unawares that they all burst into laughter. We joined, of course. Lo alone kept a straight face and replied in a gentlemanly way that they had no N.L.M. slogans or teachings.

"We concentrate upon resisting Japan and building up a new spirit, a democratic spirit, among the students."

Lo was a tall, lanky man in his thirties, with a small, intelligent face almost too gentle for the director of a military academy, and shoulders as narrow as a boy's. He looked pale and his right hand was bandaged. He had been wounded at the front some time ago, he admitted reluctantly, and the thing had not yet healed. It was only a few weeks later, when he came to the missionary hospital in Wuchang, that we learned how badly he had neglected the wound because of his work. Gangrene had set in, and amputation seemed unavoidable. Dr. Logan Roots, who had arranged for his coming, put his soul into this case, as he did in many other desperate cases.

"It is one of the worst cases of undernourishment I have seen," Logan told us, "and one of the most amazing manifestations of will power."

He saved the hand by a miracle and the two became friends for life.

K'ang Ta, formerly Red Military Academy, was founded by Lin Piao, one of Chu Teh's youngest and ablest tacticians, who had won in September 1937 the Battle of Pinghsingkwan, which can now be found mentioned in almost every military reference book as a classic of guerilla warfare.

Approximately 1600 students were enrolled at the academy. With teachers, professors, instructors and staff members, the campus housed about 2400, all in caves. The girls' company had a compound in town.

Economic conditions were deplorable. The Eighth Route diverted NC $15,000 of the monthly allowance it received from the Central Government to K'ang Ta, and furnished the uniforms.

The average expense per month per person, Commander Lo told us, was seven Chinese dollars — including food. Here are the details: —

Petty cash for student	NC $1.00
Vegetables	2.10
Noodles and millet	3.00
Balance for notebooks, pencils, etc.	.90
	NC $7.00

The students had begun a drive for funds on their own initiative, but as yet without results.

Here, as in Shen Pei, thousands of candidates were waiting for admission. Money was needed to enlarge the campus, in addition to bettering the standard of living.

A few days after our interview with Commander Lo, we were invited to attend an athletic meeting and guerilla maneuvers in the surrounding mountains, which gave us a taste of the "real thing." The climax was the storming of a "Japanese-occupied village." The "Japanese" had asked the farmers of a picturesque hamlet huddling against a mountain slope please to stay away with their families for the afternoon, lest anyone be hurt, and had "occupied" the place. Japanese flags waved from walls and roofs. Three guerilla columns were to storm it, we were told by the group of commanders watching the maneuvers. Then Charley and I were let loose on the terrain, to find those three hidden columns. We couldn't see a darn thing. The commanders laughed. One blew a whistle, and Charley and I were nearly trampled down by a good hundred boys of the center column, who had been camouflaged all around us, covered with grass and branches. The other two columns came from the hillocks right and left. There was terrific hand-to-hand fighting. There were more "Japanese" defenders than we had thought. They threw many attackers down the walls and roofs. In the red glow of the setting sun, and with the wild howling of the attacking guerillas, the scene made a formidable realistic impression. The guerillas finally captured the "village," tore down the Rising Sun and planted the Chinese flag on the roof. Charley had filmed most of it and later sent it to America.

A few hundred feet up another hill was the Yenan Nursery for babies whose parents were at the front. They lived in caves, like their elders. Three young mothers in uniform had volunteered to take care of them. They were not trained nurses, but they said they would bring them up just as they brought up their own youngsters, and the Yenan Government supported the nursery as best it could. The ages of the kids ranged from six months to two years then. The place had just been established. Later on Madame Sun Yat-sen's China Defence League adopted and supported and took a real interest in it, as it did in the Northwestern schools, hospitals and co-operatives.

Some of the tiny tots greeted Charley and me with the customary "*Chin lee.*" They wore heavily quilted robes and planted themselves with their little legs well apart before saluting, lest they lose balance when raising the arm in salute. They were a sweet, meditative bunch, as though they also realized the importance of being Chinese. They were quite pudgy and suntanned, but the volunteer fostermothers told us a sad tale of the effect of an uninterrupted millet diet upon these children. Up to the age of eighteen months, hardly any of them grew a tooth! They were weak and sickly, and the least bit of cold knocked them out, and often proved fatal. . . . Could we ask Hankow friends to send them evaporated milk, cod-liver oil, and — if this was not too immodest — some toys? they asked.

There was a wide, sandy terrace in front of the nursery caves — a loess cliff overhanging the valley at a height of some 500 feet. While we talked with the nurses, I happened to look back and saw a little boy, hardly two years old, standing at the very ridge, and quietly contemplating the landscape. I dared not yell or move or even breathe. I just pulled the nurse's sleeve in alarm. She could not understand my nervousness. "Why," she said with a smile, "we've never had any accident. As soon as a child knows how to walk, he realizes the danger. Look, this boy does not jump around, because he knows if he fell he would be dead; he just stands still and looks; he does this quite often — Who knows? Perhaps he will be a poet someday."

Two traitors had been caught somewhere in Shansi or Shensi, and mass meetings were organized throughout the Northwest to place the matter before the population and to demand their execution.

In Yenan some 8000 — children, peasants, students, and soldiers — attended. They came with banners and slogans, tablets and spears — a picturesque, interested, animated crowd.

There were many Chinese speakers, representing the Borderland Government, the Army's Political Department, the student body, the press. The three foreign speakers were Charley, a Japanese prisoner of war, and myself.

We had seen the Japanese before — he was free to walk around the town, had a sunny room in a farmer's house, which Chinese friends had helped him furnish "Japanese fashion" — that is, with floormats to sit on, and a very low table, cushions, flowerpots. He studied from two to four hours daily with some of the Japanese-educated members of the Political Department, who also lent him Japanese books.

Charley and I sat on the speaker's bench, between Ma Hai-teh and Dr. Jettmar, who looked rather worried because he had come without realizing that this was a "political" meeting — in other words taboo so far as international League officials were concerned. He emphatically made it clear he would not speak — though no one had even suggested it. Ma Hai-teh interpreted the speech of the Japanese to us. The man spoke about the traitors of the people in Japan: the military who had engineered the war. He told of the hair-raising propaganda and the lies about China and the Chinese inculcated into the people of Japan from the cradle on. He described how terrified he was when the Eighth Route surrounded his company, how he tried four times to commit suicide. He was unconscious when they captured him. He hated the doctor and the nurses who took care of him, and lived in mortal fear that they were patching him up in preparation for a particularly fiendish torture.

"By and by I realized I was among brothers," he said. "Not a day goes by without some neighbor visiting me. Neighbors like those in my country — simple folk, with the same joys and sorrows, and with the same love for the soil and hate for the oppressors, for the traitors of the people. And yet the people here are different; they have something which the Japanese people have not yet heard of — the will to emancipate, to grow into a democracy. When my teacher came the first time, I still harbored the bitter thought that he just wanted to spy on me and make a turncoat out of me, and I would not speak to him. In reality he has taught me to love my people and my country better than I did before. He and you, all of you brothers, comrades, have shown me what democracy does for people. I am studying eagerly now; I know that everything I learn here will someday serve to liberate my country from the yoke of oppression, from the rule of traitors. And when this time has come, and the war is over, I shall devote all my efforts to cement the friendship between our two peoples. Long live the Chinese people! Long live Democracy! Down with Japanese Imperialism! Long live Chinese-Japanese friendship!"

And the audience shouted in reply: "Long live the Japanese people! Down with the traitors in China and Japan! Long live Chinese-Japanese friendship!"

It was my turn to speak, but I just sat there and swallowed so hard and so fast that Charley stepped forward. We hardly listened to his preliminary sentences. Then his sonorous baritone rose in forceful, compelling indignation: —

"Comrades, *t'ung-dzhe-men*, those two traitors caught flashing information to Japanese airplanes, selling your secrets to the enemy, are not the only traitors. Every Chinese capitalist who makes his millions out of the sweat and blood of the people, and places his ill-gotten gain in American and British banks, is a traitor whose judgment you must demand. . . ."

Ma Hai-teh and I stared at each other with utter surprise. "He's got it in him . . . that lad is wonderful," he murmured; *"c'est bien dommage de vouloir en faire un prêtre."*

The day finally came when Generalissimo's rewards were distributed to the wounded Eighth Route Army men, at Erh-shih-li-pu Military Hospital, twenty li from Yenan. The story behind it was so typical of the divergent views of Hankow and Yenan that it is worth while mentioning.

The practice for all armies was to draw up a list of their wounded, with names and rank. J. L. Huang and his staff made a complete card index of them, using the system employed in the Henry Ford factories. Thereupon they got the corresponding sum out of Generalissimo's private funds: ten dollars for each soldier, thirty dollars for officers up to the rank of captain, fifty dollars for those up to colonel. Each man then got an envelope with his name and rank on it and the bills inside; and had to leave his thumbprint on the receipt, in lieu of a signature.

The Eighth Route had complied with the order to furnish a list of men wounded "in the present war," i.e. not during the civil wars. But when it came to the distribution of the money, commanders and men were unanimous that it was impossible in a democratic people's army (*a*) to ignore the comrades wounded and crippled during preceding campaigns, (*b*) to "reward" a fighter with the exorbitant sum of ten dollars for simply having done his duty to the country; and (*c*) to act on the principle that the blood shed by a commander was three or five times the price of the common fighter's blood.

The Eighth Route therefore made its counterproposal to General Yang, as Generalissimo's representative: The Eighth Route would receive the lump sum of the rewards and distribute them equally among all wounded and crippled men, regardless of rank. This would be about one dollar per man, and would mean much to them as a just token of Generalissimo's appreciation of their good behavior.

After days of laborious negotiations, the two parties arrived at a truly Chinese solution. The Eighth Route treasury got the lump sum, for distribution as they saw fit, but each man was presented with the prepared empty envelope, and had to "sign" for the receipt of ten, thirty, or fifty dollars.

Walter Yang made a moving patriotic speech. The chief of the Health Service introduced him and asked him to convey the thanks of the hospital and the Generalissimo. The convalescents stood at attention, raised their clenched fists in anti-Japanese salute and cheered Chiang Kai-shek.

After the ceremony a simple lunch was served in the cave of the young doctor, head of the hospital. It was the first time any Centralers and Reds sat down to a meal together — the beginning of a better era. We chatted like old friends.

The cave was light and as bare as any other cave, with nothing but a *k'ang*, our tiny square table and six stools. Yet, above one end of the *k'ang*, in this mountain cave so remote from civilization that it almost seemed to be in the midst of nowhere, the most unexpected thing was pinned to the wall: a page torn out of an American magazine — all pink and blue and golden curls — Shirley Temple, with "To my Friend" printed underneath. Souvenir of a year's studies in the United States . . .

Time was flying fast, and we had not seen Mao Tse-tung. No one suggested it, and whenever we spoke of asking for an interview, Maybe-better-not told us "Maybe better wait." Finally Charley and I wrote to Mao a letter expressing the hope that he might be able to give us a few minutes of his time.

We waited two days, hardly daring to leave the house for fear we might miss a message, but nothing came. With heavy hearts we gave up hope and went over to Ma Hai-teh's cave in the evening, to hear the Paris and London broadcasts over his pathetically crackling prehistoric radio, which he took down systematically for the foreign news information bulletin. We left our bodyguard and interpreter behind — here we did not need them.

That evening at nine, our bodyguard came up to the doctor's house panting: Mao Tse-tung had sent a secretary for us; we were to see him at once.

We galloped home (I rolled down part of the hill), grabbed our presents for the great man: some "Pirate" cigarettes, which Jim Bertram had said he liked, and a Cantonese ham we had bought in Sian. "You take the ham," I whispered to Charley, "you've got to break the ice of his reserve."

We hurried through the dark streets, brandishing our flashlights. At the entrance of Mao's compound a sentry armed to his teeth, with a flashing saber strapped to his back . . . At the door of his cave, another fierce sentry . . . We wondered at this unusual display of protection.

Our guide opened the door. Mao stood in the middle of the room to welcome us — tall, broad-shouldered, placid, in a disheveled padded uniform, with a zigzagging mane that clamored for a haircut, and over the crumpled, unbuttoned collar the most wonderful face I had ever seen. I had looked forward to seeing a man — a great revolutionary, but a man just the same. I had not expected to find myself face to face with the Chinese nation incarnate.

Mao Tse-tung combined all the characteristics of the Chinese people: their wisdom, in his high, square forehead; their patience and untold suffering in those sparse, painfully knitted brows; their dreams, and their keenness, their shrewdness and irony, in his large black eyes, under those heavy eyelids that one lowers when it becomes necessary to put a wall of impassivity between one's own and the outer world; their energy and pride in his strong, high-bridged nose; their determination, in his high cheekbones; their epicurean tastes, in his pale, mat, delicate complexion; their sensuality in his full lips; their sensitiveness to beauty in those nervous, finely shaped ears; their tolerant, mellow kindness in the soft curve of his chin; and their sense of humor in the corners of his eyes and of his mouth.

There are moments when life unexpectedly gives us a fleeting glimpse of eternity. That is what I felt at the first sight of this imposing, timeless, erect figure. Peasant, poet, philosopher, revolutionary and statesman in one — rooted in a legend, grown out of China's history of sorrow and glory, matured in our days into a living part of China's destiny, and leading his people out of bondage into freedom, into the future . . .

I stood still, pressing the cigarette tin to my heart, hardly daring to breathe. Not so Charley: holding the ham on his upturned palms, as though it were a velvet cushion with the keys of the city on it, he strode clear up to Mao.

"Well, Mr. Mao," he bellowed jovially, "we've brought you a present." It nearly touched the padded uniform. Instinctively, Mao held out his hands and received the ham just as Charley let it drop.

Mao tossed his head back and laughed out loud. He put our gifts on a shelf in the wall. We laughed and shook hands. The ice was broken.

Two burning candles and an open box with a variety of cigarettes from the four corners of the globe stood on the large table. We settled round it, Mao and his interpreter between the two of us.

Mao asked what we should talk about. "Not China," I replied. "We have heard a lot about it from Chu Teh, Chou En-Lai, and other Reds and Blues. Tell us what you think of the other countries, of the international situation."

He smiled, amused. "Well, let us take your country, Poland, first. What do you think of Josef Beck's last speech before the League?" And before I knew it, we were deeply involved in discussing the policies not only of this unsavory gentleman but of the other reactionary members in the Polish "Cabinet of Colonels," who had sold out to Hitler. Mao Tse-tung knew about their lives, characters and tendencies as though he had met them. He was perfectly familiar with the activities of the various political parties and their spokesmen, the different attitudes towards such internal problems as the Ukrainian issue and the oppression of Jews and other national minorities. At moments, I had an impression of being cross-examined; there was no doubt that he was in closer touch with my country than I. Mao was frank; Poland was the dark spot on the European map, he said — with a handful of corrupt militarists ruling and betraying the country, the great majority of the people totally indifferent to international politics, and with no outstanding personality, or group of persons, available to rouse the people and lead them either to democracy or to socialism or to communism. He believed in the revolutionary potentialities of her masses, but feared that the Colonels would do a lot of harm before the people would shake off their apathy.

Then Charley was cross-examined about America's labor unions, their leaders, the attitude towards the Sino-Japanese war. The two went into a huddle over some Congressmen and Senators I had never heard of. They spoke of strikes and scrap shipments to Japan, and the independence of the Philippines.

From his cave in a mountain in Shensi Mao Tse-tung kept in close touch with everything that happened in the world, just as he read the old Greeks, and European and American philosophers, and just as he kept abreast of contemporary world literature, reading summarized accounts when the work was not yet translated into Chinese.

Manchuria and Abyssinia were the beginning of a world-wide conflagration, he said, and the war in Spain was its last preliminary. There Hitler and Mussolini cemented their alliance, which would cost the world a great amount of lives and sorrow. He feared for France. France, he said, was the hope of democracy. The French people were democrats in their hearts; their minds, their philosophy were democratic; they had vision and the common sense that makes for a people's government. Neither Léon Blum nor any of the other blundering politicians could change the course of historical development. But he feared that France's military power was greatly overrated, and that the Maginot Line was a cardboard fortress to screen this fact. He did not believe it would deceive Hitler, who had a colossal war machine ready to attack the world. The Nazi theory of world domination by a master race coincided with that of the Japanese militarists. The League of Nations and, in particular, the governments of Great Britain, France and the United States still seemed to believe that war could be averted by appeasement. Mao feared that they would be attacked unawares and unprepared.

Mao Tse-tung spoke with great calm and simplicity, and so distinctly that we could understand almost every word he said. He had a fine cultured voice. The only sign of his highly strung nerves was the fact that he lit cigarette after cigarette. Here and there he would underline a phrase with a gesture of his white, expressive hands.

We wanted to know what he thought of the latest development in Great Britain. We had been following over Ma's radio the news of Neville Chamberlain's latest move towards rapprochement with Mussolini and the Reich. Anthony Eden had just handed back his portfolio as Foreign Secretary and had attacked the Prime Minister's policy. Mao believed the situation was very serious, as, with Eden gone, Chamberlain, Laval, and their satellites in both countries would open the door wide for the Rome-Berlin claims and appease the fascists at the expense of the democracies.

He deplored the absence of unity among British labor and the lack of a sound, comprehensive program. The British people lagged far behind the peoples of France and of the United States, so far as a clear conception of democracy was concerned; in his opinion, Great Britain would have to go through a purgatory, perhaps through many purgatories, before reaching the stage of enlightened democracy.

When we left Mao Tse-tung late at night, he promised to call

Jen Pei-hsi, Mao Tse-tung and Chou En-lai

Guerilla cubs in front of their cave nursery in Yenan

us before our departure, so that we could photograph him. Two days later he let us come. Chou En-lai had come up by plane from Hankow — how delighted we were to see him again! And Jen Pei-hsi, the political Director of the Eighth Route Army, was with them; he looked almost like a Russian and spoke perfect Russian. They were busy studying sets of maps, but came out to be photographed in front of Mao's cave.

"Let me at least button your collar, so that you make a better impression," said Jen to Mao Tse-tung — lifted his chin unceremoniously, and buttoned the collar.

I raised my Leica. "Ai-yah, wait, you can't take me," cried Jen. "I have a hole in my shoe, see?" The white-socked big toe peeked through.

"Never mind," Mao and I cried in unison, "the photo need not show the feet." I stepped forward and snapped the three great men down to their knees. (Charley, who stood farther away and had not heard the conversation, has a record of that white toe on his film!)

Those two fiercely armed bodyguards that had puzzled us at night were no more there. And that same evening we saw Mao minus any protection in the midst of a crowd of spectators at the Spanish Catholic Mission Church, which had been transformed into a theater. He stood up and waved a greeting in our direction. On our way home through the dark streets, lit only here and there by a little oil-lamp — mostly a wick swimming in a teacupful of oil — shining from the table of a peanut vendor, someone hailed us. Mao again, with a couple of peasant friends. He wished us a pleasant journey home. Next morning we left Yenan.

Our trip had taught us an astonishing thing: notwithstanding all statements to the contrary, the Chinese people were ripe for democracy. Given a chance, they understood and practised it. In the Borderland, each citizen, man and woman, over eighteen, had the right to vote, and to elect most of the public functionaries. The people participated in the government. Taxes were imposed in accordance with a rational fixed schedule, and collected exclusively by the treasury, who accounted for the revenues and expenditures in public statements. All citizens were equal before the law. No one was jailed or punished without public trial. There was freedom of religion, freedom of speech and press, freedom of assembly. More, everybody had the right to free education and to free medical treatment; literacy had increased already from one per cent to twenty per cent, the highest ratio of any place in China, and, notwithstanding the extreme poverty of the region, the standard of hygiene and public health was much higher here than in the rest of the country. The government did not oppose but encouraged and helped the establishment of rural and industrial co-operatives, of local defense corps, of social and cultural groups. It furthered constructive initiative in every field.

Every step we made brought us proof that democracy worked. It worked to the point of a miracle: *Not one person died of famine*. There was a bowl of millet for everyone, including the tens of thousands of people who came to study democracy at its root. Not one person questioned the integrity of the government. Not one person advocated a compromise peace. The people of the Borderland had a clear conception of their rights, their duties, and their goal: Resist the Enemy, Uphold the United Front, and Build a New Democratic China.

Again we were perched high up on a military truck, our legs squeezed in with impossible twists between trunks, canteens, and bedding rolls. Charley and I were the only foreigners, I the only woman, among some twenty soldiers and graduates from Shen Pei. The icy wind was almost unbearable. Our driver was in a particular hurry to reach Sian; he made as few stops as possible anywhere on the road, mostly in some God-forsaken village.

It was during this trip that I felt for the first time what lack of privacy can mean in China. One day I shall never forget. We had slept eleven abreast on a cold *k'ang* in an unheated room of some obscure wayside inn. The driver woke us at 4 A.M.; he wanted to take advantage of the full moon. Hot water was brought in for the customary morning ablutions, and hot tea was served. I drank four cups to get warm, and we filled our thermos bottles. Then I slipped out into the small square courtyard, which had been so conveniently dark in the evening; now, alas, bright moonlight flooded every corner. Disappointed, I scrambled on the truck with the others, hoping for an early stop.

Once or twice we stopped in the open field — just long enough for some of the boys to climb down, stretch their legs; they did it discreetly behind the truck. Charley could join them, but not I.

About 11 A.M. we halted in a village for a scanty meal of noodle soup. I asked the innkeeper's wife for the *bien suo* — "ladies' lounge" would be the polite Anglo-Saxon equivalent for it. The good lady laughed and made a sweeping gesture towards the fields. I walked out bravely. But when the whole village moved to escort me, curious to see how a foreign woman would go about it, I gave up, turned back, wiped my brow, and sat down to watch Charley eat. I could not swallow a bite, just a sip of hot tea.

The same thing happened at 3 P.M., when we stopped to get some stale bread and tea. Then up on the truck again. Only a woman who has traveled on a military truck across a frozen, arid country, dressed in four pairs of heavy woolen pants, her inside full of hot tea, and not a bush in sight, can possibly imagine my plight. During the following three hours I suffered agonies. My whole body ached; my heart was full to burst. When we stopped just before dusk, my self-possessed pride broke down.

"Charley," I said in husky, hurried tones, "missionary or no missionary, for godsake find me a nook where I can be alone for a moment."

"Why, sure," he said obligingly, "you order the chow while I reconnoiter. I'll be back in a jiffy."

Presently he returned: "Turn to your left, then again to your left; there are some walls around. The villagers are just starting with their evening meal — you won't be disturbed."

I ran. Left, then left again. Nobody followed me. I was alone in a tiny square place, with mud walls shielding me from any curious eyes. Oh, the blessings of privacy. I heaved a deep sigh of relief and relaxed, blissfully looking at the rosy clouds above, in closest communion with Nature — when suddenly a sound reached my ear that made every hair stand up under my fur cap. *Khrrrrkh, khrrrrkh* — a hog was approaching slowly . . . No, not a hog; that sound of something heavy being dragged over the sand must be a sow . . . brushing the ground with its heavy, flabby belly. Horrible . . . Here it came, through the only narrow passage. . . . Chinese swine are frightful beasts — huge, clumsy, filthy black, with bristles that seem to have a vicious permanent wave. They run around loose, the only quadrupeds duly respected for their many values; I loathed their insolent familiarity. At any other time, I should have screamed and fled. But my reason for staying was compelling. . . . I braced myself with superhuman courage.

The snorting monster eyed me with astonishment. It drew near, nearer, sniffing me — so near that I could feel its breath on my right ear.

"*Tsü*," I yelled, which meant "Scram."

The surprised animal shrank back, looking at me fixedly with its beady eyes. Pigs have stiff necks; they can neither raise nor turn their heads. That thing kept moving away backward, sideways, never losing sight of me, until it was halfway around on the opposite side of the courtyard, some two yards away. And then, staring me in the face with an expression of utter disdain, it squatted down and did exactly the same thing that I was doing. I am sure I had trespassed on its "ladies' lounge."

I reached the passage before the pig and galloped back to the restaurant, laughing frantically.

"What have you been up to?" asked Charley, surprised by my unexpected mirth.

"Charley, *t'ung-dzhe*, nothing funnier has ever happened to me. I've got to tell you — Charley, forget once more that you're a missionary — just listen to this: . . ."

Charley's laughter brought the house down.

"Ralf," he roared, "Ralf, this is a story you should tell at the Bishop's table!"

IX

Back in Hankow

ONE OF THE first people I called upon on my return to Hankow was Dr. Hollington Tong, and one of the first things he asked me to do was to write a report on my trip. I replied that I was not yet prepared to put pen to paper.

"I have never asked you for anything, Dr. Tong," I proceeded. "I have never troubled the Generalissimo for an interview. Could you arrange for an appointment now?"

Holly fidgeted: "You know the Generalissimo is very busy. . . . What do you want to see him about?"

"About the United Front and conditions in the Borderland."

"There *is no United Front*," he reminded me nervously, emphatically, "there is only a United Chinese Nation. . . . I will try my best and ask the Generalissimo, but I am afraid . . ."

Seeing that nothing would come of it, I interrupted him: "You don't need to ask him. Thanks. All I wanted was an authoritative interpretation of the United Front. Your attitude is official and representative enough so far as I am concerned. I'll abide by your version that there is no United Front here. But let me tell you there is one in the Northwest. People go there from all provinces because they believe in it. I have seen it work. It is the most hopeful thing I have seen in China."

"Won't you sit down, Miss Sues," he said cajolingly. "We need an able, well-informed publicity agent in Europe so badly. You said you would go back after your trip. Let us talk over the details of your appointment."

I was in no mood to continue the discussion, and promised him a written reply. I went home and wrote Holly a very nice letter, praising his excellent work, and explaining why I could not accept his generous offer: —

If I went as your agent and told the people in Europe about the United Front, all the thunders of the Kuomintang would fall on your head. I should be unfair to you. If I used exclusively your official propaganda material, which gives only part of the picture, I should be unfair to the Chinese people. You know me well enough to realize that I will talk about the U. F., and about the Chinese people, because I believe in them, and that I should be an utter failure if you asked me to make propaganda for any personality. Under these circumstances it would be dishonest to be on the payroll of the Government. I feel that I can serve China better by remaining independent.

We learned that three days after we had passed the Shansi border on our way to Yenan, the Japanese had taken Linfeng and were now blasting Tungwan from Fenglingtu across the Yellow River, disrupting railway communications. Chu Teh was right: without cannons, the guerillas could not hold the nine towns. The Japanese were organizing their slow march on Hankow. In the meantime we had almost daily bombing raids; they were "softening" us up. Hankow was jittery. The Government had ordered the evacuation of the heavy machinery from some factories. The city was full of refugees. For miles up and down the Yangtze, the quais on both riverbanks were black with people living on the sidewalks for weeks, waiting for transportation. The international train from Hankow to Hong Kong was bombed and out of commission most of the time. Foreigners complained bitterly of lack of butter, coffee, condensed milk, and other commodities, and when a shipment came, prices sky-rocketed and there was a mad rush on the two or three shops which still carried imported goods. But the worst thing was the lack of medical supplies and medicine. The few planes in service could hardly carry the most urgent necessities, even if they were loaded with them to capacity. They were loaded to capacity, but with passengers and luxuries: high officials and war profiteers had the power and the money to bribe their way through. Wounded soldiers and civilian victims of the bombings had to be operated on without anesthetics; there were not enough bandages to go round.

And on one of those days a member of a voluntary Red Cross committee, wife of an attaché of the French Embassy, called on the wife of a prominent banker, hoping that she might use her influence to ameliorate the situation.

"The door to the dining room stood open, and I saw the immense banquet table heaped full of mangoes," she told me. "Madame X told me she could not do without this delicious fruit, so she had ordered a planeful of them. I was indignant. 'The wounded are dying for lack of the most urgently needed medical supplies. It is horrible to see their suffering . . .' I started, but she interrupted me with that unbearable haughtiness of hers. 'That is not going to spoil my appetite,' she snapped. 'Who cares for coolies? They are better off dead than alive, anyway. And man power is the one thing abundant in China.'"

My friend never put her foot again into that apartment. But she was not the only one indignant. The X's were transferring their precious vases, rugs, and other household goods to Chung-king in Red Cross ambulances, for greater safety. China had less than fifty ambulances; eight had just arrived as a gift from Canada; the field service at the front was clamoring for them. Yet, for weeks, there was always one of them standing on the Bund, in front of their residence. This gave rise to more comment among the men-in-the-street than the fact that a group of financiers were playing havoc with Chinese currency and buying up all available rice and grain "to assure equitable distribution."

Thanks to China's unchallenged magnates, today anyone who can afford to pay NC $4000 for a bag of rice can buy it; people with fixed salaries and the rest of the population must do without. According to reliable reports by foreign doctors in China, some of Generalissimo's armies are losing from thirty to fifty per cent of their soldiers owing to undernourishment and ensuing epidemics. In Honan Province alone, famine takes a toll of 60,000 civilian lives per day. On his recent visit here, George Fitch, of Indusco, admitted to a group of us, reluctantly, that "this is a man-made famine" and that no one would need to starve in China if the Government compelled the hoarders to open their granaries and sell the crops of the past three or four years(!) at reasonable prices.

Popular demand for democratic changes in the Government was growing stronger and the Government had to do something about it. An ingenious scheme was evolved whereby the Kuomintang could both eat its cake and have it. As a first step, the "Little Parties" were assured that they had a right to exist, just as the Communist Party had its right to exist. None of them would be recognized legally, but they could send their representatives to the People's Political Council, "the first step toward democracy." When the P.P.C. was convened, its 200 delegates comprised 70 members of the Kuomintang's central executive committee, 7 members of the Communist Party, about the same number from each of the "Little Parties," and representatives of professional groups. The people had no voice in the choice; all 200 delegates were handpicked by the Government; the very title "People's Political Council" was somewhat ambiguous, as the people had no voice in the matter; and the Council was in reality a counsel or advisory body, as it had no executive power. The one-party rule continued. The one great value of the P.P.C. lay in the fact that it afforded the first public platform where views could be aired and ideas exchanged which otherwise might never have come to the nation's attention.

I saw a lot of Smitty, Tex Allison, Scotty, and others of the International Fourteenth Air Squadron. Appointments in those days were always made "air raid permitting." We met afternoons at the only elegant little Russian bar, where good drinks were served by pretty blondes, and two colorful slot-machines were in operation. We met evenings at the Navy Y, where most of the American pilots, bombardiers, and mechanics lived. Whenever the sirens blew, the boys would jump into their little yellow cars and speed hell-for-leather to the distant airdrome. The Russian pilots lived on the airdrome and kept strictly to themselves.

The roof of the *China Press* Building grew to be quite a social gathering place during air raids. Colonel Chennault came up often, as it was the only height from which he could watch his boys' performance. Captain McHugh, J. L. Huang, press correspondents and members of the diplomatic corps crowded the place.

The Japanese raiders had their fixed height — 11,000 feet; and their fixed hours of raiding — usually lunchtime or early afternoon, and at night as soon as the moon was up and bright. Hankow had four searchlights and a splendid American expert in charge of them. As soon as a plane neared, one beam would pick it up, a tiny silver dot in the black sky. The other beams would cross, and hold it while it moved past in the sky, a splendid, gleaming target for antiaircraft. But no Hankow gun could shoot so high. The white, red and green streaks of the tracer bullets of the very few batteries stopped short before ever reaching it. The little white explosion clouds looked like a carpet pattern underneath the planes.

China had so few planes that it would have been useless to attempt defending Hankow. Whenever any new planes arrived, Chennault would try to meet the invaders before they reached the city. Then the boys often succeeded in bringing some down and forcing the rest to turn tail. Otherwise the small force was used only to raid Japanese-held towns and positions. When the sirens howled in Hankow, the pilots had to take the ships up and hide in the sky. When the All Clear sounded, the airdrome gave them the green light signal to return.

Unexpectedly one day the Japanese changed their tactics. They came in force around 1 P.M., dropped a very few bombs, and disappeared.

"We are through for the day," said Colonel Chennault, and that's what we all believed.

Smitty and the others came to the bar rather late, fagged out and ready for a good stiff refreshment and a quiet evening.

"We've loaded the Martins," one of them said cheerfully. "Boy, are we going to knock hell out of them tomorrow!"

The Martin bombers were the pride and the love of the squadron.

"Good luck and Godspeed," I said. We raised our glasses and stopped in mid-air: THE SIRENS. No one took a sip. Two seconds later blonde Tania and a dozen full glasses were alone in the bar, waiting for the boys to return.

Walking over to the *China Press* — there was usually ample time before the second signal — I wondered what the Japs were up to; the town was bathed in rose-and-lavender light — never before had they come at sunset — never before had they come twice. Would the boys get there in time, to take off? . . . My God, I suddenly remembered, petrified, the Martins are loaded. . . . Even if they could take them up, they could not land at night with bombracks full. The "danger" siren set in, panting, enervating, barely ten minutes after the "alarm." I ran the last two blocks, though the police had orders to shoot anyone moving outside after the second signal.

On the roof everybody was tense. None of our fliers had taken off. I looked for Colonel Chennault; he was not there. Probably on the airdrome, too. . . . Now we could hear the faint, whining sound of Japanese bombers. Dusk was closing down upon the city, hemmed with a dark purple streak in the West, when the first formation of three appeared. They came in lower than usual, slowly, deliberately, as though they had nothing to fear. They picked their targets on the airfield. First stick of bombs . . . routine explosions, columns of dust . . . nothing hit.

Another stick of bombs . . . thundering explosion . . . flames and belching billows of thick, black smoke . . . they hit an oil tank. . . . The three black birds sailed past unmolested. Shells burst all around them without doing any harm. Antiaircraft defense was pathetically ineffective. The best of the few obsolete Italian and "new" Czechoslovak Skoda guns fired a maximum of four shots, then had to stop awhile for reloading.

Other raiders came, six and nine at a time, always in perfect formation, impudently self-assured, flying low, dropping their bombs on the airfield, and disappearing in the distance.

It was dark by now. All oil tanks were ablaze, buildings were burning. Then came a terrific explosion, followed by a second, a third: the Martins. The Martins were loaded . . . The fire was spreading fast. More raiders . . . More bombs . . . And suddenly there was a deafening burst, and a colossal luminous fountain shot hundreds of feet up into the sky, fanning out like a magnificent pyrotechnical bouquet. . . . "The ammunition dump!!" The stifled cry came from J. L. Huang's lips. He covered his face. . . . Out of the roaring sea of flaming oil, over the dark-orange tongues licking sharp zigzags into the billowing blackness, rose a gigantic phantasy of infernal beauty: sheafs of golden rockets turned loose against the universe; millions of white and green and red tracer bullets exploding in bunches, unfolding, like magnificent, prehistoric flowers; clusters of shells bursting into fluffy smoke like the ripe heads of cotton-plants. Hundreds of high-powered bombs tearing erratic holes into this luminous floral design . . . Volleys of flares, hurled into space, and floating slowly back to earth like pleiades of baby moons, illuminating the pandemonium below with their dazzling cold white light . . .

We watched the gorgeous spectacle, enraptured, dazed, desperate. I don't know how long we stood there, J. L. and others with tears streaming down their cheeks. The biggest arsenal of China's air defense, built up under heartbreaking difficulties, was no more.

The fireworks stopped. Down on the ground the holocaust continued.

The boys — what had happened to them? I went over to the Navy Y. It was late. The dining room was empty, except for two tables. The guests sipped their soft drinks demurely. Hankow was not yet aware of the disaster. I ordered a lemonade. None of the fliers had yet come back, said the waiter.

Time dragged on with horrible slowness. Finally the first of them came in, a fair-haired lad, muddy, disheveled. "Seen any of the others?" he asked me nervously. "No one's back yet," I replied. He paced up and down the floor. Others drifted in, dirty, oil-smeared, exhausted, their uniforms in rags. They greeted each other with panting, abrupt words, a pat on the shoulder, a telling handshake. "Not a scratch? Fine. Worst hell ever. . . . Where's Butch? Last I saw of him was flying headlong through the air." Butch came in with nothing missing but one leg of his pants, blown off by a concussion. The buddies nearly squeezed him dead for joy. Tex and Mumm and Scotty and Dutch, and finally Smitty — all alive, and glad to see the others. And each telling his part of the story.

They had arrived at the field when the first raiders were dropping their bombs. The pilots ran to their ships as soon as the three were a little distance off. The bombardiers and mechanics tried to unload the Martins. The intervals between the Japanese formations were too short. The boys had to rush for cover, back to their planes, back for cover again. . . . Impossible to take off . . . They tried to scatter the planes as far apart as possible, to save at least some of the craft. Then came the blazes and explosions. They helped fighting the fire.

"And the Martins?" I asked.

"All gone."

There was an ominous silence.

"Thank heaven no lives were lost!" I tried to cheer them up.

"We have lost one man." Smitty took off his cap, and those

who had caps did the same. "Young Liu tried to take off at any cost. His ship was next to the Martins. I yelled to warn him. He just grinned. The Japs were coming back. He took her up a few feet. She nose-dived right into a Martin. That set the Martins off, one after the other. Liu must have been hurled out with a terrific force. He made a hole in the ground with his head, two feet deep; we had to dig him out. Poor kid. He was a fine flier."

A few weeks later the International Squadron was disbanded. It was rumored that there had been a leak somewhere, between rum and whisky and Russian blondes. But no one seemed to know for sure.

Madame resigned from the strenuous post of Secretary General of Aviation on account of delicate health. A Chinese general was placed in charge; Chinese and Soviet fliers assumed responsibility for the defense of Hankow. The number of ships was increased rapidly.

Everybody expected the Japanese to stage a major show on the birthday of their Emperor, and we were not deceived. Round noon, the sirens went. All planes took off and hovered above Wuchang, high up, invisible. Twenty-seven Japs came in over Wuchang, at 11,000 feet, as usual. To reassure them that no Chinese fighters were around, the antiaircraft guns went into action, but stopped after a few seconds. Then the pursuits swooped down on those twenty-seven bombers and we watched the most exciting and brilliant ten minutes' dogfighting Hankow had ever seen. The whole blue sky over Wuchang and the Yangtze seemed studded with parachutes and falling, burning, smoking planes. The Japanese lost twenty-one bombers to Hankow's eight pursuits, and most of the Chinese airmen jumped to safety. The city went wild with joy.

Next day we learned a horrible thing. One of the Soviet aces who had jumped and landed safely on a meadow had been massacred by Chinese peasants, who took him for a Japanese!

The Ministry of Mass Education maintained a "safety zone" round Wuhan where mass education was prohibited.

Bishop Roots and his family were preparing to leave China for good. He had reached the age limit and his successor was to be Bishop Gilman, who was "anything but pink and tolerant" according to the consensus of opinion.

Dr. Robert Lim was organizing his front service medical corps as a quasi-autonomous unit within the Red Cross. F. C. Yen and his old-timers made fun of him and placed every possible objection and obstacle in his way. Agnes Smedley, Borciê, Eric Landauer and a number of doctor friends helped with advice or actively. I shall never forget the zeal with which Bobbie Lim and Agnes prepared the sample one-pound first-aid kits — with sterile pads, bandages, and four codein tablets — which each soldier was to carry with him, and the ten-pound kits for trained first-aiders. Hell broke loose around them for trying to pamper the coolies.

About that time Captain Evans F. Carlson came to Hankow from Wutaishan, an inaccessible mountain stronghold of the Eighth Route Army, beleaguered for many months by a three-line-deep Japanese force. Captain Carlson accompanied China's armies as an observer for the U. S. Navy Department with an assignment to "study Japanese mentality in hand-to-hand fighting." Hand-to-hand fighting on a big scale was a specialty of the Red guerillas, and Wutaishan their most fiercely defended area. This had decided his choice. Friendly partisans had guided him and his escort of thirty Eighth Route men through the Japanese lines.

The skinny, bony six-footer with his tanned, deep-lined face, his strong nose, his kindly twinkling eyes, became part and parcel of our little group. Anyone who looked at Carlson once could not possibly miss the rust-colored riding breeches, the rough tweed jacket over a thick handknitted pullover, and the big pipe which he either puffed or handled as a Chinese storyteller handles his fan to express an idea, a thought, a situation. Carlson had the tough health of a trapper, the staunch heart of a soldier, and the pure, sweet soul of a saint. Add to this a deep love for mankind, freedom and democracy, and a well-tempered sense of humor, and you will have a more or less complete picture of the man who, after Pearl Harbor, trained the first 1000 American guerilla raiders, became the hero of Makin Island, and knocked hell out of the Japanese at Guadalcanal.

He came back from Wutaishan with wonderful stories of courage, and horrible accounts of conditions there. Lack of ammunition, lack of virtually everything a human being needs to continue alive — food, clothing, blankets . . . No doctor, no medical supplies to take care of some 3000 wounded or of the desperately undernourished population . . .

He had an appointment with Chiang Kai-shek. He went to Headquarters full of hope, to present the case and get some help for the heroic outposts, strategically so important. Success was rather doubtful, we warned him. But, after all, as America's official observer his suggestions might carry some weight.

He came back from Wuchang utterly discouraged, almost aged. The lobby of the Terminal was full of people. He put his big hand on my shoulder, towering over me.

"Let's have a drink in the dining room. I'm chilled to the marrow of my bones. He and the Madame listened to me with that impenetrable, icy indifference. . . . They won't do a thing for Wutaishan."

We sat down and he ordered an "old-fashioned." I had never heard this name before; neither had the barman.

"Never mind, it's a good drink and I'll teach you how to mix it. Get me . . ." (Here followed a list of ingredients.)

The barman watched Carlson's manipulations attentively, and took the first sip with us. The cocktail was delicious.

"Please what name say again?" he asked, and before Carlson could open his mouth, I replied, "United Front cocktail." Carlson flashed a startled, merry look in my direction and confirmed, "That's right — United Front cocktail." The name appealed to the barman. We tipped off some friends, and soon the new drink was in fashion.

Carlson did not give up. He spoke privately to anyone who would listen about the need in Wutaishan. The Northwestern Partisan Relief Committee in Hankow and the China Defence League in Hong Kong made it their concern. Soon Dr. Richard Brown took a leave of absence from his mission and volunteered to take any medical supplies and equipment up to Wutaishan and care for the wounded during a few months. The funds of the Northwestern Partisan Committee had been expended. We had no money to buy anything for Wutai. Agnes had an idea. She called together the few bodyguards of the Eighth Route Hankow office, explained things to them.

"Has any one of you got a Japanese officer's or soldier's coat? Our Committee wants to make a raffle, sell one-dollar lots. The winner will get the coat. The people in Hankow have not seen many Japanese coats. I am sure we would get a lot of money for Wutaishan this way."

Two lads immediately gave their own captured coats: an officer's and a soldier's coat, one even with a hood. It became the first prize.

The raffle was a success. With some additional outside contributions, the Committee was able to equip Dr. Brown. He got through the Japanese lines just as Captain Carlson had, with Eighth Route and partisans' aid, and did excellent, hard work for some three months. When he came back for more help, Dr. Norman Bethune, of the Medical Unit sent by the American and Canadian Leagues for Peace and Democracy, which had already served the people of Spain, decided to go to Wutai with him. In the meantime Madame Sun Yat-sen, the soul of the China Defence League, had mobilized lovers of peace and freedom in both hemispheres. In July, 1938, the world conference of the International Peace Campaign decided to establish the International

Peace Hospital at Wutaishan. The initial £2450 came from the China Campaign Committee of Great Britain. Dr. Bethune became director and chief surgeon and rendered invaluable service to the whole region until the day of his untimely death. In its Report for 1938–1939, the China Defence League gave the following information: —

Working on a minimum budget, the hospital is now treating approximately 1000 wounded. Two or three hundred patients are looked after every day in its outpatient department. Of the ten fully qualified doctors and thirty trained nurses, some work in the hospital while others go out into the villages to treat the sick and wounded in the huts of the peasants. The hospital treats fighters and civilians without distinction. It is the only modern medical center in a region which has a population of 10,000,000 people.

Bishop Gilman came to Hankow to take over the diocese a few days before the Roots family left. He asked our Comrade Bishop to tell Agnes and me that he did not want any "Reds" or nonmissionaries on the compound. We could see how badly our old friend felt. We saw him and Frances off, and cleared out. Fortunately, Chou En-lai gave us a room each in a house in the Japanese Concession which the Mayor of Hankow, K. C. Wu (who is now Vice-Minister of Foreign Affairs) had given over for army and administrative personnel. The house must once have been as meticulously clean as all Japanese houses, but there was little trace of it after Chinese troops had bivouacked there. All floor mats were torn off and had disappeared, together with pieces of plaster from the walls, doorknobs and other fixtures. The beautiful black-and-white-tiled family bath — almost as big as a swimming pool — and all modern washbasins were out of repair. No running water either there or in the toilets . . . Filth and horrible stench, and mice that overran the house. Here, for the first time in his life, Guei-Guei saw and caught a mouse in my room. He was very proud and active with it, but I could not stand the sight and spent two hours of the night squatting in the corridor in front of my room, until he had eaten it up — tail and all.

Agnes and I had a washstand in the corridor, hidden by a screen. At night I crawled into my sleeping bag and slept on three bambo chairs. Po Ku and Chou En-lai dropped in occasionally, also two young men from the Propaganda Section of the Military Affairs Commission of the National Defense Council. This Propaganda Section was the first intelligent approach to publicity, perhaps because it operated outside any Kuomintang influence. It was a United Front combination between Generalissimo's own General Ch'en Ch'eng as director, Chou En-lai as vice-director, and the liveliest, most progressive, intelligent bunch of young intellectuals one could encounter round the capital.

Kuo Mo-jo, one of China's outstanding poets and writers, was the head of the Broadcasting Department, and C. L. Chang and C. C. Yeh, two of his young collaborators, came up one day to ask whether Agnes would take over the English broadcasts. She refused. I was their second choice. I had never seen a mike in my life and it took them some time to persuade me. They asked me to do it just once to help them out — next Wednesday.

C. C. Yeh, a tall, smiling, open-faced youngster with charming manners, and a fine capacity for intelligent work, came on Wednesday morning with a batch of news bulletins. I had to pick out and arrange my material, adding or dropping any items I saw fit. C. C. translated the stuff, I put it into proper English. I had to be my own announcer, too.

The Hankow Short-Wave Station was a simple three-story house, with a few rooms padded and insulated. The sentry made a great fuss before letting us in, but the charming director and personnel made up for everything.

My "studio" had a double desk with a big clock and a flimsy

little old-fashioned microphone. Opposite me sat a young lady playing the recorded music; records were stacked up neatly on shelves behind her.

I trembled with mike-fright.

"Hello, hello, this is Hankow calling, this is Hankow calling, over station XGOW . . ." I read my paper as monotonously as they had asked me to (that was the official style), watching the clock. I finished "on the nose" at 9:15. *Oof*, thank heaven, that was over. My heart had nearly jumped out of my mouth for fear. But everybody, including Madame, Donald, and the Military Affairs Commission, had listened in and liked it. And Saturday morning C. C. Yeh came with another batch. "But I don't want the job. Didn't you find anyone else?" I protested.

"We did not look any further. Kuo Mo-jo leaves you complete freedom in the choice of your program. You need not even come over to Wuchang Headquarters. I will come to your place three times a week, work with you, escort you to the Station. Don't you want to work with us?"

Could I say no? I put my heart into the work. And C. C. was a fine collaborator, chummy and full of fun. That Saturday, when we were through with the English text, he said, "And now the French broadcast." I spoke French, didn't I? Well, there was Indo-China, and the French in China that got no direct news bulletins in their own language. Maybe even France could hear me? The Commission knew for sure that London and San Francisco heard Hankow Station. I could either translate the English news or make a selection of what interested the French in particular.

This time I was not afraid. Both broadcasts went off fine, from 9 to 9:30. And it was fun to be able to tell the world three times a week not only the news from the fronts but also anything I knew about the war effort of the Chinese people. I liked the job.

A week or so after I had started, Chang and Yeh came to

my room rather stiffly, with such solemn faces that I rose. They stood at attention, and Chang spoke: —

"This morning General Ch'en Ch'eng has announced publicly your appointment as official foreign broadcaster with the rank of colonel."

I burst out laughing, sure that the kids were joking, but there was no response; they continued to look terribly official.

"I am very flattered," I said with a bow, "but why should I have the rank of colonel? Must I wear a uniform too?"

"You have the right to wear a uniform, and it may be wise to do so, because this would give you all the privileges of a military: entrance everywhere, and transportation facilities. As for the military rank, you had to have one because the National Defense Council does not accept voluntary service. From now on you are on the payroll; you will get NC $200, minus taxes, that is NC $146 per month. That's what a colonel gets. And you are a colonel because of your age and your five languages and the broadcasting . . ."

"And because you are a foreign devil," added C. C. wryly. "Chang is only Lieutenant Colonel, and I am Major, and we work twelve hours a day, seven days a week."

Chang poked him in the ribs, reprimanding him in a whisper.

We were still standing. That nomination had done something to them. They would not sit down in the presence of a colonel! I had to use all my persuasion.

"Look here," I said finally. "I haven't asked for the honor, and so far as I am concerned, Ch'en Ch'eng can keep his title. Either he agrees to degrade me, or I resign. Dammit, I'd rather keep your comradeship than accept any colonelship."

That did the trick, they sat down and we remained friends.

I never had a uniform made. Uniforms were for those who risked their lives. I wanted no unearned privileges. Instead, Chang gave me a "pass," a three-by-one-inch red silk ribbon badge, with my name and rank in black ink, and the chop of the Military Affairs Commission. "With this you will never get into trouble, and all doors will open before you," he said. Just like Aladdin's lamp. I put it in my bag and forgot about it until the day I wanted to see someone at Wuchang H. Q. and the sentry at the entrance poked a bayonet into my stomach. Then I showed him my pass. Did he salute and yell! Not only "*Chin lee*" but a whole litany. I had to hold up my pass so that all the officers and soldiers on the way — and it was a military camp! — would salute and shout. I am sure I was as red as that magic ribbon of mine, saluting and not knowing what to do with myself. I never let anyone see my pass again.

But what Chang showed me that day was well worth while. We went through the Enemy Propaganda Department, where our colleagues prepared leaflets and "passes for any Japanese who will surrender," promising good treatment. They had worked six weeks in secret, drawing cartoons of Japanese military leaders oppressing the common soldier, of Chinese and Japanese soldiers shaking hands, and making peace, and getting rid of the bad Japanese boss. They had made millions of leaflets in Japanese, Korean, Mongolian, and Chinese (for the occupied territories). Recently a squadron of Chinese fliers had paid their one and only visit to Japan, scattering not bombs but propaganda material over a number of cities, to prove that they could bomb Japan but did not do so because the Chinese Government had no grudge against the people of Japan and did not want to murder civilians.

My work with the Military Affairs Commission went on smoothly, with but two little incidents. The first came when C. C. brought me a statement proving that Chinese currency had lost nothing of its value. I was to broadcast this. Actually the Chinese dollar had just registered a drop of about thirty-five per cent on the international market. I turned to C. C., who was watching me read it.

"Whom are they trying to fool now? Great Britain? France? Wall Street? Or us? Take this back with my compliments: I don't broadcast lies."

C. C. turned pale: "But it is the Ministry of Finance . . ." he stammered.

"The Military Affairs Commission cannot sponsor misstatements of fact. For God's sake, don't make such a silly face. What's the next item?"

"Ralf," pleaded my young collaborator disconsolately, "of course you are right, but . . . We cannot refuse to broadcast this statement. . . . They will break me. . . . I am the one responsible — "

"The hell you are," I retorted. "You are only a lousy major. I am a colonel. I am *your* colonel. And I take the responsibility for refusing to broadcast lies detrimental to China's prestige. *Ming-pe pu ming-pe?*" ("Is this clear?")

"*Ming-pe.* You take the responsibility as colonel?" he asked, visibly relieved, yet still incredulous.

"Yes, Major. And you will phone Headquarters immediately, explaining my objections. These are orders."

That call lasted about fifteen minutes. I stood watching my "subordinate." At first he was all clouds and perspiration, talking nervously and very fast; then a lot of talk and back-talk; he listened attentively, holding his breath. Then he covered the mouthpiece and asked me, "What would you substitute for this statement?" "The role of Chinese women's organizations behind the front," I whispered. And a moment later the sunbeam of a smile broke through the clouds. C. C. hung up. "Headquarters see your point and approve, Colonel," he reported officially, and then, with his usual boyish candor, "Ralf, you are a hell of a fellow. . . ." We had a good laugh and never heard about the matter again.

The other incident came when I entered the studio one night, as usual, two minutes before nine, and heard the tune of the "*Horst Wessel Lied*" preceding my broadcast. I signaled to the girl to stop the record. She stared at me blankly; such a thing had never happened to her before.

I turned the switch. The station went dead. "This is the anthem of Nazi Germany," I explained to the dazed girl. "Quick, put on '*Ch'i lai.*'"

The radio director and C. C. burst into the room in a frenzy. "What has happened?"

"I won't broadcast after the '*Horst Wessel Lied.*' Make her play '*Ch'i lai.*'" Obviously not one of them knew the tune. The girl found the "*Ch'i lai*" record.

"But it is nine o'clock . . ." they whimpered; "the Generalissimo . . ."

"Put the blame on me. Hurry up. I'll read faster."

"*Ch'i lai*" was played and I finished on the dot. After the broadcast I told them to break the Nazi record. No can do — it was government property. The girl put on the records in consecutive order, without knowing any one of the foreign tunes, and without being able to read the labels.

"Then paste a white strip of paper across this one and don't use it for the duration," I suggested. This was done.

Headquarters had noticed the slip-up and demanded an explanation. They laughed when they got it — what a joke!

Then came a day when an official circular was passed round to the staff of the Military Affairs Commission. The Government was to evacuate to Chungking. As all transportation facilities were already overtaxed, carrying the wounded, children, machinery and supplies to safety, the staff was to march the 1500 miles together with the army. Every official was invited to "consult his own conscience whether he was physically and morally fit to stand the strain," and to submit his reply to the Commission.

I was in no physical condition to match the endurance of the Chinese soldier. Heartbroken, I tendered my resignation personally to Kuo Mo-jo, a cultured, kindly man, who discussed with me the propaganda possibilities in Europe and asked that

I send him periodically any printed material and suggestions of interest to the Commission's foreign publicity section.

I borrowed money for my passage, bade China and all my friends farewell, and left by the "last" international train for Hong Kong. There was a "last" train every few weeks, in between the bombings.

The trip lasted five days. We were four women in our compartment. One of my fellow travelers, the wife of a German military instructor, had a dachshund with her. He stared at my cat, and my cat stared at him. They seemed to think things over; this was war and one had to put up with all kinds of inconveniences, with all sorts of funny creatures. Without any coaxing or interference on the part of their masters, they kept peace, ate and drank out of the same bowl — first the dackel and then the cat. Guei-Guei always sits back in watchful dignity and lets the other fellow get his fill first. And before long they even took a nap side by side.

X

Hong Kong

NO FOREIGN SERVICE in the Orient was better informed, more reliable, and more helpful than that of the representatives of the United States Treasury Department. Mr. Campbell, U. S. Treasury Attaché, was a charming, cordial man, clearheaded and philosophical. We found that we had common friends, and agreed on many points. There was opium again, of course. Tu Yueh-sen had transferred his headquarters from Shanghai to Hong Kong and was shipping drugs to the four corners of the world. The British authorities said they had not enough money to cope with this clandestine traffic, and Mr. Campbell was worried over this lack of co-operation. He had booked my passage on the French S.S. *Athos II*, and reserved a room for me at a Hong Kong boarding house. And he let me have his car several hours each day, so that I might get a good glimpse of this most lovely of all islands.

I called on Mrs. Selwyn-Clarke, honorary secretary of the China Defence League. Dr. Selwyn-Clarke, her husband, was the Medical Director of the Crown Colony, and one of the few Britishers who foresaw Japan's attack and had no illusions as to the possibilities of defense. They had a sweet four-year-old daughter.

"My wife's belongings are packed. I want her and the child to evacuate at the very first sign," he said. "I shan't take the risk of seeing our baby bayoneted by a Japanese soldier. If Japan attacks, we can't hold Hong Kong more than three days. . . .

And if Singapore lasts longer than three weeks, it will be a miracle. . . ."

Mrs. Selwyn-Clarke, modest, active, and devoted with all her heart to the work of the China Defence League, took me up the Peak, where Madame Sun Yat-sen lived in a little two-room apartment, incognito, as Mrs. S. C. Ling.

A little old amah opened the door, and we stood before the One Who Loves China. No title could be more fitting, and if Soong Ching-ling ever gave any thought to titles, I am sure this is the only one she would accept. She was beautiful. Yet her beauty did not have a breath-taking quality. Quite on the contrary, in Madame Sun's presence one could breathe more freely, one felt the abundance of life and kindness and purpose. She was so small, so simple in her black dress, with that jet black hair brushed back straight and rolled into a knot in her nape. She was so exquisitely lovely; the fine oval of her face, the delicate complexion, the high forehead, those large deep, pensive eyes, that sensitive mouth of a child who has eaten too much bitterness. And when she smiled, she had dimples in both cheeks. Yet any description of her must be painfully inadequate, because the great harmony of her personality, the warm light she radiates, the whole atmosphere around her, cannot be expressed in words. It can only be felt.

Madame Sun welcomed us with quiet Chinese friendliness. We sat down in the dining-sitting room, which was furnished very simply but with taste, and I had to tell her the latest news from Hankow and the Northwestern Partisan Relief Committee. Dr. Robert Lim, she said, was expected in Hong Kong the following day, with a report on the development of the Chinese Red Cross Medical Relief Commission and its newly opened Training School. We discussed the possibilities of raising funds for the China Defence League in Switzerland and France; Madame Sun gave me a list of persons I was to contact there and promised to send me the C.D.L.'s Newsletters, reports, photos and articles for distribution among interested organizations. She hardly ever said, "I," it was mostly "we," identifying herself with the C.D.L. There was no categorical "I want it," no authoritative "This has got to be done," but constructive suggestions, usually introduced by a very gentle "Do you think we could?"

This modesty became still more apparent when the other members of the Central Committee of the C.D.L. arrived to hold the usual weekly meeting. We pulled up our chairs and sat informally, in a circle, sipping tea and listening first to the report of the Treasurer, Prof. N. H. France, then to the publicity report by John Leaning, then to one of the most interesting general discussions I had ever attended. I had had no idea of the amount of hard work, organization and initiative of this tiny group. With the exception of young Leaning, who had to earn his living, all members worked on a voluntary basis. There was no overhead except the cost of printing and postage. Accounts were kept meticulously and audited regularly by chartered accountants. The China Defence League had mobilized friendly democratic organizations in the United States and in South America, Canada, England; in a number of European countries; in India, the Dutch East Indies; and it had encouraged the creation of China Aid Campaigns and China Aid Councils and branches of Friends of China. In Hong Kong, it collaborated with Bishop Hall, with Christian and Chinese Women's Associations. It received contributions from many parts of the world: smaller and larger sums, medical supplies, clothing, blankets, milk, vitamins. The total was far below what was needed, but it was a beginning. It was thrilling to see the genuine excitement and joy of Madame Sun and her friends when one of their members — Dr. Liao, if I am not mistaken — announced that he had obtained 400,000 quinine tablets at the Java market price, which was much lower than the cartel's quotations in Hong Kong.

Whom did the C.D.L. support? The criterion was serious, honest, democratic work. The International Peace Hospital in

Madame Sun Yat-sen

Wutaishan, the Yenan Base Hospital, the Medical Service of the New Fourth Army, and Dr. Robert Lim's Training School stood at the head of the list, because they were the nuclei of a permanent system of medical relief in China.

It worked with the Chinese Industrial Co-operatives which were rebuilding Chinese industry on democratic lines — every worker laboring for himself and for the country.

It supported and enlarged the Yenan Orphanage and opened another one in Sanyuan, because the children were the future of China.

It supported K'ang Ta Military Academy, which had enlarged its scope, was now accepting students from the whole country and turning out 10,000 in every course.

There were problems, there was heartache. Who needed the portable X-ray machine most? Two of the five cases of cod-liver oil must go to the children, the other three to Wutaishan. The wool received from Australian friends could go up to the Shensi Co-operatives in one of the ambulances, contributed by friends in India, which is taking blankets, surgical instruments and powdered milk to Yenan.

"And still we cannot send Dr. Bethune the two sterilizers and the microscope and the typewriter he so urgently requires," Madame Sun worried. "He is so overworked that he has been unable to send us reports and photographs we need for the new drive. Do you think we could ask Jim Bertram to go to Wutai and help with publicity?" The Committee agreed and shortly afterwards Jim and other reliable friends toured the country regularly, investigating needs, distribution, development of the various institutions, and reporting to the C.D.L.

Madame Sun did not believe in charity but in helping people to help themselves, to fight the enemy under better conditions, and to build a better China.

The following day Dr. Lim, Mrs. Selwyn-Clarke and I had dinner at Madame Sun's. She herself opened the door this time. "I crave your indulgence for the meal you will be served," she said with her sweet smile. "Sunday is amah's day off, so I have roasted the chickens and prepared the salad myself." She had arranged the table beautifully, with flowers, and fruit. Teapot and all accessories were well within reach, so that no one might be uneasy and we all could enjoy the food and the conversation. What a thoughtful, tactful, perfect hostess!

Dr. Lim spoke of the development of the various projects with C.D.L.'s help. Three branches of the International Peace Hospital, of 250 beds each, were being established in Yenan, in Southeast Shansi, and in Southern Anhwei, this latter as part of the Medical Service of the New Fourth Army, in part behind enemy lines, on territory reconquered from the Japanese. (A few months later, Jack Belden wrote in the *Shanghai Evening Post and Mercury*, January 12, 1939, about his visit to the New Fourth Army medical service: "The hospitals established by some armies to care for the wounded are so rotten that it comes as a shock to find something so up-to-date and yet so simple as the hospitals established by the New Fourth Army. The actual hospital service in the New Fourth Army is probably better than any other army in China possesses.")

The problem of recruiting young patriotic men and women as students for the Emergency Medical Training School had been solved temporarily. The Blue Shirt elements in Hankow had succeeded in getting through an order suppressing all non-Kuomintang youth organizations, so all their members were mobilized for ambulance units under Dr. Lim. They were put through the training school then at Changsha, 120 at a time, with an intensive six-weeks training in first aid right at the front, with divisional headquarters, all equipped with stretchers. Seven units were already at the front. (A year later, there were seventy-seven.) Canton and Shanghai had been asked to send 150 students per month each. In addition the school was training doctors, surgeons, and nurses. Dr. Eric Landauer had joined Dr. Lim, and Jean Chiang, a remarkably active and devoted young woman doctor, whom I had met at Hankow, was appointed director of the Maternity Section of the Yenan Base Hospital.

Those two visits with Madame Sun and her collaborators were for me the most wonderful farewell to China. Here was living, throbbing, undeniable proof that the United Front was growing in the hearts of honest patriots throughout China, and that they banded together to work and fight for it, shoulder to shoulder with the One Who Loves China and hardly ever says "I."

XI

New York

WHEN THE WAR came and country after country was invaded, international activities ceased. Geneva, where I had been trying to work, was a dead city. Nobody wanted to hear about China. But I was homesick for her. I was ready to live on millet and a dollar a month and work for the C.D.L. I left for America en route to China.

It took me ten weeks to get through war-torn, visa-mad Europe, and I reached New York in the first days of January, 1941. By then I was pretty well out of touch with events in China. A little notice in the *Times* startled me: W. H. Donald had told an A.P. reporter in New Zealand that he was sailing on his yacht to Tahiti, to write his memoirs. This could mean one thing only — the reactionaries had grown strong enough to impose their will in Headquarters. What would happen to the United Front? And what would happen to Madame?

A few days later the news broke that government troops had ambushed and attacked the New Fourth Army in southern Anhwei, killed 4000, captured 2000, including Commander Yeh Ting. The details were that War Minister Ho Ying-ch'in had ordered the New Fourth to leave the area south of the Yangtze River which it had recaptured from the Japanese, and where it had established a number of effective guerilla bases, and to move north of the Yangtze. The New Fourth objected at first that such a move would leave the area at the mercy of the Japanese;

then, reassured that government troops would replace them, and instructed by Chu Teh and P'eng Teh-hwai to obey the order, they moved northward, following the route fixed by the War Zone Commander. Most of the Fourth Army had already crossed to the north bank when the rearguard of about 10,000 — composed of the staff, the political department, doctors, nurses and ambulance corps, guerillas and partisans — was suddenly encircled by some 80,000 troops of the National Armies. Fighting took place from January sixth to thirteenth, until the ammunition of the New Fourth unit was exhausted and their food supply cut off.

Chu Teh and P'eng Teh-hwai sent a telegram of protest to the Government. Parts of it read as follows: —

. . . Now it is obvious that, while our Government seems comparatively unconcerned about action against the enemy (Japan), against *our* army it seems to have tried to achieve a position from which it can annihilate us completely . . .

We are compelled to ask, Who is responsible for these criminal acts? For the widespread preparations to attack our Eighth Route army offices and to victimize Communists all over China, for the intensification of blockade against the Northwest; for the concentration of more than twenty divisions of Central Troops in Central China in order to launch a general offensive against us?

What sort of situation is now developing in China, when our Eighth Route and New Fourth Armies are receiving blows from the Japanese in the front, and are being attacked by our own national forces from the rear; when all those who obey military orders receive the official praise of the Government in the form of an attempt to wipe them out; when those who are faithful to an anti-Japanese policy are rewarded by murder and assassination? . . .

We should like now to request our Government immediately to withdraw the troops now encircling our New Fourth units in Anhwei, so that they can then move north in accordance with the orders of the Military Council across the Yangtze; to abolish the whole concentration for an "anti-Communist blockade" of the Northwest; to stop this policy of nation-wide victimization and slaying of Communists and Communist suspects; for we firmly believe that this is the only way to save our nation in this perilous situation . . .

Though this was strongly worded, it was still based on a United Front policy. As Chu Teh had told us, the war against Japan, the war for national survival, was the vital issue; all other questions were secondary. Certainly, we had understood; but who would have believed that they would accept even treason and death and still maintain the United Front?

All friends of China were heartbroken. About that time I met Johannes Steel, one of New York's foremost radio commentators; the Lend-Lease Bill was under discussion in Washington, and we both felt China's cause might be helped if the United States strengthened Generalissimo Chiang Kai-shek's hand. We went on the air together on February 13, 1941. Here are a few quotations from this interview: —

STEEL: How do you interpret the present situation in the Far East?

SUES: As a very grave crisis for China and for the democratic world, as a whole. If the split between Chiang's troops and the Communists deepens, China will face disaster, and Japan is bound to win the war.

STEEL: Who is, in your opinion, responsible for the break?

SUES: Indirectly, the United States and Great Britain, because of their reluctance to send China adequate supplies, and to stop shipments of war material to Japan.

Directly, the Tokyo–Berlin Axis. Japanese and Nazi Agents are very active, within and around China. They use the same "fifth column" methods that have proved effective in France and in other countries.

Up to the outbreak of the European war, Germany was China's

largest supplier. The United States came second, Russia * third, and Great Britain fourth.

Steel: And where does Chiang Kai-shek stand at present?

Sues: He seems to be very badly advised by men who have been in disgrace during the early part of this war, and who have now come back to power. He is completely isolated and seems to be getting only information misinterpreting the real state of affairs.

Steel: Is there a possibility of civil war in China?

Sues: Most emphatically yes. Chiang Kai-shek and the Communists are still trying to patch things up, but a group of high officials are ready to make peace with Japan, even on unfavorable terms. They do not want any democratic China. They want fascism. But they cannot possibly make peace so long as the Communist armies, and with them all democratic elements in China, resist Japan. The Communist armies are the keystone of anti-Japanese resistance. This is the real reason why government troops have disarmed part of the New Fourth Army.

Steel: Who are the personalities involved in this peace movement?

Sues: General Ho Ying-ch'in, China's Minister of War, for instance. It is he who ordered the attack upon the New Fourth Army. He is notoriously pro-Japanese. Then there is the C.C. group, a fascist party under the two Chen brothers: Chen Li-fu, Minister of Education, and Chen Kuo-fu . . .

Steel: Could civil war be prevented?

Sues: Maybe there is still time to prevent it. Action should be taken immediately by the United States Government. I believe that, if the right contacts are sent to Generalissimo Chiang Kai-shek, to convince him of the democracies' sincere wish to collaborate, and if adequate financial help were extended, and sufficient supplies dispatched without further delay, the situation might be saved. Chiang Kai-shek's hand should be strengthened. He should be urged to eliminate the hostile fascist elements by the most drastic

* The U.S.S.R. was the only country which did not, at the same time, send war supplies to Japan.

means, and to maintain his good relationship with China's magnificent guerilla armies.

"What did we say that was so extraordinary?" Johannes Steel asked me with a smile a few days later. "I keep getting calls and letters asking for a verbatim copy of our interview. . . . The whole of official Washington seems to have listened in."

"I mentioned names," I explained. "Here nobody thinks anything of mentioning personalities in public life, but in China it simply is not done."

I went to Washington to see T. V. Soong, but was received instead by Dr. Ludwik Rajchman, who had succeeded in getting into the Chinese Government's War Supplies Purchasing Agency, as T. V.'s Number One adviser.

Rajchman used his intimidating tactics, and I must say that his shouting stumped me for the first five minutes. Then we had a regular fight, in the course of which I learned that I was China's Enemy Number One; that I had insulted Generalissimo by pretending that he was a puppet in Ho Ying-ch'in's hands; that Ho had done nothing that was not ordered by the Generalissimo, who was fed up with the Communists anyway; that the whole United Front was bunkum and sentimental tripe for missionaries and other high-minded nitwits. And that I had better not put my foot on Chinese territory, for I would be shot on sight, as I well deserved. . . .

The broadcast had been wired *in extenso* to Chungking.

In the meantime, publishers had asked Steel whether he thought I had "the stuff for a book" in me. I said "NO!" He said "Yes" and "Don't-be-an-idiot-you-can-do-it." And that's how *Shark's Fins and Millet* was started.

Buttonholing some reliable people who came from China, I learned that Donald had left the Chiangs, slamming the door when reactionary pressure had reached its peak and when

Madame had been forbidden to write and broadcast that "China was lined up with the democracies." She was the only one with whom he shook hands. Then he left for a cruise in the South Seas. Madame went to Hong Kong and stayed there, while the Chinese Gestapo chief Tai Li and the reactionary clique left no stone unturned to estrange Generalissimo from his wife.

When the Lend-Lease bill was signed and Lauchlin Currie was sent to Chungking by President Roosevelt, Madame Chiang went up with him. It was always the same thing: the United States was the barometer — when America helped, Madame was on top; when America failed China, she was under fire.

In October and November of 1941, *Asia Magazine* published the first two installments of Donald's *Memoirs*. Then Donald and his manuscript disappeared. No one seems to know what has happened to him. Clark Lee, author of *They Call It Pacific*, seems to have seen him last, when Donald was on his way back from Tahiti to China. The freighter was four days out of Manila when the fighting started there. Donald is said to have refused to ask the American authorities for plane accommodation to Australia. He said he would take his chances where he was — "If necessary, I will take to the hills later." This sounds like Donald all right; maybe he is still alive, somewhere in the Philippines? But other accounts were far less optimistic. Hollington Tong, whom I saw in New York during Madame's recent visit, told me: "We have searched for him everywhere. We lost him somewhere in the Philippines. We don't know whether he has been captured or killed by the Japanese." This came as a shock to me. And yet, it did not sound convincing. If the Japanese had caught Donald, the most important Britisher in China, and Chiang's chief adviser, they certainly would not have kept it secret but would have shouted it all over the world. Unless, of course, they had not discovered his identity, which is pretty improbable. There were so many other people who hated Donald: the corrupt, the jealous, the dainty, and all those who feared the publication of his *Memoirs*. War in the Pacific was an ideal alibi. Donald had vanished into thin air. But far more mysterious was the fact that not one of his friends made an issue of it!

After Donald's departure, Madame's influence in Headquarters decreased to the point of being negligible. Her antagonists blamed her for every setback China suffered internationally. The trip to America was to her an all-important affair. The question was "to be or not to be." She had to prove that, where all others failed, she with her personality and prestige could succeed. She had to wrest *the* big support from Washington or abdicate forever. The time was ill chosen, and so were her political advisers.

Madame Chiang's address to Congress in 1943 came as a shock. She criticized and attacked the war strategy of the United Nations, to which the United States, Great Britain and Russia were pledged — namely, that in a total war of this magnitude, the nearest, strongest, and most dangerous enemy — Nazi Germany — has to be defeated first. She said: —

. . . Now the prevailing opinion seems to consider the defeat of the Japanese as of relative unimportance and that Hitler is our first concern. This is not borne out by actual facts, nor is it to the interests of the United Nations as a whole to allow Japan to continue, not only as a vital potential threat but as a waiting sword of Damocles, ready to descend at a moment's notice.

Let us not forget that Japan in her occupied areas today has greater resources at her command than Germany.

Aside from the danger such statements contained of splitting the united effort and losing the war, a challenge of this sort was singularly tactless. Madame Chiang pitted herself against President Roosevelt, who, less than two years before, had fought tooth and nail against America's isolationists and obtained Lend-Lease aid for China. She sided with, and appealed to, these very isolationists who had relentlessly advocated the appeasement of

Japan and opposed aid to China, up to the Pearl Harbor incident, and who were now demanding that Hirohito be defeated first.

All too soon it became apparent — not to America's congenital fans who idolize any glamorous personality, be it a pitcher, a crooner, a strip-teaser, or the First Lady of China, but to many observers — that Madame was a different person from what they had been told. Newspaper columnists began to comment upon the rousing welcome America had given her, and the cool relations between her and the White House.

Madame came to New York a few days later, visibly out of sorts. Holly told me the doctors had said that her trouble was not organic but nervous. When she had her fainting spells during the rally in Chinatown, I knew something had gone very wrong. I felt sorry for her: she was obviously incapable of handling the situation without Donald's advice. He alone dared tell her "Don't talk nonsense," and she could trust him. What I feared most was that if she continued airing her resentment, China would be the one to suffer. Somebody had to send her a reminder. That evening, an hour before she spoke at Madison Square Garden, I sent her a note accompanied by a bouquet of sweet peas. It read as follows: —

Dear Madame: —
Just a word of cheer to remind you that although W. H. Donald is not around, his spirit is still with you. Be big, take courage, and you may yet win. God bless you.

Respectfully yours . . .

"Be big" was what Donald had always stressed. I expected no reply. There was no response.

That night, speaking before a sympathetic audience of 20,000, with the whole world listening in, Madame Chiang missed the biggest opportunity of her life to identify herself with her country and her people, and to bring China nearer to America. She read a lengthy dissertation tending to prove that the Roman

Empire was a democratic republic! The majority of those present raved about her mastery of the English language, her beauty and her charm. But many people asked, disappointed: "Was it really worth while flying all the way from Chungking to give us a lecture on ancient history?"

At the press conferences she was witty and noncommittal and — as in China — it was forbidden to quote her. At official receptions she sat cool and distant on a thronelike elevation, roped off from the common mortals. She spoke to no one; the public was allowed to admire her five minutes in her fine dresses and priceless fur coats; then she rustled out of sight, escorted by her nephews and secret-service men. Madame hurt the feelings of many true friends of China when she was too weak and too busy to visit any of the organizations which had fought her fight and sent millions of American dollars to China, but found time and strength to watch the Dodgers training at their Bear Mountain field.

Soon the press linked her name with fashion and glamour more often than with China. There were even some sarcastic references to her extravagant shopping tours.

Thus Madame Chiang's visit to the United States was unfortunate for China and for her own prestige. When General Stilwell and General Chennault finally came to Washington and obtained a number of planes and weapons, so urgently needed, friends of China sighed with relief because now Madame could fly back to Chungking on an American bombing plane.

Madame Sun Yat-sen is in Chungking, carrying on her life's work under constantly growing difficulties.

Dr. Robert Lim has been ousted by political pressure and is no longer director of the Emergency Medical Training School which he created.

The Wutaishan International Peace Hospital had to move three times and is now operating in Hopei Province, far behind Japanese lines.

Bird's-Eye View of China Today

THERE ARE today two camps in China. Many divisions of the Central Army have been blockading the territory of the Eighth Route Army (now called the Eighteenth Group Army) for the past three years. The Central Executive Committee of the Kuomintang passed a resolution on September 13, 1943, accusing the Chinese Communist Party of subversive activities, expressing the hope that it would "refrain from committing acts undermining national unity and obstructing the prosecution of war," and calling upon the Communists to abandon their movement, dissolve their government, and disband their armies. This news caused anxiety among the United Nations. Eminent commentators point to the growing danger of civil war in China. The disastrous effect such an event would have upon the entire war effort is too evident to be discussed here.

The two camps, however, are not the Kuomintang camp and the Communist camp facing each other in party rivalry. Neither is the blockade line in the Northwest the frontier between two hostile Chinas divided by irreconcilable ideologies. The issue is much broader; it involves the whole nation, of which both parties are only an infinitesimal part. Six years of bloody war, the migration of millions of human beings exchanging their experiences and ideas, common suffering, common effort, common hopes for the future, have brought the people together. The proximity of the Government, the acute presence in daily life of the two rival political trends within it, stimulated critical thinking. Between the promise contained in the United Front program and the threat that tyranny was to continue, the people made its choice. The overwhelming majority of the nation constitutes today the Democratic Camp, a small but powerful minority the Feudal Camp.

The "Democratic Camp" upholds the United Front program: war to the finish against Japan, wholehearted collaboration with the United Nations, establishment of a constitutional democratic government and democratic reforms. It comprises: —

(*a*) The large majority of the Chinese masses, an elemental force, politically unschooled but conscious for the first time in history of their rights as a nation and individuals;

(*b*) All liberal, democratic and progressive elements, including the "Little Parties," students' and professional organizations, and a considerable number of unaffiliated members of the middle and upper classes;

(*c*) The majority of the Army, commanders and rank and file;

(*d*) The majority of Kuomintang members, though some are still wavering;

(*e*) The Communist Party with its Eighth Route and New Fourth Armies and associated partisans.

The "Feudal Camp," though ostensibly participating in the war against Japan, is in reality pursuing contrary aims. Although it has not yet dared say so openly, it is generally known to favor the conclusion of an "honorable" peace with Japan. It is hostile to the United Nations and to the United Front. It opposes democratic reforms of any kind and defends the old *status quo* with its totalitarian form of government and strong fascist tendencies. Its powerful leaders are: —

(*a*) Minister of War Ho Ying-ch'in, a man of conspicuous singleness of purpose, whose outstanding achievements were:
(1) the Wang Ching-wei–sponsored Ho-Umetsu Agreement,

which cost China her Northern Provinces; (2) the punitive expedition to Sian which, but for adverse weather conditions, might have cost the life of Generalissimo Chiang Kai-shek; (3) the surprise attack on the New Fourth Army which cost the lives of 4000 of China's best guerilla forces; and (4) the withdrawal from the fighting front of half a million of Chiang Kai-shek's best soldiers, to blockade the territory of the Eighth Route Army.

Ho's power lies in the fact that he controls the distribution of military supplies, the drafting of manpower, and the formidable machine of army intelligence.

(*b*) Minister of Education Chen Li-fu, leader of the C.C. clique, many of whose members hold key positions in the Kuomintang Government. His powerful secret police is almost as effective as that of the Nazi Party and pursues identical aims — the suppression by force of every democratic tendency.

(*c*) A handful of corrupt financiers and bureaucrats who have a firm grip on the nation's natural resources: food and strategic raw materials. They are engaged in profiteering and speculation on a scale so stupendous that it threatens economic collapse and a further slackening of China's war effort.

Ho Ying-ch'in and the C.C. group have been biding their time hoping for the decisive German-Italian victory, for the defeat of Russia, or at least for a split between the Anglo-Saxon Powers and Russia or between Great Britain and the United States. To them every victory of the United Nations is a blow.

The present explosive situation in China, the recrudescence of terrorism, the public accusation of the Communist Party made to justify any future armed attack upon the Democratic Camp, are due to the fact that none of these hopes has been fulfilled. The feverish activities of the Feudal Camp are in reality symptoms of fear; the steadily growing forces of democracy, and the rampant dissatisfaction within its own ranks, are anything but reassuring. The desperate campaign of spreading confusion and defeatism, the wave of blackmail and coercion, are as many preliminaries to the one and only thing which could now save the Feudal Camp, namely, civil war. It would automatically weaken the resistance against Japan and leave the Anglo-Saxon Powers high and dry on the Pacific Front.

The Democratic Camp sees this maneuver but refrains from retaliation for the sake of maintaining national unity. However, the psychological factor of human patience and endurance alone cannot save the situation.

China has been openly and repeatedly criticized for her military shortcomings: lack of uniform command and trained commanders, inadequate mobilization, and diversion of her best troops to General Ho Ying-ch'in's private wars.

She has been criticized for her economic anarchy: neglect of her abundant resources of strategic raw materials which, if properly administrated, would suffice to rearm her troops and make her depend less on supplies from Great Britain and the United States; financial acrobatics and wild speculation instead of a sound investment in developing essential national and war industries; hoarding of everything hoardable, including rice, which results in famine among the civilian population and in undernourishment of the armed forces.

And she has been criticized for her political paradoxes: An anti-Japanese United Front terrorized by pro-Japanese satraps; a gallant nation heroically fighting for freedom and democracy, subjected to the absolutism of one party; a great democratic people dying for world democracy but not allowed to live for it.

What China needs to bring her war against Japan to a victorious end is first and foremost national unity, *now*. This would imply a thorough reorganization of the Army, the placing of China's war economy on a war footing, the recognition of all political parties, and the people's participation in the government. Generalissimo Chiang Kai-shek has mentioned these far-reaching reforms in many of his addresses to the nation and to the Kuomintang. But time is passing.

The world is anxious and suspicious, viewing this extremely tense situation; and question upon question is being asked: —

Will there be civil war? Will Chinese fight Chinese again? Is China to split and to become the prey of the Japanese or other foreign interventionists? Will her delegates sit at the Peace Conference representing the leading Democracy of Asia? Or will they be treated as the spokesmen of a semi-colonial or colonial State which needs "international policing"?

There is only one man who can reply to these questions — Generalissimo Chiang Kai-shek. He is the symbol of China's power, her greatness, her United Front, the hope of the Chinese Nation. Will he lean on the strong, dependable shoulders of his great people, who have carried him to his present elated position? Or will he stand on the erratic bayonets of a Ho Ying-ch'in? Will he be swept away by the rising tide of the People's War? Or will he fulfill what he promises, justify the faith of his people, and crown his spectacular revolutionary career by founding, with the entire nation, the *San Min Chu I* Republic of China?